ReFocus: The Films of François Ozon

ReFocus: The International Directors Series

Series Editors: Robert Singer, Stefanie Van de Peer and Gary D. Rhodes

Board of Advisors:
Lizelle Bisschoff (Glasgow University)
Stephanie Hemelryck Donald (University of Lincoln)
Anna Misiak (Falmouth University)
Des O'Rawe (Queen's University Belfast)

ReFocus is a series of contemporary methodological and theoretical approaches to the interdisciplinary analyses and interpretations of international film directors, from the celebrated to the ignored, in direct relationship to their respective culture – its myths, values, and historical precepts – and the broader parameters of international film history and theory.

Titles in the series include:

ReFocus: The Films of Susanne Bier
Edited by Missy Molloy, Mimi Nielsen and Meryl Shriver-Rice

ReFocus: The Films of Francis Veber
Keith Corson

ReFocus: The Films of Jia Zhangke
Maureen Turim and Ying Xiao

ReFocus: The Films of Xavier Dolan
Edited by Andrée Lafontaine

ReFocus: The Films of Pedro Costa: Producing and Consuming Contemporary Art Cinema
Nuno Barradas Jorge

ReFocus: The Films of Sohrab Shahid Saless: Exile, Displacement and the Stateless Moving Image
Edited by Azadeh Fatehrad

ReFocus: The Films of Pablo Larraín
Edited by Laura Hatry

ReFocus: The Films of Michel Gondry
Edited by Marcelline Block and Jennifer Kirby

ReFocus: The Films of Rachid Bouchareb
Edited by Michael Gott and Leslie Kealhofer-Kemp

ReFocus: The Films of Andrei Tarkovsky
Edited by Sergey Toymentsev

ReFocus: The Films of Paul Leni
Edited by Erica Tortolani and Martin F. Norden

ReFocus: The Films of Rakhshan Banietemad
Edited by Maryam Ghorbankarimi

ReFocus: The Films of Jocelyn Saab: Films, Artworks and Cultural Events for the Arab World
Edited by Mathilde Rouxel and Stefanie Van de Peer

ReFocus: The Films of François Ozon
Edited by Loïc Bourdeau

edinburghuniversitypress.com/series/refocint

ReFocus:
The Films of François Ozon

Edited by Loïc Bourdeau

To Aurélie and Clarisse

Edinburgh University Press is one of the leading university presses in the UK. We publish academic books and journals in our selected subject areas across the humanities and social sciences, combining cutting-edge scholarship with high editorial and production values to produce academic works of lasting importance. For more information visit our website: edinburghuniversitypress.com

© editorial matter and organisation Loïc Bourdeau, 2021, 2023
© the chapters their several authors, 2021, 2023

First published in hardback by Edinburgh University Press 2021

Edinburgh University Press Ltd
The Tun – Holyrood Road
12 (2f) Jackson's Entry
Edinburgh EH8 8PJ

Typeset in 11/13 Ehrhardt MT by
IDSUK (DataConnection) Ltd

A CIP record for this book is available from the British Library

ISBN 978 1 4744 7991 2 (hardback)
ISBN 978 1 4744 7992 9 (paperback)
ISBN 978 1 4744 7993 6 (webready PDF)
ISBN 978 1 4744 7994 3 (epub)

The right of the contributors to be identified as authors of this work has been asserted in accordance with the Copyright, Designs and Patents Act 1988 and the Copyright and Related Rights Regulations 2003 (SI No. 2498).

Contents

List of Figures vii
Notes on Contributors ix
Acknowledgements xi

    Introduction: In the Beginning Was the Word 1
    Loïc Bourdeau

Part I   The Politics of Form

1 Queer Tyranny and Intertextuality in *Gouttes d'eau sur pierres brûlantes*: François Ozon Pays Homage to Master Fassbinder 15
   Amy Bertram
2 François Ozon's *Sitcom* and Politics of Form 35
   Tamara Tasevska
3 Queering the Trenches: Homoerotic Overtones in *Frantz* 52
   Helena Duffy
4 The Crystal-image and Queer Ambiguity in *Sous le sable* 72
   Peadar Kearney
5 French Ozon/Global Ozon: French Specificity and Globalisation in *Jeune & jolie* 87
   Felicity Chaplin

Part II   (In)Formal Politics

6 'The Scent of a Middle-class Woman': Desire, Family and the Adolescent Imagination in François Ozon's *Dans la maison* 109
   Jamie Steele

7 Bringing Up Baby in the Twenty-first Century: *Le Refuge* and
   the Ozonian Family   125
   Thibaut Schilt
8 Transing Dynamics: Ozon's *Une Nouvelle amie*   143
   Todd W. Reeser
9 Sex Wars in *Potiche*: Womanhood Then and Now   162
   Loïc Bourdeau
10 Female Creativity, Selfishness and Monstrosity in
   François Ozon's *Angel*   181
   Fiona Handyside
11 From *Faits Divers* to *Grandes Affaires*: Giving Voice to
   Sexual Abuse Survivors in *Grâce à Dieu*   195
   Levilson C. Reis

Filmography   212
Index   214

Figures

1.1	Bath close-up	25
1.2	Léopold and Franz on the bed	25
1.3	Franz crying	28
1.4	Facing the windows	30
2.1	The burial	38
2.2	Dinner party	45
2.3	Abdu touches Nicolas	45
3.1	Frantz and Adrien in the trenches	59
3.2	Adrien's wet body	60
4.1	Vincent's presence	76
4.2	Marie at the beach	78
5.1	Isabelle on the escalator	88
5.2	Isabelle on the hotel bed	93
5.3	Isabelle in the car	96
6.1	In Rapha's bedroom	112
6.2	Germain emerges from the pantry	114
7.1	Mousse and an inquisitive beachgoer	127
7.2	Mousse's double reflection	132
7.3	Paul and baby Louise	139
8.1	David and Gilles in the shower	147
8.2	Claire walks in on Virginia	149
8.3	Virginia tries on clothes	152
8.4	A new family	158
9.1	Mrs Marquiset in the window	167
9.2	Suzanne is the boss	171
9.3	Suzanne among her voters	174

9.4	Suzanne hitchhiking with a truck driver	177
10.1	Angel's honeymoon	187
10.2	Angel and Esme embrace in the rain	188
10.3	Angel massaged by Nora	192
11.1	Alexandre reads a newspaper	202
11.2	Flashback to boy scout years	205

Notes on Contributors

Amy Bertram is Lecturer in Motion Pictures at Belmont University, Tennessee.

Loïc Bourdeau is Associate Professor of French and Francophone Studies at the University of Louisiana at Lafayette.

Felicity Chaplin is a scholarly teaching fellow in French Studies at Monash University.

Helena Duffy is a collegium researcher in Literary Studies and Creative Writing at the University of Turku (Institute of Advanced Studies).

Fiona Handyside is Associate Professor of Film Studies at the University of Exeter.

Peadar Kearney is a final-year PhD candidate in French Studies at Maynooth University and an Irish research council scholar.

Todd W. Reeser is Professor of French and Gender, Sexuality, and Women's Studies at the University of Pittsburgh.

Levilson C. Reis is Professor of French Studies at Otterbein University.

Thibaut Schilt is Associate Professor of French and Francophone Studies at the College of the Holy Cross.

Jamie Steele is Senior Lecturer in Film and Screen Studies at Bath Spa University.

Tamara Tasevska is a final-year PhD candidate in French and Francophone Studies at Northwestern University.

Acknowledgements

Growing up in an *HLM* apartment (government subsidised housing) in the *banlieue* of Limoges (a French city with a century-long political history of socialism) in the 1990s, I was unaware of François Ozon's cinema. It was not until *8 femmes / 8 Women* (2002) that I began to appreciate his films and follow his career, albeit with more or less consistency. Yet, his work, as this volume shows, spoke to me because of its generic hybridity, its investigation of desire, and its breaking down of hierarchies, especially cultural ones (between lowbrow and high-brow productions). In my early teens, an elderly neighbour gave me a robot-shaped radio set. In the confines of my bedroom, I discovered Classical Music Radio which introduced me to Mozart, Bach and Vivaldi and lulled me to sleep every night. A few years later, another neighbour lent me a DVD of *Potiche*, Pierre Barillet and Jean-Pierre Grédy's 1980 *Boulevard* play featuring the irreplaceable Jacqueline Maillan. Ozon adapted the play in 2010, and I have now written about it here. I watched the play over and over again; I still do. Thinking back on these two instances, I do not believe that I was destined in any way to write about Ozon, but I do think my background set me up to appreciate his oeuvre. Ozon's commitment to giving a voice to social outcasts and marginalised communities resonates with me not only personally but also professionally. Indeed, my previous project, *Horrible Mothers: Representations across Francophone North America* (2019), testifies to my interest in motherhood and marginality, which this current volume investigates further.

Beyond these personal considerations, putting together this volume would not have been possible without the enthusiasm and expertise of my fellow contributors. As such, I would like to thank them all for their outstanding work, patience and responsiveness throughout the process. I also thank them for their trust. In order of appearance in the book, they are: Amy Bertram, Tamara

Tasevska, Helena Duffy, Peadar Kearney, Felicity Chaplin, Jamie Steele, Thibaut Schilt, Todd W. Reeser, Fiona Handyside and Levilson C. Reis. It has been quite an honour to be joined by such excellent scholars, many of whom had already advanced the scholarship on Ozon in significant ways.

This project would not have been possible without Gillian Leslie, EUP senior commissioning editor. She quickly accepted the project and saw the potential in dedicating a new volume to François Ozon. Her professionalism, support and enthusiasm made this entire experience a pleasant one. I thank her for choosing dedicated external readers whose comments have helped me (and the contributors) to shape an exciting product. I am indebted to these readers, as I am to the series editors, Robert Singer, Gary Rhodes and Stefanie Van de Peer. The three of them also welcomed my project with open arms and provided helpful tips, feedback and support throughout. From proposal to manuscript, they read everything with attention and care and ensured that this volume would be of high quality. I would like to thank Robert Singer, in particular, for answering my queries so promptly and so kindly.

As a faculty member in the Department of Modern Languages at the University of Louisiana at Lafayette, I have received much-needed financial and mental support. My Louisiana Board of Regents Endowed Professorship has allowed me to cover important research expenses. I thank Professor Monica Wright for allowing me to brainstorm/share ideas with her and for cheering me on from beginning to end. I also owe a debt to Sarah Smith, doctoral fellow in francophone studies and editorial assistant to the University of Louisiana's peer-reviewed journal *Études Francophones*, who proofread my own work in this volume.

I would like to thank Alexandrine Mailhé for her friendship and for her critical eye over my work (not just in this volume). She lets me share my work in progress with her; her comments and encouragements are always invaluable. Overall, I feel very fortunate to have wonderful friends around me, near or far, who support me, distract me, or listen to me. I thank my mother, my dearest David and Colette, and my special someone for their unwavering love. Finally, I would like to thank Aurélie and Clarisse, my two best friends to whom I dedicate this volume. We first met, respectively, as new-borns and as kindergarteners. Thirty years have passed, and our friendship remains intact. This book is about love and the power of relations and community, and I am grateful for the beautiful people and community that surround me and brighten my own world.

Introduction: In the Beginning Was the Word

Loïc Bourdeau

Putting together a scholarly volume about a French Queer filmmaker has a peculiar resonance at a time when France is experiencing political polarisation in favour of its more conservative factions (Pétreault 2020), President Emmanuel Macron and his government are co-opting (far-)right rhetoric and (queer) scholars are blamed for allegedly 'breaking the Republic in two' (Ahmadi 2020). Words such as 'intersectional', 'feminist', 'racialist' or 'islamo-gauchiste/islamo-leftist' are thrown around like insults and have come to embody everything that is wrong with society. In 2007, François Ozon 'spoke of the danger posed to the country by [Nicolas] Sarkozy', deploring 'France's increasing renunciation of the possibility of relation, revolution or community reborn' (Asibong 2008: 8). In fact, Ozon's *Potiche* (2010) clearly draws from the 2007 elections, Sarkozy's neoliberal and individualistic agenda and offers an alternative model grounded in egalitarianism and collectivism. Socialist François Hollande's subsequent presidency – in particular Manuel Valls's term as Prime Minister – did little to reignite a radical, left social project. The same goes for Macron's 'at-the-same-time' approach to politics.

This volume, *ReFocus: The Films of François Ozon*, embraces queerness, feminism and intersectionality, which it employs in the same manner that Nick Rees-Roberts does in his exploration of French Queer cinema: 'The principal use of "queer" . . . is intended to avoid a celebratory (white, middle-class) "gay pride" rendition of French cinema, one that would necessarily exclude the primary areas of cultural contestation around race, ethnicity, migration, transgender and AIDS' (Rees-Roberts 2014: 5). These initial considerations reveal the importance and the weight of words in shaping our reality, along with the attendant power to give a voice or to silence one's lived experiences. Born in Paris on 15 November 1967, Ozon, one of France's most prolific and best-known international directors, with nineteen feature-length films (and over a dozen shorts) to date, has built a filmography that not only engages in the representation of (non-normative) sexualities, kinship and violence (Asibong 2008: 3) but which makes room for social outcasts and marginalised communities. Releasing *Été 85 / Summer of 85* (2020) in the midst of a pandemic – and noting that 'people are eager to get back to the movie theatre' (Perrier 2020) – further attests to Ozon's attachment to and conception of cinema as something that 'crée du lien' ('connects us all'); cinema is an integral part of the fabric of society.

While Thibaut Schilt, in his incisive and detailed monograph, anchors his analysis around the terminology 'fabric of desire' – inspired by the movement and theoretical potentiality of fabric in *Une Robe d'été / A Summer Dress* (1996) – to consider the fluidity and 'the complex renegotiations of desire present in all of Ozon's films' (Schilt 2011: 4), I find similar avenues of queerness in his relationship with words, text and naming. Andrew Asibong explains that '[s]till a schoolboy, Ozon, inspired by his father's Super-8 projections of the Ozon family . . . had started making short films. Between the ages of 18 and 22 he had made over thirty Super-8 productions of his own' (Asibong 2008: 2). His early work showcases 'how keen the young Ozon was to generate concrete images for his peculiarly family-orientated preoccupations' (Asibong 2008: 2); these preoccupations thus were foundational texts to create his visual productions. Looking at his later work, from *Gouttes d'eau sur pierres brûlantes / Water Drops on Burning Rocks* (2000), *Swimming Pool* and *Angel* (2007) to *Potiche* (2010) and *Dans la maison / In the House* (2012), it is likewise evident that Ozon's filmography owes much to the written word.

More recently still, in a radio interview about *Été 85 / Summer of 85*, Ozon credits both Aidan Chambers's 1982 novel *Dance on my Grave* and musical group The Cure's 'In Between Days' (1985) as inspirations for the film. Describing the song as his *madeleine de Proust*, Ozon even changed the original title, *Été 84 / Summer of 84*, to be able to obtain the rights to Robert Smith's song. Journalist Amélie Perrier also notes references to poet Paul Verlaine's 'Il faut, voyez-vous, nous pardonner les choses / You see, we must be forgiven things . . .' – having adapted the line about 'soyons deux jeunes filles' / 'let's be two young girls' to fit the film's 'deux jeunes garçons' / 'two young boys' – along with a Rimbaldian approach to death (Perrier 2020). Released a year earlier, *Grâce à Dieu / By the Grace of God* (2019) – a film that explores the sexual abuse scandals in the French Catholic Church – opens on a shot of Ozon's main character, Alexandre Guérin (Melvil Poupaud), holding a newspaper before going about his life with his family. Simultaneously, a voiceover of the character reads a letter in which he introduces himself and shares the story of the abuse he suffered in his youth. A voiceover of Philippe Barbarin, Archbishop of Lyon, then picks up and responds to Alexandre's revelations.

Critics, including the contributors to this volume, have commented on the rich intertextual nature of Ozon's oeuvre. Schilt, who highlights the workings of intertextuality throughout the short films, confirms that 'this cinema of reference continued into Ozon's full-length film career' (Schilt 2011: 28). Furthermore, his practice also exhibits self-referential tendencies. In that regard, Douglas Morrey argues that:

> if Ozon's work, and *Swimming Pool* in particular, bears the influence of the New Wave, it is perhaps most clearly in the film's acute self-consciousness, the pointed way in which it addresses the accursed vocation of the auteur. *Swimming Pool* is, in short, a 'self-portrait of the filmmaker as writer'. (Morrey 2020: 196)

Fiona Handyside's contribution to this volume likewise proposes that we see Ozon in Esme, the main protagonist of *Angel*. I would add that self-consciousness not only provides insights into his filming processes or even his intimacy – for instance, critic Charlotte Linpinska notes that *Été 85 / Summer of 85* is 'an eminently personal film' (France Inter 2020) – but also denotes Ozon's awareness of his film's reception. Just as novels, songs, news ('faits divers') and letters become scripts, film reviews and commentaries seem to permeate his stories. Levilson C. Reis starts his chapter with references to Alice Stanley's unpublished doctoral thesis in which she argues that Ozon enthusiastically tackles major societal issues, yet refuses to offer 'politically engaged stor[ies]' (2009: 48). For Reis, however, the lack of engagement does not equate to political neutrality. In my own chapter on *Potiche*, I show how a conversation between two characters brings forth the very question of engagement along with the political nature of the arts: here, the film comments on itself. Moreover, it is clearly imbued with feminist sensibility, regardless of its comedic or non-realist take.

Yet one should bear in mind that, as with the public reception of films, scholarship forms a similarly heterogeneous body and oftentimes yields contradictory readings and perceptions. Though such a remark may be stating the obvious, it is a reminder that nothing is sacred, untouchable, even queer cultural products or individuals that give a voice and a visibility to marginalised groups. In *Disturbing Attachments*, Kadji Amin offers an excellent study of Jean Genet and his privileged and idealised status within Queer studies. Amin argues that although 'Queer studies without idealization would not be Queer studies at all' (Amin 2017: 4), the field must nevertheless engage in de-idealisation if it wishes to maintain its edge, embrace the 'unease' or the 'bad object' and seek 'to locate the source of the rub' (Amin 2017: 31), because bad objects 'may generate surprising theoretical and historical insights' (Amin 2017: 176). In the context of Ozon's oeuvre, of interest here, Morrey notes that a similar process of idealisation might be at play. He writes: 'Kate Ince has suggested that a fundamental misunderstanding, or refusal, of the thematics of queer desire in Ozon's work has led to "some damagingly judgmental dismissals" and "inadequate appreciation" of his films' (Morrey 2020: 195). In return, he posits that 'film criticism must retain the ability to judge some films more aesthetically successful than others, if it is to remain criticism at all' (Morrey 2020: 195).[1] The present volume does not quite concern itself with aesthetic success, perhaps because each contributor chose a film they enjoy (either personally or for the theoretical possibilities it offers or both). Yet, the volume includes nuanced readings that aptly point out shortcomings whenever necessary. As a final comment on the matter, Schilt reminds us that as a university student, Ozon produced a significant number of shorts and 'call[ed] himself a "bulimic" filmmaker (Goudet, "Court métrage" 94)' (Schilt 2011: 11). As such, in a large pool of creations, aesthetic success is not always a guaranteed outcome. Like the character of Angel, Handyside tells us, whose first book was published unedited, Ozon, in his continued bulimic tendencies sometimes releases pieces which perhaps required more attention, thus giving way to more or less memorable films. Having said that, if 'Ozon must be understood as a filmmaker who has formally analysed film . . . and as a *cinéaste* who has . . . delighted in displaying his brilliant knowledge of cinema' (Asibong 2008: 5), he may well be an artist who also uses his medium to address the critical reception of his work.

The epistolary exchange at the heart of *Grâce à Dieu / By the Grace of God* proves a fitting metaphor for the exchanges and network of communication that exist throughout Ozon's work. Asibong, among others, speaks of the director's 'clear fondness for Fassbinder's [work]' (Asibong 2008: 5), which Amy Bertram's chapter explores in more depth, as well as the work of Pedro Almodóvar, Stephen Frears, Alfred Hitchcock or John Waters. I previously mentioned the influence of novels and music, too, thus attesting further to the hyper-referentiality of his oeuvre. Ozon's own work must be included within this system of influences. Reviewing *Été 85 / Summer of 85*, Peter Debruge sees in the 2020 production a return to the late 1990s when 'Ozon's movies were unabashedly queer, hotblooded and hormone-driven affairs, explorations of jealousy and desire' (Debruge 2020). Beyond the repeated use of key tropes such as beaches (see, for instance, Handyside's 2013 study: 'Ghosts on the Sand: François Ozon's Haunted Beaches'), Ozon's films speak to one another. Debruge notes the 'cheeky cross-dressing gag [in *Été 85 / Summer of 85*] that recalls his scorching 1996 short "A Summer Dress"' (Debruge 2020). Additionally, the film's 'subliminal evocation of AIDS' (Hammond 2020) recalls *Le Temps qui reste / Time to Leave* (2005), 'a film about illness with a gay protagonist, that does not make AIDS its overt subject' (Wilson 2006: 18). The outdoor sex scene, the voyeurism and the shower scene in *Les Amants criminels / Criminal Lovers* (1999) echo, respectively, *Une Robe d'été /*

A Summer Dress and *Une Nouvelle Amie* / *The New Girlfriend* (2014). Sexual violence and pregnancy complications in *Angel* resonate with the earlier *5x2* (2004). On the one hand, these few examples underline Ozon's 'ability to sustain a personal signature across different genres and production contexts', which for Morrey is 'the most unequivocal sign of the auteur' (Morrey 2020: 194). On the other, these cinematic conversations problematise the question of artistic growth and maturity. Ince, for instance, discards 'a Manichaean opposition between Ozon's "youthful" and "mature" film-making' (Ince 2008: 112). Indeed, stylistic and thematic trends emerge throughout his career, but maturity seems somewhat irrelevant. Analysing *5x2*, Rees-Roberts (rendering Jean Douchet's impressions) remarks on how the film 'denaturalises the linear chronology and cultural archetypes of heterosexual coupling and kinship' (Rees-Roberts 2014: 10). At the macro level of his oeuvre, it seems, too, that Ozon denaturalises the linear and normative chronology of the human and artistic experience, according to which maturity comes with age and is to be celebrated; on the contrary, for Ozon, no style, no topic, no genre is ever out of bounds. Given the breadth of the existing scholarship on Ozon's work, to which this volume and each of its chapters owes a debt, I have also opted for a non-chronological approach. Rather, the volume consists of two main parts wherein articles attempt to communicate with and expand on one another as Ozon's films do. And, the director's prolific output makes it evident that we have yet to be able to produce a definitive study of his filmography from beginning to end – he is already working on his next film, an adaptation of Emmanuèle Bernheim's *Tout s'est bien passé* about end-of-life care. Ozon has previously adapted Bernheim's work, including *Sous le sable / Under the Sand*, *Swimming Pool* and *5x2*.

I return to the title of this introduction, 'In the Beginning Was the Word', to take some time to consider the term 'queer auteur'. For Ince, Ozon is 'France's first mainstream queer *auteur*' (Ince 2008: 113). Schilt unpacks the 'provocative' and 'seemingly antithetical terms' (Schilt 2011: 34) – mainstream (e.g. Hollywood blockbusters), auteur (e.g., French New Wave) and queer (i.e., anti-patriarchal domination) – in relation to historical developments in cinema and concludes 'that in Ozon's case, they are no longer at odds with each other' (Schilt 2011: 34). Both Tamara Tasevska's and Amy Bertram's chapters explore the formal politics of New Queer Cinema in relation to Ozon's filmmaking. In the French context, these terms also carry their share of tensions or incongruencies considering the country's reluctance to acknowledge 'identity politics in the name of universalism' (Schilt 2011: 35–6). In the aforementioned interview about *Été 85 / Summer of 85*, Ozon himself presents Aidan Chambers's story as a 'simple and universal love story between two young men'; homosexuality in Ozon's film is not political, 'it is sentimental' (Perrier 2020).[2] If this puzzling rhetoric, which seeks to somehow depoliticise the film, further illustrates

French universalist ideals and discourses, Schilt contends that 'Ozon is [nevertheless] much less reluctant about the relationship between gender, sexuality, and authorship' (Schilt 2011: 37). One could also argue that refusing identitary labels is, in fact, quite queer. At the cinematographic level, Alistair Fox and Morrey, among others, have commented on 'the blending of genres and styles that has become the hallmark of Ozon's oeuvre' (Fox 2015 in Morrey 2020: 194), and which, to some extent, also typifies queer artmaking. Contemporary literature, for instance, exhibits numerous examples of queer writers who deconstruct and play with generic conventions.

Ozon's approach to cinema via the literary word conjures up questions of adaptation, fidelity and infidelity. Although some chapters in this volume touch on the subject, (in)fidelity does not represent a major concern or interest here. Handyside has already explored the question in 'Queer Filiations: Adaptation in the Films of François Ozon', where she 'argue[s] that Ozon's self-conscious use of adaptation as a trope draws attention to the radical queer potential that is at the heart of the adaptation process' (Handyside 2011: 54). Queer, from the high German *quer*, meaning oblique (or perverse), indeed proves quite apt insofar as Ozon constantly deviates from the original text, or takes an oblique approach to it. He goes where no one expects him and, along the crooked way, breaks down 'another binary opposition beloved of French cinema – that of "popular" and "art-house"' (Handyside 2011: 64).[3] The successful *Potiche* is one such example of popular culture (i.e., *Boulevard* theatre) whose adaptation fully embraces the feminist potential (present in the 1980 production) and deviates at times from the original, thus making it a queer film.

* * *

This volume brings together eleven contributions, each focusing specifically on one of Ozon's films. While parts of his filmography remain unexplored here, such as *8 femmes* / *8 Women* (2002), *Ricky* (2009)[4] or *L'Amant double* / *Double Lover* (2017), the contributors engage in a significant number of comparative analyses to place their main object of study within the larger frame of the director's oeuvre. Since Schilt's 2011 monograph, which continued Asibong's 2008 endeavour, Ozon has released eight films, most of which are discussed here. Moreover, the existing and rich scholarship – often cited across the chapters – not only offers readings of his films, it also attests to Ozon's overall clout among film critics and scholars alike, making him a continued object of scrutiny. Bringing together scholars of Film Studies, Gender Studies and French Studies, and engaging with current theoretical developments (from female selfishness with Lisa Downing to Trans* studies), *ReFocus: The Films of François Ozon* aims to expand our understanding of specific films, Ozon's filmmaking, French cinema and French culture overall.

Part I of this volume, entitled 'Politics of Form', combines five chapters that primarily investigate François Ozon's stylistic choices and locate his work within the larger scale of cinema. In Chapter 1, 'Queer Tyranny and Intertextuality in *Gouttes d'eau sur pierres brûlantes*: François Ozon Pays Homage to Master Fassbinder', Amy Bertram tackles the connection and influence of German filmmaker Rainer Werner Fassbinder on Ozon's 2000 feature film. Bringing forth the stylistic components of Ozon's queer cinema, Bertram engages in more detail than previous studies with some Fassbinder source material, thus offering a new understanding of *Gouttes d'eau / Water Drops* as a complex and evocative piece. Drawing on Laura Mulvey's theory of cinematic scopophilia, the chapter underlines the way in which Ozon's style augments the queerness of the narrative and the visual pleasure. Indeed, for Bertram, the use of high-colour saturation of the production design and costumes, in addition to the campy overtones, give way to queer cinematic pleasures. Bertram also provides a historical account of New Queer Cinema (NQC), which Tamara Tasevska investigates in great detail in the subsequent chapter. Indeed, 'François Ozon's *Sitcom* and Politics of Form' looks at Ozon's filmmaking in conjunction with the formal politics of NQC. Here, Tasevska discusses the use of queer within a French context, Ozon's reworking of the mechanisms of cinema and the ways in which he in fact challenges the structure of heteronormative, mainstream cinema. The chapter shows that *Sitcom* (1998) – with its excessive *mise-en-scène* and use of perversion – not only yields queer attachments but also experiments with social value, beyond patriarchal culture.

Chapter 3, 'Queering the Trenches: Homoerotic Overtones in *Frantz*', provides an extensive analysis of the 2016 drama and one of Ozon's most recent and successful films. An unusual film within his oeuvre, given its setting outside of France, for the most part, and the use of black-and-white, *Frantz*, Helena Duffy argues, interrogates hegemonic masculinity – with the help of Kaja Silverman's conceptualisation of historical trauma and overall work on marginal masculinities – and the notion that it should be crystallised by war. In doing so, the director unsettles heteronormative conventions. Further, Duffy pays particular attention to Édouard Manet's *Le Suicidé* to identify connections between homosexuality and the death drive (established by the painting). Peadar Kearney, in Chapter 4, 'The Crystal-image and Queer Ambiguity in *Sous le sable*', tackles what many critics and scholars note about Ozon's work, that is, his blending of fiction and reality. Here, the chapter brings forth the film's singular treatment of subjectivity, the blurring of the distinction between diegetic reality and fiction and the overall sense of ambiguity that pervades the narrative. Adding to the scholarship on *Sous le sable / Under the Sand* (2000), Kearney turns to Gilles Deleuze's crystal-image and queer theory and reminds us that ambiguity, ambivalence and indiscernibility are crucial to deciphering Ozon's films and open up concepts of space, time and identities. The final chapter in this section, 'French Ozon / Global Ozon: French Specificity and Globalisation in *Jeune & jolie*', serves to bridge both parts. Indeed, Felicity Chaplin anchors her analysis of the 2013 feature within the frame of French cinema, culture and traditions. Yet Chaplin argues that *Jeune & jolie / Young & Beautiful* occupies an interstitial space between French specificity and globalisation. Drawing on a rich scholarship, including the work of Ginette Vincendeau, Alistair Fox, Kate Ince and Frederic Jameson, this chapter provides a close reading of Ozon's style and use of pastiche (also discussed later by Handyside) and confirms that his characters are at once French and postmodern.

Part II, '(In)Formal Politics', continues to explore the director's style, while placing the social and political dimension of the films at the heart of each analysis. If Chaplin underlines Ozon's references to the French education system to make his work typically French, in Chapter Six, '"The Scent of a Middle-class Woman": Desire, Family, and the Adolescent Imagination in François Ozon's *Dans la maison*', Jamie Steele explores Ozon's filmmaking style and approach to institutions at the centre of the French national imaginary, such as the school system. By questioning these structures, *Dans la maison / In the House* (2012) subverts heteronormative assumptions of Western European society and culture. In particular, Steele investigates desire and how it permeates the depiction of the school and the family institutions. Finally, this chapter confirms that it is reductive to consider Ozon's films only through the representation of homosexuality, even if the topic is at the heart of many productions. Chapter 7, 'Bringing Up Baby in the Twenty-First Century: *Le Refuge* and the Ozonian Family', continues the exploration of family structures. Here, Thibaut Schilt first situates the 2009 film within Ozon's existing oeuvre and highlights its innovative aspects. Then, after an analysis of the ways in which *Le Refuge / The Hideaway* further complicates visions of motherhood and kinship structures, Schilt – using references to *Les Amants criminels / Criminal Lovers* or *8 femmes / 8 Women*, among others, – discusses the film's portrayal of fatherhood through the figure of Paul, an openly gay man and surrogate father to his deceased brother's child. Finally, the chapter takes into account the French socio-political context and contemporary debates over LGBTQ rights in which the films seems to intervene. Todd W. Reeser, in the following chapter, 'Transing Dynamics: Ozon's *Une Nouvelle amie*', likewise analyses family dynamics, in this instance through the lens of a transgender character.[5] Reeser uses Jean Baudrillard's work, not to take a position on his conceptualisation of 'transsexuality' per se, but rather to consider how *Une Nouvelle amie / The New Girlfriend* (2014) bridges conflicting conceptions of gender. It seems that Ozon's film is representative of the French intellectual tradition of signifying play as defined by Baudrillard and tells the story about the phenomenon of the seduction of 'transsexuality', literally and metaphorically.

The personal emancipation at the end of *Une Nouvelle amie / The New Girlfriend* echoes that of the titular character of *Potiche* (2010), which Chapter 9, 'Sex Wars in *Potiche*: Womanhood Then and Now', investigates. Here, I seek to analyse Ozon's strategy to represent French womanhood and to bring forth his criticism of gender expectations and the political and queer dimension of the film. I argue that Ozon manages to empower the 'trophy wife' with the very means of her submission: credulity, candour and maternal responsibilities. Adapting a 1980 *Boulevard* play and drawing on the 2007 presidential elections, Ozon relies on the ghost of the past, of women's liberation, to comment on contemporary matters. This work is grounded in recent feminist scholarship, such as Lisa Downing's *Selfish Women* (2019), which also inspires Chapter 10. Fiona Handyside's 'Female Creativity, Selfishness and Monstrosity in François Ozon's *Angel*' indeed posits the lead character, Angel, and her commitment to a fantasy life as a perfect case study of female selfishness. While the 2007 film may not be as radical and anti-patriarchal as Ozon's earlier films, it does make room for a deliberately unsympathetic female figure who prioritises her instincts and interests over the kind of self-sacrifice that women have been trained to perform (as Downing explains). Along the way, Handyside explores Ozon's use of pastiche and highlights the self-referential dimension of the film, thus reflecting on Ozon's approach to filmmaking. The last chapter, by Levilson C. Reis, 'From *Faits Divers* to *Grandes Affaires*: Giving Voice to Sexual Abuse Survivors in *Grâce à Dieu*', offers one of the first studies of Ozon's 2018 production. Reis contends that *Grâce à Dieu / By the Grace of God* illustrates Ozon's evolution both in terms of aesthetics and representational politics, rather than a sudden change of direction. Cinema, as a tool, asserts its ability to transform the secretive and the unspeakable. By making these stories of abuse seen and known, Reis argues, Ozon has created a social justice film.

As a final note, I would turn to François Ozon's attachment to filming on 35mm or on Super-16 rather than using digital cameras. He explains that new technologies have a 'tendency to make things insipid and extremely clear or neat' (Perrier 2020). This volume shows that beyond technical considerations, Ozon's storyworld exists entirely in opposition to clarity and neatness; it is also far from insipid. And, if he embraces the full potential of ambiguity and ambivalence, this volume hopes to bring the necessary clarity to better understand his oeuvre as a queer auteur.

NOTES

1. Morrey's analysis of *Swimming Pool* is an example of de-idealisation. First, he underlines Ozon's problematic representation of Sarah Morton (Charlotte Rampling) 'as a narrow-minded stereotype of a repressed middle-aged Englishwoman', and how 'the language he uses to describe these women [female British crime writers] betrays an extremely

judgmental and outdated binary view of gender' (Morrey 2020: 198). With regard to the younger character, Julie (Ludivine Sagnier), she 'is constantly presented as a figure to be looked at' (199) and the object of male gaze. The argument that Ozon blurs fantasy and reality 'becomes a weak excuse for exploitative gendered representation' (202). Finally, Morrey shares an interview with Sagnier about Ozon's intense and domineering filmmaking and writes that 'she has learned that this is not the only type of professional relationship possible on set and is more inclined to favour egalitarian working relationships' (202) Schilt also recounts Ozon's interest in filmmaking 'that directors, unlike actors, were the ones with the "true power"' (Schilt 2011: 11). In these respects, Ozon's approach leaves much to be desired for advocates of equality/equity and the breaking down of hierarchies and systems of domination.
2. Although HIV/AIDS is not the focus of the film, it echoes current French productions such as Robin Campillo's *120 Battements par minute / Beats Per Minute* or Christophe Honoré's play, *Les idoles/Idols* that have shed new light on the 1980s health crisis and lasting trauma.
3. In this regard, Morrey writes: 'Critics noted that *Swimming Pool*'s narrative . . . combines the "noble" references (Hitchcock, Buñuel, Chabrol) with "popular" ones' (Morrey 2020: 194).
4. *Ricky* represents an interesting film within Ozon's work and French cinema overall insofar as it exhibits qualities of the horror genre, as Jason Hartford proposes. In doing so, he argues that the film 'poses problems . . . both for critical consensus and, beyond that, for conceptions of genre that do not account for affect and cognition' (Hartford 2016: 32).
5. Soon after the release of the film, Levilson C. Reis published a piece on this film, which informs Reeser's analysis. See Reis (2020).

WORKS CITED

Ahmadi, Irène (2020), 'Macron juge le "monde universitaire coupable"', *Les Inrockuptibles*, 11 November, <https://www.lesinrocks.com/2020/06/11/actualite/societe/macron-juge-le-monde-universitaire-coupable-davoir-casse-la-republique-en-deux> (last accessed 20 October 2020).
Amin, Kadji (2017), *Disturbing Attachments: Genet, Modern Pederasty, and Queer History*, Durham, NC and London: Duke University Press.
Asibong, Andrew (2008), *François Ozon*, Manchester: Manchester University Press.
Debruge, Peter (2020), 'François Ozon's "Summer of 85": Film Review', *Variety*, 14 July, <https://variety.com/2020/film/reviews/summer-of-85-review-ete-85-1234706311> (last accessed 20 October 2020).
Downing, Lisa (2019), *Selfish Women*, Oxford: Routledge.
France Inter (2020), '"Été 85" de François Ozon: un des grands films estivaux', *France Inter*, 27 July, <https://www.franceinter.fr/cinema/ete-85-de-francois-ozon-un-des-grands-films-estivaux-a-voir-d-apres-le-masque-la-plume> (last accessed 20 October 2020).
Hammond, Nick (2020), 'Summer Love', *Paris Update*, 22 July, <https://www.parisupdate.com/ete-85> (last accessed 20 October 2020).
Handyside, Fiona (2011), 'Queer Filiations: Adaptations in the Films of François Ozon', *Sexualities*, 15: 1, pp. 53–67.
Handyside, Fiona (2012), 'The Possibilities of a Beach: Queerness and François Ozon's Beaches', *Screen*, 53: 1, pp. 54–71.
Handyside, Fiona (2013), 'Ghosts on the Sand: François Ozon's Haunted Beaches', *Continuum: Journal of Media & Cultural Studies*, 27: 5, pp. 663–75.

Hartford, Jason (2016), 'Angel Wings, Chicken Wings, and the Boundaries of Horror: A Cognitive Analytical Reading of *Ricky* (François Ozon, 2009)', *Studies in French Cinema*, 16: 1, pp. 32–47.

Ince, Kate (2008), 'François Ozon's Cinema of Desire', in Kate Ince (ed.), *Five Directors: Auteurism from Assayas to Ozon*, Manchester: Manchester University Press, pp. 112–34.

Morrey, Douglas (2020), *The Legacy of the New Wave in French Cinema*, New York and London: Bloomsbury.

Perrier, Amélie (2020), 'François Ozon: "les gens sont contents de retourner dans les salles"', *France Inter*, 10 July, <https://www.franceinter.fr/emissions/l-invite-de-7h50/l-invite-de-7h50-10-juillet-2020> (last accessed 20 October 2020).

Pétreault, Clément (2020), 'Pourquoi la France est encore plus à droite', *Le Point*, 23 July, <https://www.lepoint.fr/politique/pourquoi-la-france-est-encore-plus-a-droite-22-07-2020-2385183_20.php> (last accessed 20 October 2020).

Rees-Roberts, Nick ([2008] 2014), *French Queer Cinema*, Edinburgh: Edinburgh University Press.

Reis, Levilson C. (2020), 'Goodbye, "Temporary" Transvestites – Hello, New Girlfriend! Ozon's Transgenre and Transgender Crossovers in *Une nouvelle amie* (2014)', *French Screen Studies*, 20: 1, pp. 42–66.

Schilt, Thibaut (2011), *François Ozon*, Urbana, IL: University of Illinois Press.

Stanley, Alice (2009), 'Representations of Sexuality in the Films of François Ozon', PhD thesis, University of Warwick, <http://go.warwick.ac.uk/wrap/3195> (last accessed 20 October 2020).

Wilson, Emma (2006), 'Time to Leave (Le Temps qui reste)', *Film Quarterly*, 60: 2, pp. 18–24.

PART I

The Politics of Form

CHAPTER 1

Queer Tyranny and Intertextuality in *Gouttes d'eau sur pierres brûlantes*: François Ozon Pays Homage to Master Fassbinder

Amy Bertram

Handsome and domineering in François Ozon's third feature film *Gouttes d'eau sur pierres brûlantes / Water Drops on Burning Rocks* (2000; hereafter, *Water Drops*), Léopold Bluhm (Bernard Girardeau) epitomises the simultaneous sexual allure and endless tyranny of his namesake from Rainer Werner Fassbinder's early play, *Tropfen auf heiße Steine: Eine Komödie mit pseudotragischem Ende / Drops on Hot Stones: A Comedy with a Pseudo-tragic Ending*. Fassbinder never published his first play, written in 1965–6 when he was nineteen (Fassbinder 1999: 121). Neither did he adapt it to the screen, considering it too immature and autobiographical (Asibong 2008: 64; Schilt 2011: 116). Yet, this first theatrical text already incarnates many of the themes to which Fassbinder would return throughout his theatre and film career: (hetero/homo/bi)-sexual seduction, cruelty and/or betrayal by sadistic men or women, sexual and social dysfunction, and suicide. Ozon adapts the obscure German play to create a masterpiece, adding uniquely cinematic touches and making a few key changes that further queer the already transgressive story. Ozon evokes the troubled and tyrannical characters and pays homage to Fassbinder elsewhere, but *Water Drops* is at once a tribute to, and an intertextual engagement with, not only this early Fassbinder play but also certain late-career films, most notably *Faustrecht der Freiheit / Fox and His Friends* (1975; hereafter, *Fox*) and *In einem Jahr mit 13 Monden / In a Year with 13 Moons* (1978; hereafter, *13 Moons*). This chapter seeks to elaborate on the connection to, and influence of, Fassbinder's work on *Water Drops* while also tracing the stylistic components that inform the evolution of Ozon's queer cinema.

TABOO, TRANSGRESSION AND EXTREMITIES: CONCEPTUALISING QUEER IN THE 1990S

B. Ruby Rich coined the term 'New Queer Cinema' (NQC) in 1992, inaugurating a new era of film criticism focusing on queer content. She recognised that these films were not uniform and did not 'share a single aesthetic vocabulary or strategy or concern', but rather that they 'are nonetheless united by a common style. Call it "Homo Porno": there are traces in all of them of appropriation and pastiche, irony, as well as a reworking of history with social constructionism very much in mind' (Rich 2004: 16). Reformulating Laura Mulvey's 1975 postulation of scopophilia and the male gaze as primary spectator (pleasure receiver) on the female as object on screen (pleasure provider), queer cinema recognises a multiplicity of subjects and objects of visual pleasure (Mulvey 2009: 15). NQC not only showcases a wide variety of sexual identifications, but also inherently entails fluidity and resistance to or rewriting of what is considered to be normal, 'untethered from "conventional" codes of behaviour' (Aaron 2004: 5). Queer identity is a distinctly anglophone term and has been appropriated for use in French film criticism in its English form. NQC was identified by Rich to include almost exclusively American filmmakers, including Tom Kalin, Gregg Araki, Todd Haynes, Sadie Benning and Jennie Livingston (Rich 2005: 15–16). Shortly thereafter, French film scholars, such as Martine Beugnet and Nick Rees-Roberts, describe a tendency towards the inclusion of extremely subversive and sexually transgressive content in contemporary French Queer Cinema from the late 1990s and early 2000s, including in films by Ozon, Bruno Dumont, Catherine Breillat, Gaspar Noé, Virginie Despentes and others (Beugnet 2007: 14–15; Rees-Roberts 2008: 2–10). Fassbinder's films challenged the norms of his day and have been claimed as queer by twenty-first-century scholars. Michele Aaron builds on Rich to indicate that having a 'new' means having an 'old' and determines that 'Old Queer Cinema' includes Fassbinder, Jean Genet, Andy Warhol and John Sayles (Aaron 2004: 5). Davide Oberto analyses Fassbinder's cinema as queer in a distinctly contemporary sense, focusing particularly on *Fox and His Friends* (1975) and *Querelle* (1982).[1] He concludes his study with a clear explanation of this queerness:

> ... dans le sens de déviant et extrême. Comme ses personnages, ses œuvres aussi cherchent à créer des identités nouvelles, des identités 'filmiques'. Fassbinder a toujours aimé, et a presque toujours réalisé, des films de *genre*: le film noir américain, le mélodrame; cependant, dans son cinéma, le *genre* devient fluide et radical, il n'est pas la répétition de canons fixés, il est absolument contemporain aux histoires, aux tentatives de dépassement et à la recherche d'une identité (d'un *genre*) de Querelle, Fox, Elvira, *tous les autres et toutes les autres*. (Oberto 2005: 153, emphasis in original)[2]

The German filmmaker's subversive and transgressive subjects in Ozon's hands become queer in the sense of NQC due to the further amplified fluidity of sexuality and gender, as well as performative qualities of the stylised melodrama, high-colour saturation, and perfectly choreographed, campy dance sequence.

Ozon's films have always contained a queer aesthetic, but contrary to the brutal violence or extreme sex acts contained in some other Ozon films and in many films by NQC filmmakers, *Water Drops* does not contain gore or overly transgressive sex scenes. Ozon featured homosexual characters prior to *Water Drops*, but not normalised as they are here. His early shorts, such as *Victor* (1993), *Une Robe d'été / A Summer Dress* (1996) and *Regarde la mer / See the Sea* (1997), plus his first two features, *Sitcom* (1998) and *Les Amants criminels / Criminal Lovers* (1999), showcase taboos and overtly subversive, even mortally transgressive, subjects and themes. For example, in his first feature, *Sitcom* (1989), gayness is excessive, while in *See the Sea*, a queer character turns murderous. Other more recent Ozon films have distinctly queer locations that punctuate the narrative, such as the hardcore S&M dungeon scene in *Le Temps qui reste / Time to Leave*, in 2005.

FASSBINDER'S WORKS TURN QUEERER STILL WITH OZON

Scholars and critics have mentioned some relationship of *Water Drops* the film to the original play, though Evelyne Szaryk's *Cinematic Queerness* provides perhaps the most comprehensive exploration of the connections between Fassbinder's work and *Water Drops*. She importantly signals the predilection for emotive close-ups of faces as Deleuzian affection-images, creating intimate spaces based on the body and making the need for dialogue 'superflus' ('superfluous'; Szaryk 2008: 230). I build on her study of this Ozon film by further considering deviations from, and additions to, Fassbinder's play, as well as specific influences from Fassbinder's filmmaking that exceed her analysis, as well as further investigating the use of close-ups and their affective impact. Deleuze cites work by masters of the close-up, including Dreyer and Bresson, to determine that the 'close-up makes the face the pure building material of the affect' (Deleuze 2006: 103). Though the action and dialogue follow closely what is in the play, Ozon takes advantage of uniquely cinematic elements of the camera and the sound design to increase the affective qualities of the narrative and create fleeting emotive moments. Using frequent tight framing, camera techniques that include an often slowly moving, even hovering, camera, and well-paced, creative editing, Ozon, his camerawoman Jeanne Lapoirie, and editors Laurence Bawedin and Claudine Bouché maintain precise control over what and how the spectator sees. The insistent close framing in *Water Drops* creates affection-images that punctuate the entire film, and the most important ones will be discussed below. More than the other characters, Franz is frequently the subject of these tightly framed shots. A range of emotions on his face communicate his uncertainty, euphoria, or angst clearly and poignantly as immensely affective moments that exceed the dialogue. Deleuze explains multiple ways these spaces arise, with one being 'shadows, whites and colours which are capable of producing and constituting any-space-whatevers, *deconnected or emptied spaces*' (Deleuze 2006: 120, emphasis in original). Franz is sometimes shown in such tightly framed shots that the surrounding no longer matters, only the emotion on his face, as he floats in detached close-ups that are suspended in Deleuzian any-space-whatevers.

Water Drops presents a beautifully wrapped cinematic package of queer identities and psychological abuse. The structure in four acts, the use of the original four characters, the German single interior setting and most of the dialogue derive directly from Fassbinder's play. The characters, Léopold Bluhm, Franz Meister, Anna Wolff and Véra (no last name given in the play), have the same names in the film as in the play, all without surnames except for Léopold Bluhm. In Act I, Léopold seduces Franz (Malik Zidi). Most of this act proceeds almost verbatim from the exchanges in the play, other than being translated into French, though cinematic elements augment the sexual tension in the film. One major change is having Léopold be fifty rather than thirty-five, as he is in the play, a choice determined by the casting of Bernard Giraudeau (Schilt 2011: 127). In Act II, six months has passed, their relationship has evolved and devolved, and Léopold's cruel dominion is laid bare. By the third act, the two men function well only on the sexual plane, as evidenced with the provocative opening sex scene, a tightly framed cinematic and homoerotic addition to the play. This act is the only one in the play with two scenes, signified in the film with a cut to black. After this moment of mutual enjoyment until Léopold leaves on business mid-act, the two men clash just as they do in the play, driven by Léopold's dissatisfaction and disdain, and Franz's increasingly sardonic and despondent reactions. In Act III Scene 2 of the film, Franz reunites with former fiancée Anna (Ludivine Saignier) when she comes to visit during Léopold's absence. She appears as she does in the play, as an innocent, though sexually curious, young woman hoping to reunite with her former lover, whom she professes to still love. Though Véra (Anna Thomson), Léopold's former lover, derives from the corresponding character in the written work, she is no longer a cisgender woman (though played by one), but a transgender woman instead. In the play, Véra speaks more with, and is much harsher to, Léopold, from stating her desire to have children with him when they were together to outright condemning him for his cruel and unfaithful behaviour. She appears in the final act of the play with Léopold, at his bequest and begrudgingly, not of her own volition. In the film, Véra more closely resembles a later Fassbinder character: long-suffering, transgender Elvira (Volker Spengler, a cisgender man) from *13 Moons*.³ Unlike in the play, Véra appears at the apartment door twice, in Acts II and III, before arriving alone in Act IV, when all four characters are together for the first time (both texts).

Many scenes in *Water Drops* reference particular framing choices, camera movement, settings, costumes and acting styles in Fassbinder's films, especially *Fox* and *13 Moons*. The title character in *Fox*, Franz Bieberkof (nicknamed Fox and played by Fassbinder himself; hereafter called Fox) appears to be a slightly older version of Franz Meister from Fassbinder's first play, who is no longer naïve, but comfortable as a homosexual man. Bright wardrobe colours, especially Fox's satin turquoise button-down shirt and the style of suits worn by many of the upper-class men, seem to directly influence Ozon's choices for Franz and Léopold's costumes in *Water Drops*. The lilting accordion music heard as *Fox* opens, while the camera pans the crowd at the street fair, corresponds with the initial upbeat music that plays in the first few moments of *Water Drops* as a series of eight colourful 1970s postcard-like images of an unnamed German city appear on screen featuring the film credits. One notable replication of a shot from *Fox* arrives early in the first act of *Water Drops*, as Léopold asks if Franz wants to play a game. From a close-up on Léopold's face, he stands to give a close-up of his crotch.

Instead of cutting or camera movement, Léopold's physical shift changes the content of the frame. Szaryk notes the queer significance of the close-up crotch shot that pairs with Léopold's provocative question to Franz, 'Vous voulez jouer à un jeu? ('Do you want to play a game?'), which also composes part of her article's title. However, though she repeatedly insists on Ozon's connections to Fassbinder's cinema, she surprisingly does not suggest a direct relationship here (Szaryk 2008: 229 and 231). This type of shot is used in *Fox* during a sequence at Eugen Thiess's (Peter Chatel's) flat shortly after he and Fox meet. Snooty, opportunistic and usurping Eugen hosts a gathering of like-minded bourgeois elitists who show disdain for Fox until learning of his recent lottery windfall. As Eugen looks across the room, a cut to Fox's pelvis framed in close-up signals his sexual desire for Fox. The corporeal close-up is not on a face, but the crotch, making this tight shot in both films a sensual affection-image symbolising lust and exploitative intent. Deleuze recognises that most affection-images derive from close-ups on faces, but recognises that other body parts, or even objects, can also carry an expressive impact. He indicates that, '[a]lthough the close-up extracts the face (or its equivalent) from all spatio-temporal co-ordinates, it can carry with it its own space-time' (Deleuze 2006: 108). In this sexually tense scene in *Water Drops*, the close-up on the crotch becomes a metonymic moment at once signifying lust, foreshadowing the sexual encounter at the end of the act, and also visually situating the exact locus on the body of this desire. Ozon incorporates close-ups of faces and provocatively framed body parts throughout the film.

Arguably the greatest connection to *Fox* lies in the sheer normalcy of the homosexual relationships portrayed in *Water Drops*. Fassbinder's observations in an interview at Cannes in 1975 about *Fox* are equally pertinent for *Water Drops*:

> It is certainly the first film in which the characters are homosexuals, without homosexuality being made into a problem. In films, plays or novels, if homosexuals appear, then homosexuality was the problem, or it was a comic turn. But here homosexuality is shown as completely normal, and the problem is something quite different, it's a love story, where one person exploits the love of the other person, and that's really the story I always tell. (Braad Thomsen 2004: 180)

Being homosexual is accepted as normal, with gay-friendly settings, and, elsewhere in society, homosexuality seems to be socially accepted as well. *Water Drops* has a heteronormative setting with the apartment in the suburbs, far from gay night life, though homosexuality appears to fit with the realm of the conventional here, too. While dysfunctional, the relationship that Léopold and Franz share for the first two-thirds of the film is like that of many heterosexual couples: one partner works, one keeps the house and both live a conjugal life together under one roof. However, as with Fassbinder's declaration about his routine engagement with the theme of exploitative love, Léopold is manipulative and verbally abusive of young Franz, as written in the play and again in Ozon's film, though seductive and kind often enough to maintain the relationship.

Unlike the stylistic similarities in costume and production design between *Fox* and *Water Drops*, *13 Moons* differs in look and feel. Colours are generally drab, settings are often sombre and cluttered, and the narrative progression is jarring and confusing. Fassbinder's insistent and continual Brechtian distanciation intentionally prevents any sympathising with characters and evokes instead feelings of despair, disgust and melancholy. One strategy Fassbinder uses to distance the spectator in *13 Moons* is to incorporate a series of very long takes with overlapping lengthy monologues by characters not necessarily speaking within the frame and in strange settings. Elvira serves as much more than just inspiration for a transgender character. Franz and Véra are both informed by Elvira, especially her submissive demeanour with her boyfriend, Christoph Hacker (Karl Scheydt), and her obsession with Anton Saitz (Gottfried John). Christoph is cruel and overbearing. He only appears in the second scene of *13 Moons* and is never seen again after he abandons Elvira and drives away. Anton is an unrequited love crush whom Elvira has not seen in years and who inspired her to have a sex change, and, ultimately, commit suicide after finding him kissing her friend, Zora (Ingrid Caven).

Ozon incorporates one key line verbatim from *13 Moons* that further queers the original play and strengthens the association between Elvira and Véra, as well as links Anton and Léopold. Towards the end of *13 Moons*, Elvira ascends to Anton's office and obtains entry by guessing the password. Deep inside the expansive suite, she finds the eccentric, boyish, yet devious man she had once loved, encircled by his faithful servants/guards. He relates to his cadre of men that Elvira 'cut his dick off in Casablanca' in order to try to please him. In *Water Drops*, Léopold says these exact words to Franz and Anna in Act IV about Véra, who is vulnerable and melancholic like Elvira, and unwavering in her love for Léopold. Early in *13 Moons*, Elvira pathetically tries to placate her lover, Christoph. From their first words to each other, he expresses nothing but hostility towards Elvira, while she acts pitiful and plaintive. He is quickly cruel, dragging her towards the mirror by her hair to mock her for being fat.[4] Elvira is well-dressed, though never fully convincing as a woman, nor comfortable when dressed as a man. Home after a lengthy absence, Christoph decides on the spot to leave Elvira for good, after a seemingly long time together. When Léopold returns from his business trip early in Act II, he is similarly moody and stern with Franz, who does everything to try to please him, including dressing in boyish lederhosen and pampering him, all to no avail. Léopold even suggests they should not continue living together. Franz resembles Elvira in being lonely in both his lover's absence and presence, but his distress is raw due to the relationship being newer. Elvira's suffering and eventual suicide relates to Franz and his future if he were to stay with Léopold, leading him ultimately to choose death by poison, the same choice made by Elvira.

OZON'S ORIGINALITY EMERGES ACROSS TEXTUAL CHANGES AND AFFECTIVE CLOSE-UPS

Though certain aspects of the framing and composition seem to have been inspired by *Fox* and *13 Moons* as discussed above, most of the cinematographic and editing choices in *Water Drops* have a distinctly Ozonian touch. His characters speak to each other within the frame in well-paced dialogue inside an attractive space that visually entices spectators. After the opening colourful postcards, the lights come up inside the stylish apartment, with its 1970s chic mod decor and the two handsome, well-dressed men. The exquisite design by Pascaline Chavanne, combined with the increasingly tightly framed cinematography within the *huis clos* setting, enclose, contain and trap the characters, and, for a time, also the spectators. What is often lugubrious, torturous and oppressive in Fassbinder's works is, in this Ozon film – at least initially and periodically – beautifully tense. Ozon's stylised and colourful production design adds to a greater sense of melodrama, while also increasing a sense of distanciation. Fiona Handyside explains the lineage and relationship of Douglas Sirk to Fassbinder to Ozon with regard to setting up a dialectical exchange for the spectator within especially doubly framed shots (for example, by a doorway or window, as well as by the camera). She explores the complexity of such shots, noting that this use of space is:

> a classic Sirkian technique also exploited by Fassbinder. Here the image doubly distances the spectator: they are distanced as they would be in the Fassbinder original but here the very reference to Fassbinder (and arguably his self-conscious use of Sirk) holds the scene at one further remove. (Handyside 2007: 211)

This type of double distanciation also leads to sites of affection-images when the doubled (or even tripled) frame encloses an emotive facial close-up. The remainder of this chapter will consider Ozon's cinematic style across *Water Drops*, its relationship to the play, and the visual impact of the multiplicity of close-ups as affection-images, as well as of shots with extra internal framing via doors, windows, and mirrors.

In the theatrical text, Fassbinder conveys multiple auditory indications, from the omnipresent record player used in most acts, to times when Franz sings. Ozon maintains a strong sense of musicality as part of the diegetic and extradiegetic fabric of the film, though he changes most of the songs. Herbie Mann's jazzy 'Summertime' in Act I of the play is traded for Gustav Mahler's Symphony No. 4 in the film as part of the sophisticated atmosphere of seduction Léopold sets for Franz as he fixes them each a drink after entering the apartment. Sometimes the already close camera subtly moves even nearer to its subject(s) while music plays. Several times in the play, either Léopold or Franz puts Handel's 'Hallelujah' on the turntable. Ozon drops Handel and instead includes Giuseppe Verdi's 'Requiem Dies Irae' to augment tensions between Léopold and Franz. He also makes two other major additions of songs. The first is Françoise Hardy's haunting and evocative 'Traüme', which plays in Act III as Franz comes to terms with the idea of leaving Léopold. This song has a reprisal at the end of the film as Véra holds her hands against the windows she is unable to open. The other is Tony Holiday's 'Tanze Samba Mit Mir', the catchy, sexy number to which the four dance in Act IV. Besides music, Franz recites poetry in the film, though he does not sing at all, whereas he sings several times in the play. The song lyrics and poem remain in untranslated German in the film, just as the German songs and poems remain in the original language in the French translation of the play. Additionally, each of the first three acts ends in the bedroom with either Léopold or Franz in a trench coat, acting out the childhood dream fantasy Franz describes to Léopold during the initial seduction in the first act. First Franz, then Léopold, then Anna lies naked on the bed at the end of the first three acts, respectively, waiting for their lover, as music box-like notes play. The scenes cut from a wide shot of each lover on the bed to a low-angle tight shot that tilts from feet to head (or the inverse) of Léopold, then later Franz, twice. In the play, each of these three acts ends with the insinuation that sex is about to take place through verbal cues, but no one takes off their clothes, wears a trench coat or lies in wait on a bed, and no music is indicated. These hyper-performative, melodramatic act-ending additions in the film contribute to a campiness that briefly interrupts the increasing tension and melancholy with light-hearted moments of playful sexual anticipation and incongruous childlike musical notes.

In Act I, Léopold is suave, alluring and attentive. Still, subtle verbal cues and facial expressions reveal that he is likely stern, demanding and hard to please, such as when he says he 'gets so little pleasure' out of life, first in Act I, then again in Act II. By contrast, Franz is young, innocent, inexperienced and intrigued. The two enter through the glass-paned door to Léopold's apartment and go to the adjacent black stone-walled living room. Léopold plays host to his new prey, pouring drinks, playing Mahler on the turntable, and sitting on the couch beside Franz to talk and eventually ask his seductive question, as discussed earlier, matched with the provocatively framed crotch close-up. Once Franz loses a match of ludo, the board game they play after Léopold's literal (though laden with seduction) question, the two men move to the next, mainly empty room and stand in front of the windows. The camera gets closer to each man as the sexual tension builds, until Léopold begins to circle Franz. The camera moves in the opposite direction from Léopold, with both circling Franz. This movement is juxtaposed with the stillness of the figures in the next sequence as Léopold elicits Franz's sexual history at boarding school and then relates some of his own homosexual encounters. The men face two different windows and remain immobile while they talk. The camera frames them first from behind, then moves to the exterior of the apartment building for the first of only five such occurrences during the film. From outside, the camera slowly approaches the windows from a slightly low angle. While the camera only moves to medium shots, not close-ups, their emotive faces still create affection-images. A close-up on Léopold reveals his sexual intention as he asks the even more provocative question of whether Franz has ever considered sleeping with a man for real. The act wraps quickly after these confessional moments with the wordless, campy act-ender described above. The older man directs Franz to take off his clothes and lie on the bed, where the young man lies face up, hands covering his genitals. As the camera pans up Léopold's body in the trench coat, the low-angle close-up on his face indicates both his desire and his control. A quick close-up on Franz's face shows his gleeful anticipation.

Léopold's true nature emerges slowly at first, almost as imperceptible to his latest victim, Franz, as to the unsuspecting spectator. But by the end of the first act, this well-dressed gentleman has seduced and is about to sodomise his heretofore (mainly) heterosexual young prey. After luring the spectator in, much as Léopold ensnares Franz, who, as in the play, quickly succumbs to the older man, the remaining three acts function more to push the spectator further away in an Ozonian engagement with distanciation. The tinkling music ends the scene and the act with what turns out to be a false sense of playfulness and fun. The following act will not be sex-filled and lascivious, but instead will expose Léopold for the cold manipulator that he is, laying bare his increasingly cruel treatment of, and detachment from, Franz.

Six months later, Act II opens with a close-up of Franz alone soaking in the bathtub. He solemnly recites the poem 'Die Lorelei' by Heinrich Heine in German, though the poem is not identified, nor are the words translated. The poetic interlude occurs in the play, but the location of delivery changes from the living room to the bathroom in the film. That Franz quotes this particular poem adds a dimension of understanding that he has been lured in and trapped by a siren's song. Though solemn, Franz appears relaxed and content, if pensive. He seems to enjoy soaking in the tub, eventually smoking a cigarette. Malik Zidi/Franz's red hair and pale skin contrast beautifully with the baby blue tub surrounded by shiny black tiles. The beginning of this act has been described as the feminisation of Franz (Schilt 2008: 117; Szaryk 2011: 232). Franz calmly progresses through his rather feminine-style grooming routine in preparation for his lover's eventual return: he bathes, blows his hair dry, cuts his toenails, plucks his eyebrows. The sequence in front of the three-way mirror is the first of several occasions when Franz faces himself in triplicate, creating a reflective, multiply framed, affective space. He is the only character to spend time alone in the apartment, and his time in the bathroom, particularly the closest shots, provide key moments of complex affection-images (Figure 1.1). The triple mirror multiplies the frames around the three images of Franz and the impact of his emotive face. He eventually dresses in surprisingly youthful green lederhosen that resemble the traditional garb of a schoolboy. For the rest of the film, he eschews black, his former favourite colour to wear, and dons a variety of vividly coloured items, usually a long-sleeved red or green shirt paired with briefs only, no trousers.

Once Léopold returns from his business trip, the tone immediately shifts. He is surly and implacable from his first words. Though Franz waits on him like a doting housewife, even wearing a feminine apron in the kitchen, Léopold does nothing but criticise and provoke Franz into reciprocating with sarcasm and defensiveness. Here is the first glimpse for the spectator of Léopold's cruelty and an indicator to Franz of how life will be living with this older man. Eventually, Franz breaks down crying and Léopold consoles him, leading him to assert that their sex life was still good, to which Franz agrees. They do go to the bedroom, but not for sex. Instead, Léopold becomes vulnerable for once and confesses that he killed someone. He is actually feeling guilt for the death

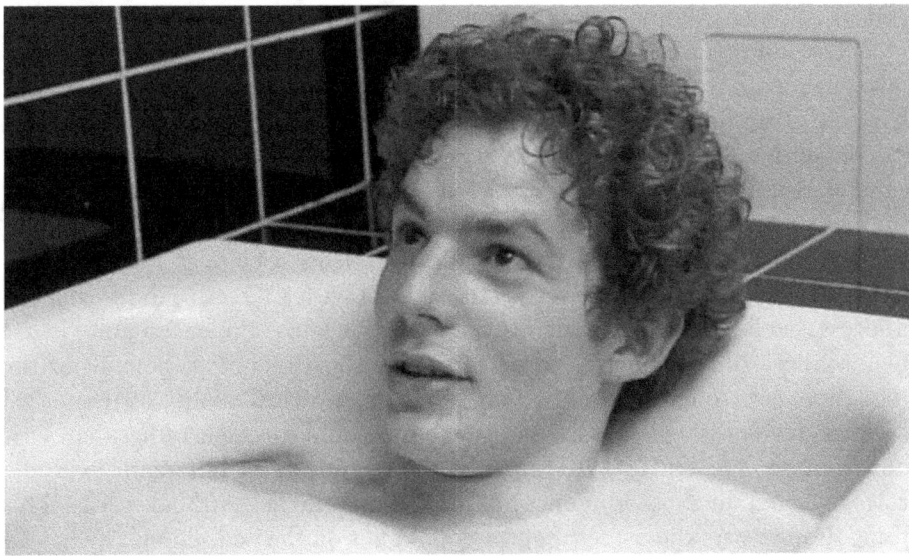

Figure 1.1 Bath close-up

Figure 1.2 Léopold and Franz on the bed

(by suicide) of one of his clients whom he swindled. The cinematography of this scene provides another affective sequence, most notably the overhead long take of a medium to medium close-up shot of Léopold and Franz lying on opposite sides of the bed with their heads meeting in the middle (Figure 1.2). The relatively tight framing captures their heads and torsos on the orange bedspread, and eventually tightens further so that their heads fill the screen in a close-up of Franz's head visually framed on top of Léopold's, forming a disconnected any-space-whatever. Never one to linger in an emotional state, Léopold abruptly sits up, and the honest moment ends. The camera returns to its conventional position facing the action. This type of overhead shot is replicated in Act III with Franz and Anna lying in bed side-by-side, then again near the end of Act IV as Franz lies dying on the floor.

The dialogue before the bedroom scene reflects what is in the play: first Léopold then Franz, respectively, ends each act with a directive to the other to undress and lie on the bed. What happens next is left to the imagination in the play, while Ozon includes these performative short scenes at the ends of the first three acts to emphasise the non-realistic, theatrical quality of the narrative, serving to distance the spectator with camp and spectacle rather than serious emotion. The end of Act II again shifts the tone to melodramatic, with the roles reversed, in another moment of pure visual cinema, without words. This time, Franz wears the overcoat and Léopold lies on the bed, though he lies on his stomach and looks over his shoulder at Franz. The camera pans, from the perspective at a lower angle of Léopold in wide shot looking up from the bed, to a close-up moving from Franz's bare ankles, up the coat, to frame his head as he smiles at Léopold. Tinkling music plays again as it did at the end of Act I, indicating anew a sense of absurd frivolity mixed with sexual foreplay. The anticipation of seeing the two actually having sex is fulfilled as Act III opens with a close-up of them in the final throes of orgasm. Though they are framed from their shoulders up, their heavy breathing and moans leave no doubt as to what is happening. Though nowhere as transgressive or taboo-breaking as many sex scenes in films from NQC, the scene is nonetheless fairly provocative as it intimately shows gay sex on screen in an aurally graphic way that allows the mind to easily fill in what is missing from the tightly framed shots. This *in medias res* visualisation of their iterations that their sex life is still good even if they do not get along well otherwise is another queer cinematic addition to what is in the play. Not only is it an extended take with no dialogue, but the shot is also a sexualised affection-image that conveys their pleasure but maintains a certain distance in its closeness, meaning that the setting becomes an any-space-whatever oozing carnal desire and fulfilment.

In Act III Scene 1, Franz reads a book and Léopold joins him after waking up later than he planned, provoking him to become quickly dour and hostile with Franz. In both the play and the film, Léopold is demanding and domineering, while Franz attends to him subserviently. In the film, the domestic discord resumes after the explicit sexual interlude that opens the act. Franz then spends time alone as he does at the beginning of this act in the play. But in the film, he also listens to the radio and answers the door when Véra rings. Franz mistakes her for one of Léopold's clients, and she insists on not leaving a message. Her dismay at Franz's presence in his red shirt and skimpy briefs shows on her face. Once Léopold awakens, he is grumpy, though Franz coddles him and runs him a bath. Franz plays Verdi on the turntable, interrupting Léopold's peace. He drips his way from the bath to where Franz, completely absorbed in the music, air conducts euphorically. Léopold's harsh admonitions end Franz's actions and enjoyment, leaving him standing alone, dejection written across his face.

Before Léopold leaves on another business trip, the two proceed much as they do throughout Act III Scene 1 in the play, with rancour, irony and friction. In both texts, Franz has written a poem for Léopold, but the callous older man is too busy trying to find a bill to pay and ignores his lover's artistic expression of love. In the film, Franz reads a book, smokes, and sits still in a chair while Léopold moves about in search of the elusive paperwork and grumbles accusatorily at Franz. The framing remains in mainly medium-long to long shots, denying the closeness of the camera that we saw in the opening of the act and symbolising the growing distance between these men. At one point, Franz is framed in medium close-up, through the closed door to Léopold's office, with textured windowpanes, at a double distance from his lover and the spectator. Even domesticated Franz cannot bear Léopold's incessant tyranny of displeasure and blame without starting to take an ironic tone, to talk back, and eventually to pack a bag, though he does not leave. In one of the single most poignant moments of the film, Franz sits with tears in his eyes, heard in voiceover saying the words that serve as a prescript in the play, a quotation by Franz Pörner: 'one day, there was something on which they could not agree, a small thing, insignificant, a divergence, but from that day on, there was no more us, nothing more in common, only divergences' (Fassbinder 2016: 10). These words end on a medium close-up of him crying, as the camera moves in to almost a close-up on his face filled with solemn despair (Figure 1.3). This shot is the single greatest affection-image of the film, occurring at the only time when the image is detached from the voice via voiceover, which acts as a visual and aural divergence that emphasises the meaning of the quotation.

In the play and the film, in the last part of Scene 1, while Léopold works in his office after they momentarily suspend their feud, the phone rings for Franz: Anna is on the line. She wants to see Franz in person. After Léopold leaves, Franz eats alone, does the dishes, vacuums, then sits in Léopold's office chair and spins, bored. In the film only, he opens the desk drawer, finds a gun, and mimics shooting himself in the head. A clever cut from him pulling the trigger to him flinging himself on the bed indicates that he was only pretending. He goes to the window as it rains outside, and the camera returns briefly to the exterior, framing him in medium close-up through the rain-soaked windowpane. Then, Anna arrives to find Franz sitting alone in the dark, crying, just as at the beginning of this scene in the play. Her girlish outfit resembles

Figure 1.3 Franz crying

Franz's earlier lederhosen, though she is not really childlike. They catch up a bit, moving from sitting on the floor to standing in front of the windows. The camera moves to the exterior again, mimicking the framing from the first act with Franz and Léopold. Here, Franz stands where Léopold did. This section again follows the play closely in terms of dialogue and action, with a third scene in the bedroom in the film only. Franz emulates Léopold in terms of harsh talk mixed with seduction that ends with him again wearing the trench coat, but with Anna lying naked on the bed in clear contented anticipation of resuming sexual relations with her former fiancé. This time, the camera pans from Franz, smiling in close-up, down to his bare feet as the music box notes play for the last time.

Act IV opens provocatively, though less so than Act III, with the naked Anna opening the bedroom curtains. For the rest of the film, she will be scantily clad, revealing her voluptuous body, which is all woman, not at all a child, from fully naked, to wearing Léopold's robe, to a blue bra and panty set. After they spend time dreaming about married life and the children they could have, much of the rest of this final act evokes Franz's sadness at the possibility of ending his relationship with Léopold. He wants to linger in the bedroom alone and asks Anna to put on a record. As 'Traüme' plays, an exquisite affection-image occurs when the camera sways back and forth in an overhead close-up of Franz, lying on the bed with tears in his eyes. The image becomes fully affective and detached from the rest of the scene, with Franz floating in an emotive any-space-whatever. To the non-German speaker, the meaning of the song remains solely the affective impact. However, 'Traüme' means 'dreams', and this dialogue-less sequence conveys Franz's dreamy contemplation of the decided-upon end of his relationship with Léopold, whom he still very much loves and is reluctant to leave without saying goodbye. He closes his eyes, and for the only time in the film, a cut to white, instead of black, occurs. A medium shot of Anna reveals her to also be pensive, standing by the shelves of records and turntable in the living room.

Léopold does not reveal the true gender of his former lover to Franz until Act IV when Véra finally enters the apartment (in the film). Her appearance at the door to Léopold's apartment twice, before we see her for a third time knocking at the door in Act IV, and the fact that she arrives alone and of her own volition, underscores her unwavering devotion to her former lover in a similar way as does Elvira's absurd quest to find and unite with Anton Saitz in *13 Moons*. In the play, Véra arrives only in the final act and with Léopold, who has apparently sought her out after thinking that Franz has probably left him to be with Anna, as indicated with one quick exchange between them:

> Léopold: Tu vois, Véra, c'est ici que je vis. (You see Véra, this is where I live.)
> Véra: Mais pas seul. (But not alone.)
> Léopold: Tu as entendu, non? Il veut déménager. Ensuite nous serons tout seul ici. (You heard, didn't you? He wants to move. Then we will be here all alone.)
> Véra: Vraiment? (Really?)
> Léopold: Je pensais qu'il était déjà parti. (I thought he was already gone.)
> (Fassbinder 2016: 74)[5]

In the film, Léopold delights in the novelty of having his former and current lovers, as well as Anna, all together in Act IV, at no point saying that he thought Franz would be gone. After having encountered first Franz, then Anna, when she rings the bell in the second and third acts in the film, Véra has no expectations of finding Léopold alone on her third trip to the apartment.

As Franz packs his suitcase, Léopold returns. Shortly after introductions to Anna, who wears nothing but the bra and panty set, Véra rings the doorbell. Léopold lets her in and bluntly introduces her to the other two with the phrase from *13 Moons*, as the one 'who cut off his dick in Casablanca'. After the four characters are together, Léopold asserts his dominance over everyone and has them doing his domestic bidding. Véra asks to play a record. As the music starts, the first shots are those in close-up of each person's samba-shaking behind. As with the crotch shot in Act I, these four close shots of their rear ends combined with the sensual samba music portend sexual interactions. The four characters perform an impromptu, but refined, sensual, and synchronised dance to the

Figure 1.4 Facing the windows

catchy 'Tanze Samba Mit Mir'. The spontaneous performance serves multiple functions, from uniting the characters in a sensual activity to distancing the spectator who wonders why the sudden visual and tonal shifts occur. The cinematographic push-and-pull of the scene is likely inspired by the chaotic, awkward tribute to a TV movie musical in *13 Moons*. Performed by Anton Saitz and his cronies, as well as a maladroit Elvira, the friends follow Anton and imitate his actions. Awkward and unsure, Elvira attempts in vain to follow along. In the samba sequence in *Water Drops*, the shots remain close, deconstructing the characters' bodies into separate sexy components (torso, shoulders, faces), and only a few times are they shown in a four-shot (Figure 1.4).

The few wide shots allow the spectator to see how fluidly Léopold, Véra and Anna move, contrasting with Franz who continually looks to the others for how and when to do something different. The angst that we see from Franz in the extremely affective overhead view of him alone in bed earlier in Act IV, listening to 'Traüme', appears anew on his face as he struggles to stay in sync with the others. Unlike the broad smile that conveys Anna's pleasure in the unexpected dancing, Franz's face foreshadows his descent into ultimate despair. Franz understands far better than the others that Léopold will never be faithful and that his tyranny is unstoppable, inevitable and unavoidable, except in death.

Though Anna and Véra squeal in delight and run for the bedroom at Léopold's abrupt song-ending order, Franz remains behind. In the play, Léopold tells Franz that he wants to talk with Anna alone in the other room, but really takes her into the bedroom to have sex. Véra leaves to buy beer and returns to Franz alone, shocked to find out where the others are. Franz has already taken the poison. The final act ends with Véra and Franz talking, with him making two phone calls, one to his mother and one to a psychiatric hospital, with him dying, and with Léopold and Anna coming out to see why Véra is screaming. In the film, several aspects of Act IV exceed or change the original text. First, the two men briefly talk to each other alone before Léopold goes to join the others in the bedroom. Upon Franz questioning whether Léopold needs him, the older man states that Franz needs *him*. Franz again spends time alone in the bathroom, and we see another triple-mirror close-up of his face. Distress momentarily turns to delight as he fantasises about going to the bedroom and shooting Léopold in the head. The women scream, framing the dying man, then a cut shows Franz from a low angle, grimace-smiling at his murderous act. Another cut brings him and the spectator back to reality in the bathroom, where he does not end Léopold's life, but rather decides to commit suicide. Before he dies, Franz does call his mother, but does not make another call, as in the play. As he is dying and after he expires, Franz lies on the floor wearing Véra's red fur-fringed jacket. He has never worn women's clothes before this moment. Franz signals his resignation via the feminine coat to being one of Léopold's creatures, but also denies his lover the opportunity to be with him ever again. Véra is scantily clad in only a black camisole and black boots. Instead of an overhead shot, the camera captures Franz and Véra as they talk sitting on the floor, in affective medium close-ups. Their expressive faces communicate their suffering to each other and to the spectator. A last overhead shot of Franz underscores his tragic choice. Véra's tears here, then her inability to open the window at the end, reinforce that the only means of escape is through death. The camera is positioned on the exterior of the building for a final time, framing Véra as she freezes as an actor would do at the end of a play, holding her position as the notes of 'Traüme' return. Shown in a medium close-up, the camera slowly pulls back from the windows, away from her angst-filled face, ending the film with another affective-image boding inescapable trauma. This tragic finish is mitigated by the reprise of the song, whose repetition of the word for dreams, 'Traüme', hints (in German) that this strange tale was possibly only a bad dream.

QUEER ROOTS BEAR QUEER FRUITS

This chapter analyses in more detail than previous studies some Fassbinder source material that is key to understanding *Water Drops* as a complex, evocative film. Ozon's developing cinematic style augments the queerness of the narrative and the visual pleasure, in an NQC-style nod to Laura Mulvey's theory of cinematic scopophilia. The beautiful, high-colour saturation of the production design and costumes, as well as the playfully provocative act-enders and campy dance sequence, provide the spectator with repeated opportunities for queer cinematic pleasures. However, the tragic trajectory of the narrative underscores the dark underbelly of human relationships in general. Without the subtitle that the play has, spelling out that it is a pseudo-tragedy, the film ends with neither resolution nor retribution. Those who are seductive tyrants continue unchecked, while those who are tortured souls succumb to self-destruction, whether by suicide or by staying. Yet, with much of the film being composed of affective close-ups, the spectator is especially drawn into the emotive state of Franz. The extreme proximity of the camera also serves to distance the spectator in an intellectual engagement of detaching from the narrative into Deleuzian any-space-whatevers of pure emotion. While this chapter has moved further in determining the nuances of Fassbinder's influence on Ozon in this film, more analysis of the connections between these two filmmakers is still necessary. The more spectators understand the associations between Ozon films and films such as *Fox* and *13 Moons*, and the more they comprehend the meaning of the poem and songs in German, the richer the experience of watching *Water Drops on Burning Rocks*, particularly for an Anglophone audience.

Ozon often queers literary texts in the creation of his films. Since 2000, he has returned to melodramatic period pieces with high-colour saturation in both the production design and costumes, most notably in his film, *8 femmes / 8 Women* (2002). In this film, he explores women and queers the original play by Robert Thomas to include several lesbian characters. With the eight famous actresses each singing a song and, at some point, dancing along, Ozon reaches a new level of hyper-performativity that engages the spectator repeatedly in the type of distanciation evoked by the surprise singular dance sequence to 'Tanze Samba Mit Mir' in *Water Drops*. In *Été 85 / Summer of 85* (2020), rather than primarily engaging with Fassbinder, Ozon's film about two young gay men on the cusp of the AIDS crisis seems to pay tribute instead to Gregg Araki's *The Living End* (1994) and other early American NQC filmmakers in a more extreme and even queerer take than *Water Drops* on the coming-of-age and coming-out narratives.

NOTES

1. Fassbinder's final film is an adaptation of Jean Genet's 1953 transgressive novel about a homosexual sailor turned assassin.
2. . . . 'in the sense of deviant and extreme. As with his characters, his works also seek to create new identities, "filmic" identities. Fassbinder always liked, and almost always made, *genre* films: film noir, melodrama; however, in his cinema, the *genre* becomes fluid and radical, it is not the repetition of fixed canons, it is absolutely contemporary to the stories,

to the attempts to surpass and to research an identity (a *genre*) of Querelle, Fox, Elvira, and all the others, male and female.'
3. In his book *François Ozon*, Thibaut Schilt analyses *Water Drops* and engages with some differences from the play. He mentions in passing the association between Véra in the film and Elvira in *13 Moons* (Schilt 2011: 127). Andrew Asibong, the author of the other monograph on Ozon, footnotes the reference to Véra, and relates that in the play she is a "real" woman (Asibong 2008: 70). Elvira is occasionally called by her former name, Erwin, in *13 Moons*.
4. In *Water Drops*, Léopold is demeaning by calling Véra old instead of fat.
5. These lines are quoted from the French version of the play, *Gouttes d'eau sur pierres brûlantes / Water Drops on Burning Stones*, translated from German in 2016 by Jörn Cambreleng. To my knowledge, the play has not been translated into English. The translations from French to English are mine. All references to the play are from the French version, though the original German text is referenced for its title and for when Fassbinder wrote it.

WORKS CITED

Aaron, Michele (ed.) (2004), *New Queer Cinema: A Critical Reader*, New Brunswick, NJ: Rutgers University Press.
Asibong, Andrew (2008), *François Ozon*, in French Film Directors series, Manchester and New York: Manchester University Press.
Beugnet, Martine (2000), *Marginalité, sexualité, contrôle dans le cinéma français contemporain*, Condé-sur-Noireau, France: L'Harmattan.
Beugnet, Martine (2007), *Cinema and Sensation*, Edinburgh: Edinburgh University Press.
Braad Thomsen, Christian [1991] (2004), *Fassbinder: The Life and Work of a Provocative Genius*, trans. Martin Chalmers, Minneapolis, MN: University of Minnesota Press.
Deleuze, Gilles [1983] (2006), *The Movement-image*, trans. Hugh Tomlinson and Barbara Habberjam, Minneapolis, MN: University of Minnesota Press.
Genet, Jean [1953] (1974), *Querelle*, trans. Anselm Hollo, New York: Grove Press, Inc.
Fassbinder, Rainer Werner [1985] (2016), *Gouttes d'eau sur pierres brûlantes*, trans. Jörn Cambreleng, Paris: L'Arche.
Fassbinder, Rainer Werner [1985] (1999) *Tropfen auf heiße Steine: Eine Komödie mit pseudotragischem Ende*, Frankfurt am Main, Germany: Verlag der Autoren (Theaterbibliothek).
Fox and His Friends (*Faustrecht der Freiheit*), film, directed by Rainer Werner Fassbinder. USA: Criterion Collection, 1975 (2017).
Handyside, Fiona (2007), 'Melodrama and ethics in François Ozon's *Gouttes d'eau sur pierres brûlantes / Water Drops on Burning Rocks* (2000)', *Studies in French Cinema*, 7: 3, <doi: 10.1386/sfc.7.3.207/1> (last accessed 13 March 2020).
In a Year with 13 Moons, film, directed by Rainer Werner Fassbinder. USA: Fantoma Films, 1978 (2004).
Mulvey, Laura [1975] (2009), 'Visual Pleasure and Narrative Cinema' in L. Mulvey, *Visual and Other Pleasures*, 2nd edition, London: Palgrave Macmillan, pp. 14–27.
Oberto, Davide (2005), 'De Fox à Querelle, le "cinéma queer" de Rainer Werner Fassbinder', in D. Bantcheva (ed.), *Fassbinder l'explosif*, Condé-sur-Noireau: Corlet éditions Diffusion, Département CinémAction, pp. 147–54.
Querelle, film, directed by Rainer Werner Fassbinder. USA: Artificial Eye, 1982 (2014).
Rees-Roberts, Nick (2008), *French Queer Cinema*, Edinburgh: Edinburgh University Press.

Rich, B. Ruby (2004), 'New Queer Cinema', in M. Aaron (ed.), *New Queer Cinema: A Critical Reader*, New Brunswick, NJ: Rutgers University Press, pp. 15–22.
Schilt, Thibaut (2011), *François Ozon*, Urbana, IL: University of Illinois Press.
Szaryk, Evelyne (2011), '"Vous voulez jouer à un jeu?": désir et manipulation dans *Gouttes d'eau sur pierres brûlantes*', in F. Grandena and C. Johnston (eds), *Cinematic Queerness: Gay and Lesbian Hypervisibility in Contemporary Francophone Feature Films*, Bern: Peter Lang, pp. 227–43.

CHAPTER 2

François Ozon's *Sitcom* and Politics of Form

Tamara Tasevska

François Ozon's cinematography has often been associated with the notions of 'cinéma du corps' / 'cinema of body' and 'cinema of excess', as well as with the umbrella term 'French gay cinema', all of which refer to an eclectic group of French art-cinema productions, sharing features such as a defiance of common representations of the body and a tendency to disrupt heteronormative, familial and institutional structures (Asibong 2008: 10–13; Beugnet 2007: 36; Palmer 2006: 22–32; Schilt 2011: 32).[1] Ozon's work has also been characterised as 'French queer cinema', notably by Anglophone critics such as Kate Ince (2008) and B. Ruby Rich (2013), whose broader consideration of discourses on gender and queer theory has attuned them to the centrality of issues of sexuality in Ozon's work.[2] In her essay 'Queer Nouveau: From Morality Tales to Mortality Tales in Ozon, Téchiné and Collard', Rich moreover compares Ozon's work to the 'New Queer Cinema' (NQC) movement, a postmodern Anglophone genre initially identified in the early 1990s that challenges traditional film structures in its pastiche of discordant, surrealist, melodramatic forms, and attempts to 'rework history with social constructivism very much in mind' (Rich 2013: 332). Ozon, like his NQC contemporaries from the other side of the Atlantic, including Gus Van Sant, Sadie Benning and Todd Haynes, largely draws inspiration from global cinematic traditions including Hollywood-style genre cinema (melodramas by Douglas Sirk), New German Cinema melodramas by Rainer Werner Fassbinder, and French New Wave musical comedies by Jacques Demy, along with the more recent 'gleam' cinema of Pedro Almodóvar, John Waters and popular entertainment forms like TV. Furthermore, Ozon plays with his experimental aesthetics in ways that make visible connections with NQC, such as imitation and adaptation (pastiche), intensified attention to hybridity (singular/everyday, phallic/fluid) objects, and a style of excess that mixes pathos with surrealism and fantasy. Both Ozon and the NQC filmmakers, as Rich contends, attempt to queer the structure and form of cinema, not only through its content but by reworking and readapting common genres in order to evoke a new form of cinema concerned with queer representation in the late-millennial, post-identificatory period in France and the Americas (Rich 2013: 332–63).[3]

Scepticism, however, exists with the use of the Anglophone term 'queer' in relation to French universalism and identity politics. Despite his status as a gay filmmaker living and working in France, there exists a doubt that Ozon himself would have used the term 'queer' to describe his cinematic strategies or to suggest an affinity with the larger group of NQC filmmakers. Nevertheless, he has highlighted instances of aesthetic affinity that voice a preoccupation with reworking cinematic language and structure that is similar to the queering strategy of NQC.[4] Throughout his career, Ozon has pointed out that he was not interested in developing story, but rather form: 'J'ai le sentiment de raconter toujours les mêmes histoire[s], en changeant la forme' ('I have the feeling that I always tell the same story, altering the form') (Ozon 1998), or 'I don't want to repeat myself' (Martin 2010). In another telling discussion, when asked about the use of perversion in *Sitcom* (1998), his response suggests that perversion relates to a formal strategy of excess: 'S'il y a une perversité, c'est peut-être de vouloir tout pousser vers l'excès' ('If there's a sort of perversion, perhaps it is the desire to push everything toward excess') (Ozon 1998). By reworking the mechanisms of cinema, Ozon points to working with form and perversion as ways to multiply the aesthetic potential of his films, which indeed are uniquely attuned to the various kinds of perversions, differences and divergences that invite us to explore the margins of conventional filmic perception and response.

In the following analysis, I would like to use this conjunction between the French filmmaker and the formal politics of NQC to ask how we might think about Ozon's work as a process of creating a new form of cinema that challenges the structure of heteronormative, mainstream filmmaking. Looking more closely at *Sitcom*, Ozon's first feature and the first of a series of increasingly stylised melodramas focusing on a classically patriarchal family, this essay comprises three sections.[5] The first shows how Ozon draws from sitcoms and classical narrative cinema in order to expose the ideological cohesion of the wholesome family environment. This will reveal Ozon's formal politics of reworking/re-inscribing the classical and mainstream narrative forms by disrupting their ideological integrity, which sees the heteronormative and distinctly white union as the sole acceptable, and most significant, model of social relation. If the function of the postwar genre film, notably melodrama, is understood either to subvert (gender and power dynamics) or to offer escapism (Elsaesser 1991: 72), Ozon's postmodern blending of such spectacular forms of narrative and his pairing of these with sitcoms simulates a refusal to play by the rules of the game of the global narrative system, by thwarting the smooth operations that govern these narrative stories and forms of popular culture. This shows how the film sets the stage for queer attachments, but also how it functions more broadly, framing global systems as a kind of laboratory experimenting with social value (to note, the white rat that suddenly appears in the film is indeed a laboratory rat).

The second section focuses on what I call Ozon's 'art of perversion', and looks more closely at Ozon's fondness for use of non-linear temporality, irony and excess as cinematic mechanisms that create simulations of models of identities, and diversify and push the limits of generic representation. *Sitcom*, as will be analysed further, is not a film of an internal analysis, since the characters have very little interiority (unlike in classical narrative cinema). The film's excessive *mise-en-scène* thus acts as a force that absorbs characters' psychology or interiority and serves to orient or open up the narration to point in different directions. In turn, perversion comes to form a queer narrativity, in which the narrative itself is oriented differently. It takes different objects, looks somewhere else, looks from within itself, and most importantly looks to escape from a system imposed by dominant ideologies. Finally, the last section will pull all of *Sitcom*'s generic threads together in order to account for Ozon's creation of a different cinematic form, one based on queering operations that elucidate the importance of reimagining a new dream and new possibilities for queer attachments apart from the dominant, patriarchal culture.

FILMING AND DISRUPTING THE DREAM OF FAMILY WHOLENESS

Sitcom's plot revises the 1968 film *Teorema*, by Pier Paolo Pasolini, in which the sudden appearance of a beautiful young man into an Italian bourgeois family leads to various sexual encounters and which reshapes the family's life forever. In *Sitcom*, situated in the late 1990s, it is a rodent pet – a white laboratory rat – that causes the transgressing of taboos and sexual norms in a French upper-class family, ultimately transforming their seemingly peaceful suburban life. Under the spell of the rat's 'negative vibrations' as they are called in the film, the nerdy and introverted son, Nicolas (Adrien de Van), discovers he is homosexual, news to which his mother reacts dreadfully.[6] His sister Sophie (and real-life sister to the actor, Marina de Van), often unnoticed by the mother and considered ugly by the father, transforms into a dominatrix confined to a wheelchair, while her macho boyfriend, David (Stéphane Rideau), becomes hyper-fragile and a prey to Sophie's masochistic role-play. This sexually triggering situation extends to the stay-at-home mother, Hélène (Evelyne Dandry), who begins to sleep with her son in attempt to cure him, as she insists,

Figure 2.1 The burial

of his homosexuality. Moreover, their new Spanish housekeeper, Maria (Lucia Sanchez), is equally affected and begins to perform sexual favours (her 'Spanish specialty') on David, while her husband, Cameroon-born gym teacher Abdu (Jules-Emmanuel Eyoum Deido), who is also homosexual, attempts to seduce Nicolas and participates in his circle orgies. The only family member immune to the rat's power is the father, Jean (François Marthouret), not surprisingly, perhaps, as he is a rigid scientist who remains detached and indifferent throughout the film even though he brought the mysterious pet home. Even if this new situation is liberating, the characters are still incapable of reaching satisfaction (both sexual and spiritual). The last scenes of the film dramatically portray the elimination of the ambivalent father/rat couple, which is blamed for the family's distress. These scenes feature the family's rebirth, symbolically figured in a swimming pool, in a scene overlaid with the father consuming the rat before literally transforming into a giant rat himself. Although the film ends with the murder and burial of the father, the image of the newly composed non-patriarchal couplings and unity (Sophie and David; Hélène and Maria; Abdu and Nicolas) is undermined again by the emergence of another white rat on the father's grave (Figure 2.1).

Unlike *Teorema*, filmed in the documentary and neorealist styles, *Sitcom* is a flashy, comical pastiche that largely mixes artificiality, pathos and stylised excess while referencing various genres, including sitcom, theatre, classical Hollywood cinema, melodrama and thriller. These numerous reference points and adaptations invite us to consider Ozon himself as a filmmaker creating his first feature, but also to more broadly question *Sitcom*'s position in relation to the film's own contemporary moment. *Sitcom* was released one year before the official recognition of the civil union between homosexual and heterosexual couples, the 'Pacte Civil de Solidarité' (PACS), voted in by the French parliament in 1999. The connection between this legal victory for homosexual couples and the film's comical staging of sexually liberated praxis and of common taboos has been noticed by the film's critics. For Thibaut Schilt, for instance, *Sitcom* frankly addresses the contemporary situation of LGBTQ cultures in France, but also in Western societies more generally (Schilt 2011: 46). For Michelle Chilcoat, moreover, the film's power lies in the queer staging of the long-standing Oedipal drama which in turn accounts for the recognition of a multiplicity of queer, feminist and 'perverse' sexual desires (Chilcoat 2008: 23), whereas for Andrew Asibong, the film powerfully points to a critique of the 'post-ideological' liberalism that had contributed to a gradual blurring of categories of political struggle in late-capitalist Western Europe (Asibong 2008: 37–8). Some of the most severe critiques came from the French press and canonical journals such as *Cahiers du cinéma* and *Positif*, which generally denigrated the film's style, condemning it as manipulative at worst, and an example of empty formalism, or a failed attempt to truly subvert bourgeois mores, at best. For them, *Sitcom* failed to articulate a clear message or motivation behind the staging of the so-called perversions.[7]

This ethos of perversion in Ozon's work proves strikingly relevant in a larger cultural and political context wherein perversion is often associated with things that go astray or lead to error. Very often, the term 'perversion' is applied to individuals whose sexual practice is considered abnormal or non-normative. However, when considered in the aesthetic context of a certain Sadean lineage, the concept of perversion carries associations with the illicit, the scandalous and indeed the excessive, which can point to a subversive force.[8] Importantly, concerns around perversion also relate to the multiple forms of sexualities and gender trouble that the term 'queer' evokes in contemporary French culture and politics, and which conservative groups consider to be threatening to both the idea of a familial wholeness and to a national fantasy of purity. As Bruno Perreau points out in his recent study, despite the significant move towards greater acceptance of LGBTQ rights and non-heteronormative couplings (PACS in 1999, and the so-called 'Marriage for All' law in 2013), movements denouncing same-sex marriage and gender fluidity continue to 'denounce the perversity of anyone who rejects traditional gender roles' (Perreau 2016: 11). These various denunciations surpass mere homophobia, often invoking claims of various kinds of (religious, racial, ethnic) foreignness.[9] As Perreau writes:

> Demonstrators against gay marriage play simultaneously on fear of the enemy within (by establishing a parallel between Judaism and homosexuality) and on racism (by placing sexual minorities in the same category as uncivilized foreigners). (Perreau 2016: 11)

Given *Sitcom*'s own historical moment, I would argue that its staging of 'unlawful sexualities' directly points to the numerous fantasies and moral tensions that re-emerged in France around the decision to legally acknowledge homosexual family units. These imaginary structures and tensions brought to the surface long-lasting concerns and reconsiderations, not only about the purity of the familial whole, but also more broadly, about the nation itself.

The first part of Ozon's strategy in *Sitcom* involves reworking the staging of the family unit itself, and its homogenously (heteronormative and white) representation that has proliferated on national TV and other forms of media, permeating both French and other societies' popular imaginaries. This issue is announced by the film's opening, which shows the title overlaid with an image of a red curtain being drawn, accompanied by light audience noise and the 'trois coups' typical of French theatrical performances. Schilt has compared this intertextual opening to 'Jean Renoir's filmic homages to the theatre such as *La chienne / The Bitch* (1931), which also opens with the parting of a curtain and ends with murder', and which also 'insists upon the fact that we are about to see a staged drama, a story we should perhaps not take too seriously' (Schilt 2011: 40). I would further argue that this opening can be interpreted self-reflectively, as it also points to the general framing and history provided by televisual family comedy or sitcom, the film's namesake. As Lynn Spiegel points out, the American-style sitcom genre was historically developed by merging live entertainment with elements of theatre, such as intimacy, immediacy and spontaneity (Spiegel 1992: 142–3). As with Ozon's *Sitcom*, sitcoms from their beginning were based on comical domestic situations, theatrically staged within the middle-class or upper-middle-class/bourgeois environment. Not surprisingly, sitcoms have generally trafficked in images of familial wholeness, typically revolving around the heterosexual/normative family lifestyle. This element, as Spiegel moreover explains, has been incorporated in sitcoms' mode of address, which usually imagines the family unit as a whole, and as its ideal audience in front of the TV set in their home (Spiegel 1992: 144). In the postwar French context, popular entertainment imagery from sitcoms, but also from magazines and advertisements, was promoting similar ideologies saturated with ideas of familial wholeness. These were inextricably linked to the state-led modernisation effort and related processes such as the 'construction of the new French couple, not only as a class necessity, but a national necessity as well' (Ross 1996: 148).[10] *Sitcom* largely draws from these generic elements of Western-style sitcoms and of popular entertainment aesthetics, wherein a negotiation with the idea of the familial wholeness, thematically and as a mode of address, are, not without irony, part of the film's overall *mise-en-scène*.[11]

Evocative of this is an early scene that begins with Maria, framed in the interior of the house, in a close-range shot next to kitchen appliances. Visibly bored, she is captured performing her role as a maid, peeling potatoes in a tedious repetitive gesture. This moment is juxtaposed with an image of an anxious, but excited, Hélène who is cooking and running around the house, smiling and poking her son Nicolas who is very noticeably reading a generic 'scientific journal'. In a comical acceleration, the camera then transposes us to the entrance door, into a framing of David, who enters the brightly illuminated room and passionately embraces Sophie, as the mother is looking at them in blissful approval, with all performing as if on stage in front of a camera.

Sitcom not only hyperbolises but also thwarts the aesthetics of popular sitcoms. For instance, the use of the name 'Hélène' for the mother is a direct reference to the 1990s popular French sitcom, *Hélène et les garçons / Hélène and the Boys*, and the casting of real-life siblings for the roles of the brother and sister intensifies the construction of familial relations. In one scene, for instance, this is figured with an image of the two siblings bathing together while evoking childhood memories. Additionally, the fact that all the characters have typical, clichéd names, and neither of them nor the family as a whole is ever addressed by their last name, advances a concept of a family of a general order, a meta-stereotype subjected to commonality and norm. While this heightens the sense of intimacy and closeness with the viewers, it also signals the maintainance of a distance.

Along with televisual shows, *Sitcom* borrows substantially from classical cinema and Hollywood genre films, such as women's pictures, film noir and melodramas. These cinematic genres are famous for their staging of an ideology of upper-/middle-class bourgeois domesticity. As critics have observed, throughout the history of cinema these genre films managed to sustain the image of the heterosexual unit as desirable and, very often, foreclosed the possibility of any imaginable alternative. Thematically and stylistically, the overall setting of *Sitcom* is underwritten by the heterosexual aspirations and hegemonic familial wholeness of generic sitcom and classical cinema narratives that are working in the film's background. A common trope in these films (which *Sitcom* furthermore transfigures into its filmic fabric) is the simultaneous staging of desirability (often relegated to the female character, the bourgeois wife, a widow, or her daughter) and the impossibility to fulfil that desire.[12] The colourful surface of *Sitcom*, as well as the use of pathos and intense emotion, reflects the way in which these genre films, and notably the melodrama, articulate a space saturated with a sense of the feminine as being pivotal in negotiating between the intimate and the outside, the familial and the social.

At the same time, *Sitcom*'s composition draws from French and American film noir, in which intensified female characters were generally framed in intimate spaces and with the use of close-ups. Ozon has claimed that his cinema has been inspired by Alfred Hitchcock and Claude Chabrol (Ozon 1998), cult filmmakers known for their suspenseful films from the 1940s and 1950s, which Mary Ann Doane in her psychoanalytic reading dubbed 'the paranoid woman's films' (Doane 1987: 124). Very often, the women in these films were portrayed as on the verge of paranoia and hysteria, and therefore associated with liminality and marginal conditions that were pointing to broader class, gender and sometimes racial oppression as well.[13] Although comical and exaggerated, *Sitcom*'s tension and heightened emotion is similarly placed on characters who, like those in the classical genre films, society would deem liminal and marginal, and whose desire would be exemplary of an impossible desire (same-sex, interracial, adultery, and so on). By drawing from these films and by disrupting the coherent whole of the family unit which reflects their structure, Ozon's *Sitcom* both acknowledges the influence of classical narrative and mainstream films and contests their uniforming tendencies in producing hegemonies.

This becomes evident from the film's outset, which shows the model American-style suburban house of the traditional and generic French family. The scene begins with a long tracking shot that follows the father's car entering a private driveway, a movement which signals a separation between the protected, distinct space of the home and the rest of the world. The father is shown getting out of the car, briefcase in hand, and entering the house. The composition of this shot separates the paternal – the patriarch and his privileged domain of production – from the domain of the house, which comes to trigger associations with domesticity and reproduction, associations both related to the feminine. This establishing shot is followed by another separation emerging on the cinematic level, when Ozon's camera, instead of following the father inside the house, fixates itself on the exterior of the house, capturing it in a freeze frame as *an image*. As this scene unfolds, we hear sounds of singing for the father's birthday and then, shockingly, gunshots, cries and the sounds of cold-blooded murder carried out by the father himself, all while the visuals remain frozen on the image of the house's smooth exterior. This episode announces the split between dichotomies such as sound/visual, surface/interior, father's law/repression which the film's form largely condenses, notably up until the moment when the father wakes up, and we realise the scene was a dream.

Key elements in this sequence involve the positioning of the father as a patriarchal figure and the staging of his encompassing dream with the use of retroactive narration and temporal condensation. The father's killing of the family in his dream plays a crucial role in the narrative structure, as it functions as a kind of 'primal scene' for the chaotic familial situation that saturates the film. Later in the narrative, when his dream is visually revealed, we also find out that its events have been intertwined with the *real* events taking place in the film, which began four months earlier with the arrival of both the rat and Maria and Abdu into the family's home. This non-linear and retrospective temporality merges the father's dream (his unconsciousness) with an omnipresent gaze (perhaps that of the rat?) that undermines the provocative sexual liberation taking place throughout the film. The symbolic power of this gaze, which Asibong, via Slavoj Žižek, has called 'empty law', is the one that consistently governs the family situation without, however, acting or doing anything about it (Asibong 2008: 37). The temporal structure evoked through the father's dream counters the one in typical sitcoms or classical narratives, in which suspenseful twists followed by a revelation very often serve to expose a hidden truth structuring the entire plot. In *Sitcom*, the father's dream is unveiled in the second part of the film, but the filmic narrative still continues to elaborate the familial transformations. In this way, *Sitcom* shows that its concern is not merely oriented towards unveiling the truth behind the ideology of the father's despotic rule. Rather, the film's techniques, such as the use of convoluted temporality but also simulation, irony and excess, point to a truth that exists on the aesthetic level, oriented towards subverting any forms of teleology and essentialism while enabling diversification and queering.

THE ART OF PERVERSION

The constant play with irony, excess and simulation are indeed prominent elements of *Sitcom*'s texture. While they dramatise psychoanalytic clichés (inevitably related to the law of the father), they also largely call into question psychoanalysis as a discipline present in the Western popular imaginary.[14] Moreover, the film extends these psychoanalytic clichés to larger issues related to racial, sexual and national identities, which in the film importantly point to the father's house as a site of undifferentiated violence. This is illustrated for instance in a scene that shows Maria cleaning kitchen knives (visibly a phallic object of violence) on a dining table a few moments after she has come into the house. At some point, she is shown eerily looking at her own reflection on the surface of the knives, creating a suspense which does not truly get resolved, but continues to exert an agency on the film's surface. As house help, Maria is framed in the backdrop, even though her overall figure, emphasised by a colourful uniform and a large cross around her neck, renders her hyper-visible in an aesthetics *à la* Pedro Almodóvar (as a meta-commentary to reference her Spanish compatriot). Consequently, Maria highlights elements of mysticism and foreignness, but also of someone belonging to the working, immigrant or marginal underclass. Captured in this way, she clearly stands at odds with the more discreetly captured Hélène, whose presence is reaffirmed by the classical Chopin music, itself evocative of harmony and bourgeois domesticity. What also remains curious in this *mise-en-scène* is how the framing, music and montage establish relation through (mostly phallic) objects, rather than through Maria's and Hélène's interiority. Thus, from the close-up of Maria's knife, we then suddenly follow Hélène who receives a phone call, a moment which will transpose the tension of the action onto the telephone call and, ultimately, the absence of Françoise, Hélène's friend (who we never get to see in the film, but whose figurative existence announces yet another absence that the filmic texture both actively and self-consciously represses).[15]

Instead of self-victimising and being assimilated into the dominant order, the film's characters who suffer the most from the father's dream are portrayed as excessive in their simulation of models of identities, which indeed points to perversions precisely because they fail to fit into the existing framework which tries to capture them. We can see this through Ozon's formal and chromatic play with differences that expose such simulation of models of identities and push the limits of generic representation. Some of these ironic and perverse simulations emerge through vestimentary codes, as we see in the scene in which Abdu and Maria arrive overdressed for the family's dinner party, in a combination of black and white. This moment provides a commentary on what Dominic Thomas has called 'the discourse on clothing as a symbol of assimilation' in France's postcolonial culture (Thomas 2007: 161). More than a marker of social and economic distinctions, Maria's and Abdu's clothing also serves as an indicator that recuperates prior colonial fantasies. Thus, not surprisingly, numerous scenes portray Abdu, the only black character, as hypervisible, notably in relation to Nicolas, who functions as his double and who had remained almost invisible until his coming out.[16] Bringing to the surface prior colonial hierarchies, Abdu's positionality is repeatedly questioned throughout the film, but not in order to safely acknowledge his status within the familial circle, like Nicolas, but rather to consistently interrogate his position as an outsider, in relation to the family and to French society more generally. This is evident in the dinner party scene, in which Nicolas's coming out is staged to interrupt Abdu's account of France's colonial history to the seemingly ignorant family (Figure 2.2).

Abdu's character also brings in a classic trope according to which black individuals are seen first as bodies, and his job as a PE teacher precisely reinforces this perception. Hence, in a scene in Nicolas's bedroom, Ozon vividly captures the muscular tonality of Abdu's naked chest in a close-up, before Abdu comically asks Nicolas to touch and embrace him.[17] The flat lighting illuminates his figure, and the overall setting is further dramatised by the use of island-themed décor in Nicolas's bedroom as well as sounds of chirping birds and breaking waves (Figure 2.3).

Although comical, this dramatic setting serves to emphasise the notions of exoticism and natural sensuousness usually attributed to black bodies, thereby reanimating what Mame-Fatou Niang calls France's 'long history of racist representations of Black bodies'.[18] After Nicolas's coming out, Abdu is 'interpellated' (to use the concept of postcolonial thinker Frantz Fanon) by Maria and Hélène to 'do something' about Nicolas's sexuality, given the fact that he is a gym teacher, and thereby supposedly well-equipped to help young boys

Figure 2.2 Dinner party

Figure 2.3 Abdu touches Nicolas

(develop their masculinity), by initiating them into sports.[19] Identified by his job and as a racial referent, Abdu's 'interpellation' also comes at the moment when he is needed to save the prospects of the French heteronormative white family, an idea corroborated in the film by the mother's dreadful claim that she would never have grandchildren (in a homophobic–traditional account that also excludes her daughter Sophie from the family's procreation). This moment reinforces the ideological hierarchies enacted by the colonial discrimination, while also pointing to the multiple ways in which Abdu's character is exploited. The most remarkable image of this idea is articulated in the scene that shows Abdu as the only character who gets bitten by the white rat, while the other characters visibly enjoy its caresses. The fact that the rat is synonymous with disease and infection also shows considerations for *purity*. Evoking a looming image of violence, here the black man, as Fanon would say, *soils* the white race and white family.

Throughout the film, Ozon further investigates circuits of aesthetic and economic value related to race, class and gender. Maria progressively appropriates a more 'black look' (with changes in hairstyle, outfit and accessories), and expresses her acceptance of Abdu's homosexuality by claiming that she also perhaps holds a lesbian tendency (given her familial tie with a lesbian aunt in Spain). While Maria's ambivalent reactions might be seen as signalling a reversal of the heteropatriarchal gaze, they also point to a connection between the film's liberatory politics and the racialised specificity of her husband Abdu. In relation to Hélène and Nicolas, who do not work but spend money excessively on diet, clothing and well-being, Maria's and Abdu's positionality is also expressed through an economic perspective. The fact that Abdu has lost his job is dreadful to Maria, and clearly points to the precariousness of immigrant workers. This disproportionate economic status also extends to the portrayal of the relation between the two gay male characters. While Nicolas is transformed into a radiant and fashion-obsessed gay man, who manifestly takes care of his body and clothing style (and typifies the interactions of sexuality and the capitalist modes of consumption), the one whose economic suffering is most dramatised in the film is Abdu. This economic power dynamic is also expressed through language in the film, which equally points to Maria and Abdu's position as a racial and foreign referent, to their economic status, and to their status as possession. For instance, in a scene in which Hélène talks to her psychoanalyst, she specifies a racial difference and possession when she evokes Abdu and Maria as 'le mari noir de ma femme de ménage' ('the black husband of my house maid'), thus underlining through logos the various layers of power dynamics within their group.

In addition to racial and economic reference, the film also comically disperses psychoanalytic signifiers and references that become largely indicative of sexual and gender oppression. This is illustrated in the dramatic scene of Sophie's suicide attempt, which begins with her experiencing pain in the genital area a few moments after the white rat caresses her. This moment exaggerates the long-standing psychoanalytic obsession with the lack of a penis, but also points to notions such as self-harm, mutilation and hysteria traditionally associated with women. Similarly, the scene in which Hélène and Sophie dramatically cut zucchini in the kitchen, while discussing Sophie's inability to experience sexual pleasure, gestures towards Sophie's fear of castration, but also to a broader stigmatisation related to women's pleasure.

As shown in these episodes, Ozon's approach of portraying his characters as subjects of racism, xenophobia and homophobia (this extends to the misogyny that is clearly inflicted on Sophie as well): the black gay/bisexual man, the Spanish maid, the white gay son and suffering daughter, takes into account the specificity of their struggles, as they are not all technically and aesthetically depicted in the same way. This itself reveals a queer and intersectional approach in his cinema. As such scenes illustrate, Ozon considers the characters' individual struggles, but not in a competing way. Each circuit of excess and form of perversion parallels other examples of identity formation among minority groups (as, for example, the case of Abdu's experience as an Afro-French gay/bisexual man) that disrupt the current hegemonic relationship between the dominant and minority positions and also account for the existence of differences and differential relationships within a bounded category.

ESCAPING THE DREAM OF THE FATHER

The film depicts subversive individuals who are subject to patriarchal suffering. They continuously refuse the values, identities and sensibilities imposed by the existing domestic and societal framework. This in turn begins to contaminate the domestic space with their new fantasy, making the father, and the dominant patriarchy for which he stands, the victim of their so-called perversion. Expressed in this way, perversion becomes a capacity, a power to contest, an art. I would argue that the various repetitions and simulations of such sexual practices, to the point of excess and perversion, hold a sort of diabolical power, precisely because they show that they cannot function within the structure that is supported by the father's dream. Rather, the failure of these practices points to the necessary evasion of that system. It is a new dream, composed of different ways to intimately relate, that begins to take shape through these protests.

This is why the scene that, very symbolically, figures the rebirth of a new form of family unity coincides with the end of the father's murderous dream. Alluding to a womb, this scene takes place in a swimming pool and directly sets the stage for the invention of other forms of non-patriarchal relations. In it, the bodies of Hélène, Sophie and Nicolas progressively become more choreographed to the symphonic score *Resurrection* by Albert Roussel. This moment initiates a new kind of intimacy which, while charged with music and affect from the melodrama, nonetheless reveals a pure potentiality of a utopian longing. Through the floating movements of their bodies, a sort of pre-identificatory desire is evoked, a desire that predates any form of sexual identity, but which is open to a new shaping. Following this, the scene depicting the murder of the father signals the final battle of rejection of the paternal law and the familial imperatives that are its principal socialising vehicles. Indeed, the film portrays this moment precisely as a battle between the father and his family. Here, Ozon shows what seems to be a momentous possibility, a new imperative: to reject the family game that the father has set in motion and has imposed on its members, the tragedy by which society has been oppressed since Oedipus's patricide, and to create new possibilities for non-heteronormative/queer attachments.

In the last scene at the cemetery, the characters are shown lined up in the new formation: Hélène and Maria at the centre, Abdu and Nicolas coupled on the right and Sophie and David on the left, as they watch the father's grave with a gaze that mirrors and undermines the father's objectifying watching that structures the film's setting. This image, however, followed by a re-emergence of the white rat, the ultimate fetish and omnipresent gaze, is an image circular in itself, exposing the struggles of the racial, transnational, gendered and sexually marginalised characters from within the film's texture. Paired with the final image of all the characters leaving the cemetery, it creates an ending which does not, however, mean that these characters flee the father's law and its persisting framework for good. Rather, it points to their ongoing struggle and the importance of remaining in motion, not settling into a world that tries to shape them to its form.

NOTES

1. Andrew Asibong describes Ozon's cinema as 'specifically homosexual', while situating him within a 'queer' legacy both in Europe and the Americas, inspired by the philosophies of Michel Foucault and Gilles Deleuze dating from the mid-1960s onwards (see Asibong, pp. 10–13). For more on Ozon's relationship to the 1990s trends in art-cinema 'French Extremity' and 'cinema of excess', see Beugnet, pp. 36, 127.
2. Kate Ince makes a case for considering Ozon as 'France's first mainstream queer filmmaker' given his experimentation with staging of fluidity of gender and sexual desire, and the continual performative transformations of identity worked within it. See Ince (2008).
3. Even if she identifies a broader affective mode of correspondences with NQC, Rich's analysis of Ozon's cinema remains grounded in a specific French historic and cinematic tradition, combining French New Wave (Eric Rohmer) with a trajectory of filming fluid sexualities (André Téchiné and Cyril Collard). In my reading, I try to look at Ozon from a perspective that considers his preoccupation with reworking cinematic form from within a larger global cinematic history.
4. It is important to note that Ozon's professional training at the prestigious French filmmaking school the *Fémis*, known for moulding auteur-directors, has contributed to his development of a personal vision attuned to cinematic history. For more on Ozon's technical training see Schilt, pp. 16–17; Asibong develops a similar understanding of Ozon as a 'filmmaker who has formally analysed film, its history, its theory, its practice, and as

a cinéaste who has, from the start of his career, [. . .] delighted in displaying his brilliant knowledge of cinema' (Asibong, p. 5).
5. This series includes *Gouttes d'eau sur pierres brûlantes / Water Drops on Burning Women* (2000), *8 femmes / 8 Women* (2002), *Potiche* (2010) *and Une Nouvelle amie / The New Girlfriend* (2014), all of which focus on reworking gender roles and familial structures within the highly familiar dynamics of the bourgeoisie.
6. Citation is from the film's official subtitles in English. See filmography at the end of this book.
7. For a more detailed discussion of the film's media reception and criticism see Schilt, pp. 42–5.
8. Asibong's discussion of Ozon's treatment of sex and sexualities is useful to note, as he connects Ozon to a specific French history and culture of transgression that goes back to figures such as the Marquis de Sade, the Comte de Lautréamont and Georges Bataille, who explore the subversive force of unlawful, perverse and evil sexualities. See Asibong, p. 13. The philosophy of Gilles Deleuze is also useful for this discussion, especially Deleuze's consideration of perversion (via Sade) as productive in thinking about desire and its active cultivation in everyday psychic and social life. I'm interested in the way the notion of perversion in Deleuze points to something that attempts to follow a different logic and defies categories of representation by rendering them 'perversive', as he puts it, meaning open to all kinds of differences and variations. See Deleuze, pp. 133, 197–9, 304–5.
9. Bruno Perreau's book *Queer Theory: The French Response* provides an excellent study of the various forms of contemporary cultural insecurities in France stemming from the English term 'queer' and its relation to the American academic discourses on gender and queer theory. See Perreau (2016).
10. In her book *Fast Cars, Clean Bodies*, Kristin Ross provides an important discussion of larger American cinematic and cultural influence in the postwar, postcolonial period in France. For more, see Ross (1996).
11. Thibaut Schilt has identified several 1990s Anglo-American and French sitcoms as *Sitcom*'s references, including *Absolutely Fabulous*, *All in the Family*, and its French remake *Maud*, as well as *Hélène et les garçons / Hélène and the Boys*. See Schilt, pp. 39–40.
12. The work of Laura Mulvey and Mary Ann Doane which intersects feminist film theory, psychoanalytic theory, and sexual and racial difference in film is important for this discussion. See in particular Doane's *The Desire to Desire* (1987), *Femmes Fatales* (1991) and Mulvey's more recent reconsiderations on her discussion on visual pleasure in narrative cinema, *Death 24x a Second* (2005) and *Afterimages* (2019). Jonathan Goldberg's work *Melodrama: An Aesthetics of Impossibility* on the notion of the 'impossibility' of desire in classical melodrama, as well as its relation to what he calls 'homoaesthetics', is also relevant. See Goldberg (2016).
13. Kate Ince relates this melodrama and the infused aesthetics of women's film to Ozon's experimentations with 'theatricality' and an aesthetics of entrapment in his films *Sitcom, Sitcom, Gouttes d'eau sur pierres brûlantes / Water Drops on Burning Women and 8 femmes / 8 Women* . See Ince, p. 129.
14. For a more detailed psychoanalytic reading of *Sitcom* and the way the film queers and subverts the dominating (heteronormative) structures that the discipline values and reinforces, see Chilcoat (2008). It is also important to note that Ozon claimed that psychoanalysis was one of his privileged areas of thinking human subjectivity. His more recent film, *L'amant double / Double Lover* (2017), in which one of the main characters is a psychoanalyst and the other is following psychoanalytic treatment, further dramatises the relationship between the discipline and the processes of subject formation and of creating (familial) intimacy. Acknowledging the importance of psychoanalytic concepts present in Ozon's oeuvre, my reading of *Sitcom* will further develop by focusing on how the film excessively uses psychanalytic clichés, thus constructing various circuits of perversion at the level of its form.

15. Françoise, who is figured through her absence or failure to show up to events, also presents as Hélène's missing, but confident, other. Combining digression and comical relief, her character is directly inherited from sitcoms.
16. Comically, in another excessive reference to Lacanian psychoanalysis, Nicolas eerily looks at himself in a mirror after his coming out, as if identifying himself as a subject for the first time.
17. This also relates to Frantz Fanon's writings: 'There is one expression that through time has become singularly eroticized: the black athlete' (Fanon, p. 122).
18. Available at <http://monitoracism.eu/on-frances-contempt-for-black-bodies> (last accessed 21 August 2020). Ozon's depiction of Abdu's sexualised body as excelling in physicality largely draws from aesthetic traditions of visualising eroticised black bodies by white gay artists. This tradition includes Carl Van Vechten's fetish studio photographs and Nickolas Muray's nudes of Paul Robeson among others, and understands the portrayal of the black body as the focus of numerous fantasies that cut across inter-racialism, homoeroticism and primitivism, but also across power dynamics such as identification and dis-identification, passive and active, and captor and victim. Rokhaya Diallo's work 'Où sont les noirs' in French cinema is pertinent for this discussion as well, as it traces a history of visibility of black actors in French cinema.
19. For Fanon, the black subject begins to exist when interpellated by the white gaze. This is what Fanon calls the 'fact of Blackness' in *Black Skin*, p. 82. Moreover, the fact that Abdu is interpellated at the specific moment when the future of the family (and by implication, France) is discussed reiterates a long-standing colonial hierarchy and ideas about France's dependence on its colonial subjects.

WORKS CITED

Aaron, Michele (ed.) (2004), *New Queer Cinema: A Critical Reader*, New Brunswick, NJ: Rutgers University Press.
Asibong, Andrew (2008), *François Ozon*, Manchester: Manchester University Press.
Beugnet, Martine (2007), *Cinema and Sensation*, Edinburgh: Edinburgh University Press.
Chilcoat, Michelle (2008), 'Queering the Family in François Ozon's *Sitcom*', in Robin Griffiths (ed.), *Queer Cinema in Europe*, Chicago, IL: University of Chicago Press, pp. 23–33.
Deleuze, Gilles [1969] (1990), *The Logic of Sense*, trans. Mark Lester with Charles Stivale, New York: Columbia University Press.
Doane, Mary Ann (1987), *The Desire to Desire*, Bloomington and Indianapolis, IN: Indiana University Press.
Doane, Mary Ann (1991), *Femmes Fatales: Feminism, Film Theory, Psychoanalysis*, New York and London: Routledge.
Elsaesser, Thomas (1991), 'Tales of Sound and Fury: Observations on the Family Melodrama', in Marcia Landy (ed.), *Imitations of Life: A Reader on Film and Television Melodrama*, Detroit, MI: Wayne State University Press, pp. 68–91.
Fanon, Frantz [1952] (1967), *Black Skin, White Masks*, trans. Charles Lam Markmann, London: Pluto Press.
Goldberg, Jonathan (2016), *Melodrama: An Aesthetic of Impossibility*, Durham, NC: Duke University Press.
Ince, Kate (ed.) (2008), 'François Ozon's Cinema of Desire', in Kate Ince (ed.), *Five Directors: Auteurism from Assayas to Ozon*, Manchester: Manchester University Press, pp. 112–34.

Handyside, Fiona (2012), 'The Possibilities of a Beach: Queerness and François Ozon's Beaches', *Screen*, 53: 1, pp. 54–71.
Martin, Michael (2010), 'Ozon Layers', *Out.com*, July 2010, <https://www.out.com/entertainment/2010/07/13/ozon-layers> (last accessed 21 August 2020).
Mulvey, Laura (2019), *Afterimages: On Cinema Women and Changing Times*, London: Reaktion Books.
Mulvey, Laura (2006), *Death 24x a Second*, London: Reaktion Books.
Niang, Mame-Fatou, 'The DiRosa Fresco and the Problematic Space of AfroFrenchness', *Monitor Racism*, European University Institute/Robert Schuman Center for Advanced Studies, Florence, June 2020, <http://monitoracism.eu/on-frances-contempt-for-black-bodies> (last accessed 21 August 2020).
Ozon, François (1998), 'Entretiens *Sitcom*', *François-Ozon.com*, April–May, <http://www.francois-ozon.com/francais/ozon.entretiens05.html> (last accessed 21 August 2020).
Ozon, François (1998), Interview with Philippe Piazzo, François Ozon: 'C'est plus excitant ainsi', *Le Monde*, 27 May.
Ozon, François (1998), Interview with Vincent Ostria, 'No fun: *Sitcom* de François Ozon', *Les Inrockuptibles*, 6 March.
Palmer, Tim (2006), 'Style and Sensation in the Contemporary French Cinema of the Body', *Journal of Film and Video*, 58: 3, pp. 22–32.
Perreau, Bruno (2016), *Queer Theory: The French Response*, Stanford, CA: Stanford University Press.
Rich, B. Ruby (1992), 'New Queer Cinema', *Sight and Sound*, 2: 5, pp. 32–3.
Rich, B. Ruby [2007] (2013), 'Queer Nouveau: From Morality Tales to Mortality Tales in Ozon, Téchiné, Collard', in *New Queer Cinema: The Director's Cut* (e-Duke books scholarly collection), pp. 332–63.
Ross, Kristin (1996), *Fast Cars, Clean Bodies: Decolonization and the Reordering of French Culture*, Cambridge, MA: MIT Press.
Schilt, Thibaut (2011), *François Ozon*, Urbana, IL: University of Illinois Press.
Spigel, Lynn (1996), *Make Room for TV: Television and the Family Ideal in Postwar America*, Chicago, IL: University of Chicago Press.
Thomas, Dominic (2007), *Black France: Colonialism, Immigration, and Transnationalism*, Bloomington and Indianapolis, IN: Indiana University Press.

CHAPTER 3

Queering the Trenches: Homoerotic Overtones in *Frantz*

Helena Duffy

Set in the small German town of Quedlinburg in the immediate aftermath of the Second World War, and filmed in black-and-white with only an occasional outbreak of colour, *Frantz* (2016) follows a young woman called Anna (Paula Beer). The older couple Anna lives with would now be her parents-in-law, had Anna's fiancé, Frantz (Anton von Lucke), not died in the war. Anna's and the Hoffmeisters' (Marie Gruber and Ernst Stötzner) mourning for the fallen soldier is interrupted by the arrival of a young Frenchman, Adrien Rivoire (Pierre Niney), who – and here comes the spoiler – has come to seek forgiveness for killing Frantz at the front. Over the next few days, Adrien, who is too afraid to reveal the actual reason for his visit, comforts the bereaved family with made-up tales of his pre-war friendship with Frantz. We are made to expect that Adrien, who becomes a sort of revenant, will take up the dead soldier's place in his fiancée's and parents' lives, but, contrary to its source text and the earlier cinematic adaptation thereof, *Frantz* rejects heteronormative standards and instead queers Adrien's feelings for the man he killed.

Frantz is at once typical and untypical of Ozon's oeuvre, for, unlike the majority of the director's works, it is set largely outside France and in a relatively distant past. Equally uncharacteristic is the film's black-and-white tonality that Ozon himself ascribes, on the one hand, to the morbid story he is telling and, on the other, to the fact that our image of the First World War has been shaped largely by archival material (Ozon, 2016). Conversely, *Frantz* shares with *Sitcom* (1998), *8 femmes / 8 Women* (2002), *Swimming Pool* (2003) and *Dans la maison / In the House* (2012) its preoccupation with death, including suicide, and with the domestic space as a stage for unsettling conventional family constellations. Additionally, as with Ozon's earlier films that, in a typically postmodern fashion, parodically engage with popular narrative conventions such as whodunit, melodrama, or *Boulevard* theatre, and with existing cultural texts, *Frantz* plays with the genre of heritage cinema or – to employ terminology used in the French context – 'nostalgia film' (Powrie 1997) or 'la nouvelle qualité française' (Sainderichin 1982: 18, quoted in Austin 1996: 144).[1] Its source text is the once successful but now forgotten play, *L'Homme que j'ai tué / The Man I Killed* (1925), by Maurice Rostand (1891–1968), an openly gay writer who was associated with homosexual artists including Jean Cocteau, Raynaldo Hahn and Lucien Daudet (Arnaud 2016: 52–5). Rostand's play was first adapted for the cinema in 1932 by Ernst Lubitsch (1892–1947) as *Broken Lullaby*, however, Ozon confesses to having discovered the adaptation only once he had begun working on his own film. While it is not my intention to enter into the unhelpful rhetoric of the (in)fidelity of Ozon's film to its source text(s), this chapter's focus requires stating that, unlike Rostand's play and Lubitsch's film, *Frantz* adopts the perspective of the defeated Germans rather than that of the victorious French. Another relevant difference is Ozon's use of deception and surprise revelation, which, besides making the plot more gripping, opens up a space for the homoerotic narrative of Adrien's imaginary friendship with Frantz.

It is Ozon's unsettling of the heteronormative story told by *L'Homme que j'ai tué* and retold by *Broken Lullaby* that this chapter will address. My main contention is that by queering the First World War and the ensuing trauma *Frantz* goes beyond Rostand's and Lubitsch's ambition to question the hegemonic narratives of patriotism and militarism, and to provoke reflection on contemporary political challenges. Namely, Ozon's film interrogates conventional masculinity and the notion that it should be crystallised by war (Christensen and Rasmussen 2015: 189; Hutchings 2008), which it achieves through linking the loss and the physical and psychological damage resulting from the war to non-normative (sexual) identities and positions. To demonstrate this, I first examine the flashbacks narrating Adrien's and Frantz's imaginary relationship, where I will pay particular attention to Ozon's unorthodox use of monochrome and colour, and to the sequences featuring Édouard Manet's *Le Suicidé* (1877–81). My discussion of the connection between homosexuality and the death drive established by Manet's painting will be framed with Kaja Silverman's conceptualisation of 'historical trauma' as a symptom of the death drive and, more broadly, with her examination of marginal masculinities. My other theoretical lens is Leo Edelman's more recent construction of homosexuality as a force opposing the dominant ethos of reproductive futurism and, consequently, identified with societal death drive. I will then shift my focus to the paradoxical interplay between Ozon's unbinding of conventional masculinities and his film's adherence to heritage cinema, a convention defined as 'an artful and spectacular projection of an elite conservative vision of the national past' (Higson 1996: 233). Heritage film thus seems an ideal vehicle for the 'dominant fiction', as Silverman dubs the meta-narrative which solicits faith in male adequacy, the unity of the family and small-town life, and which encompasses the official discourse on the war (Silverman 1992: 15). I will, nevertheless, argue that *Ozon's* inscription of heritage cinema is postmodern and therefore self-conscious and ironic, and that it supports Linda Hutcheon's and other more positive evaluations of adaptation. Subscribing to the view that, if used critically, heritage film does not have to be 'an ideologically conservative process and product', but can challenge totalising ideologies (Handyside 2011: 54), I will decipher *Frantz*, which – it needs reiterating – assumes the Germans' perspective, as a powerful questioning of the conservatism, nostalgia and glorification of national past underpinning heritage film. It is the queering of the war-induced trauma that provides the vehicle for this questioning. At the same time, it makes the past narrated by *Frantz* relevant to viewers beyond those normally attracted to cinematic adaptations and frees the film's source text from the confines of heteronormative standards abided by its gay author.

THE COLOURFUL PAST, THE MONOCHROME PRESENT

It is only fitting that a film as obsessed with death as is *Frantz* should open at a cemetery. As she is about to replace the flowers on her fiancé's grave, Anna discovers that someone has anticipated her action. From the foreign coin the caretaker produces she learns it was a Frenchman, while the man's accompanying gesture – he spits disdainfully – additionally tells us about the Germans' resentment towards the war's victors. That the sense of humiliation caused by the defeat has curdled into deep hostility accompanied by a desire for revenge is confirmed by the meetings the local menfolk hold in the hotel restaurant. During these gatherings, the men sing 'Die Wacht am Rhein' / 'The Watch on the Rhine', whose significance stems perhaps less from the historical fact that it was the German troops' favourite song during the Franco-Prussian War (1870-1) than from its role in *Casablanca* (1942). In Michael Curtiz's film, as German officers drinking in Rick's bar bellow 'Die Wacht am Rhein', resister Victor Laszlo stirs patriotic ardour in the émigrés by intoning 'La Marseillaise'. Interestingly, Ozon, too, quotes the French national anthem, however, as I discuss later, he does so to strikingly different ends. Among the men attending these gatherings are Herr Kreutz (Johann von Bülow), who embodies intransigent nationalism and machoism, and Frantz's father who, in contrast to Kreutz, gradually shifts towards a self-critical position. On first encountering Adrien, Dr Hoffmeister is still so possessed by grief, bitterness and hatred of the French that he does not even let Adrien elucidate the purpose of his visit. As he dismisses the Frenchman purely on the grounds of his nationality, he uncannily proclaims: 'Jeder Franzose ist für mich der Mörder meines Sohnes' ('Every Frenchman is for me my son's murderer'). Adrien nevertheless returns to the house, this time on the invitation of the family, who, having erroneously deduced that the Frenchman must be Frantz's acquaintance from his student days in Paris, hope that his reminiscences will stir up their own fond memories of their son. The Hoffmeisters thus impose on their visitor a heteronormative narrative of male comradery, with which Adrien meekly goes along. In the backdrop of the Frenchman's narrative, colour flashbacks silently tell a story that subverts not only the prevalent discourse of Franco-German animosity but also that of heteronormative relationships. The sequences showing Frantz and Adrien visiting the Louvre, locking their gazes as they dance with women, or engaging in violin lessons that facilitate physical intimacy are all charged with homoerotic tension. The ownership of this narrative remains, however, ambiguous, especially given the mirroring among the film's characters, and between the main characters and Ozon himself.[2] Does the fantasy belong to Adrien, as suggested by his subsequent confession of having grown to love Frantz? Or does it belong to the director alone, who uses queerness as a cipher for the contemporaneous unspokenness of non-normative masculinities, pacifism and war trauma?

Unlike the rest of the film, the flashbacks are all shot in colour, even if the level of saturation differs between the episodes imagined by Adrien and the scene of Frantz's death, which has a subdued tonality. If Ozon himself attributes the juxtaposition of black-and-white and colour to the aforementioned practical concerns or even posits it as arbitrary (Ozon, 2016), the consistency with which he narrates Adrien's relationship with Frantz both in colour and wordlessly points to his technique's deeper significance.[3] If the absence of dialogue plausibly alludes to the silencing of homosexuality in Rostand's play and, more generally, in the public discourse at the time that *L'Homme que j'ai tué* premiered, the colour underscores the sombre mood dominating the black-and-white diegetic present. One of the two other scenes shot in colour depicts Anna and Adrien resting on the riverbank after Adrien has swum in the river. The sequence's cheery tonality seems to herald a happy ending, such as the one in Lubitsch's film where Paul (renamed Adrien) and Elsa (renamed Anna) form a couple. But, instead of complying with the Hollywoodian identification of happiness with establishment/restoration of a heteronormative couple/family (Le Vay 2019: 192), Ozon offers us an alternative happy ending, one that rejects the 'heterosexual imperative' (Butler 1993: 2).[4] The film's final scene, also shot in colour, shows Anna overcome her depression, throw off the shackles of small-town bourgeois mentality and embark on an emancipatory journey in Paris where she can accede to experiences unavailable to a small-town woman.

Just as Ozon subverts the Hollywoodian bundling of happiness with the heteronormative, he challenges the tradition of combining colour and black-and-white, where the former is habitually the dominant tonality (Misek 2010:

96). Moreover, if, conventionally, black-and-white has been codified as a signifier of the past (Misek 2010: 90), in *Frantz* it serves to narrate the present, whereas the (imagined) past is filmed in colour. Ozon's inversion of the customary visual signifiers of the past and the present may have been motivated by the connection of black-and-white to documentary authenticity and the black-and-white flashback's consequent limited potential for ontological ambiguity. Indeed, '[a] flashback that involves lying, misremembering, uncertainty, or distorted consciousness . . . cannot be black-and-white' (Misek 2010: 91). With his cinematic technique the queer director may have also wished to signal his imposition of a homoerotic narrative on a heteronormative story, a suggestion invited by the fact that in *Frantz* colour is attached to homosexuality and, more largely, by the recognition of saturated colours as a token of camp queer (Waldron 2010: 75).

In the first of the flashbacks, which is set in the Louvre, Adrien and Frantz pause in front of *Le Suicidé*. At this moment, replicating verbatim Rostand's description of a Gustave Courbet painting, Adrien speaks of 'ein Bild eines jungen Mannes mit dem Kopf nach hinten' ('a picture of a young man with his head thrown back'). The silent visual narrative reveals, however, a painting with a much more dramatic content: in a sparsely furnished bedroom, an elegantly dressed man has just shot himself in the stomach. This substitution, which the director himself explains with Anna's story's need for a more violent intertext (Ozon, 2017), must be contextualised with Ozon's sustained interest in the phenomenon of suicide.[5] This interest is also manifest in *Frantz*, where Manet's painting foretells Adrien's and Anna's attempted suicides and, more broadly, helps to thematise war-induced psychological injury. The scene immediately following Adrien's revelation of his identity as Franz's killer restages *Le Suicidé* with Adrien replacing the anonymous male figure. Later, during her stay in Paris, the painting gives Anna the idea about Adrien's poor mental health and inspires her to search for him in a hospital. Her visit to Val-de-Grâce and consequent encounter with the widow of Adrien's late uncle, who, having lost both legs at Verdun, has taken his own life, foregrounds the physical and mental wounding produced by the senseless conflict, and reinforces the film's anti-war message. Finally, Manet's painting foreshadows Anna's own attempt to take her own life, which results from her conflicting feelings for her fiancé's killer, before Ozon ultimately reinvests it with positive meaning. Anna's concluding remark regarding *Le Suicidé* – 'il me donne envie de vivre' ('it gives me the will to live') – transforms the canvas from a signifier of a self-destructive revolt against the rigidity of socially defined identities into one of liberation from such crippling constructs. Just as paradoxically, the painting, as cast in the film's final sequence, repositions Frantz's death as the trigger of Anna's emancipation from the conservatism of the provincial bourgeoisie and of her attendant entry into metropolitan and cosmopolitan life.

Yet, as well as signifying Anna's rebirth, in *Frantz*, *Le Suicidé* offsets the idea of heroic death for one's country, which, as Ozon's film makes it plain, continues to hold sway on both sides of the Franco-German border. The French director's critique of militarism is most palpable in the scene set in a Parisian restaurant, in which the arrival of war veterans in uniform elicits a rendition of 'La Marseillaise' from the diners. Unlike in *Casablanca*, which endows the French national anthem with unquestionably positive connotations, *Frantz* puts the military song that glorifies death in battle on a par with 'Die Wacht am Rhein', condemning it as an expression of war-mongering nationalism. My reading of *Le Suicidé* as an intertext subverting the heroicisation of death derives its thrust from Ulrike Ilg's interpretation of Manet's canvas as marking its author's break with the academic tradition of associating suicide with heroism, sacrifice or idealism, and of restricting its representation to the field of history painting (Ilg 2002: 181).[6] Given that, as he worked on *Le Suicidé*, Manet himself was traumatised by the violence he had witnessed during the Prussian siege of Paris (1870) and the Paris Commune (1871) (Rubin 2012: 119–38), Ozon's choice of this iconoclastic painting clearly ties in with his film's ostensibly pacifist and anti-nationalist narrative.

RECTUM IS THE GRAVE

Le Suicidé's presence in Ozon's film can be further illuminated with Leo Edelman's reframing of queerness as resistance to the viability of the social order and its consequent positioning in the place of this order's death drive (Edelman 2004: 3). Although scores of gay men and women wish to and indeed raise children, the queer, states Edelman, is incompatible with reproductive sex and, consequently, stands for a sexuality that is pure pleasure and that our culture does the best to conceal. Put otherwise, the queer is equated with non-reproductive narcissistic enjoyment understood as 'inherently destructive of meaning and therefore as responsible for the undoing of social organisation, collective reality, and, inevitably, life itself' (Edelman 2004: 12–13). Identified with negativity, queerness also refuses 'every substantialisation of identity' and rejects the hope for reaching meaning through signification: '[T]he queerness of which I speak would deliberately sever us from ourselves, from the assurance, that is, of *knowing* ourselves and hence of knowing our "good"' (Edelman 2004: 5). Edelman then attaches this 'good' to the ideas of 'normalisation' and 'generalisation', and contrasts it with 'the stubborn particularity' marking the queer (2004: 6). Reconsidered in this light, *Le Suicidé* becomes a fitting backdrop for Adrien's and Frantz's homoerotically charged friendship that negates the heteronormative social order. More specifically, the two men refute 'hegemonic masculinity', which is the configuration of gender practice ensuring the domination of patriarchy (Connell 2001: 77) and which is linked to military culture as characterised by 'stoicism under hardship', 'absence of emotion', and 'rational calculation' (Barrett 2001). Adrien and Frantz's negating position finds expression in their shared pacifism, in Adrien's profound traumatisation resulting from the war and, considering the assimilation of gayness with what is 'symbolically expelled from hegemonic masculinity' (Connell 2001: 79), in Adrien's implied homosexuality. And so just as Manet's painting silently speaks of a socially unacceptable death, Adrien's homosexual fantasies are articulated wordlessly. The synonymy between pacifism and homosexuality thus insinuated by Ozon's film has a particularly strong resonance in the German context, where, on the eve of the First World War, Pan-Germans equated the pacifism of Wilhelm II and his inner circle with unmanliness or even homosexuality, and believed that only conventional, belligerent masculinity could assure Germany's imperial expansion (Domeier 2014: 746).

Recast in Kaja Silverman's terms, *Le Suicidé* becomes a cipher for Adrien's mental crisis resulting from his killing of Frantz, where Adrien's implicit homosexuality serves to stress the impairment of his masculinity as part of what Freud called 'war trauma' and what, extending the term's application to other crises, Silverman rebrands as 'historical trauma'. Experienced individually but influencing the collective, historical trauma triggers the suspension of belief in the 'dominant fiction' into which we are ushered by the positive Oedipus complex and which hinges on our faith in the unity of the family, in small-town life and in the adequacy of the male subject (Silverman 1992: 55). While the discourse of war linking masculinity to mastery is integral to the 'dominant fiction', war effectively becomes experienced as disintegration of 'a bound and armoured [male] ego' that is predicated upon control, cohesion and denial of castration and otherness (Silverman 1992: 11, 62). Following Freud, Silverman identifies the death drive as the force behind the historical trauma, and sees it as both directed outward through the killing of other soldiers and turned against the (psychologically) wounded soldier's self (Silverman 1992: 60). In *Frantz*, the faith in the 'dominant fiction' of patriotism, militarism and unity of the nuclear family is shown to have been dented by the war, whose ravages are externalised by the surviving men's physical and/or psychological mutilations. By emphasising the fathers' responsibility for their sons' demise, Ozon's film also isolates the Oedipus complex as the driving force behind the 'dominant fiction', the paterfamilias finding embodiment in Dr Hoffmeister, whose austere demeanour and name which literally translates as 'the estate master' only confirm his role. However, Hoffmeister's exposure to Adrien's traumatisation softens his original entrenchment in the dominant ideology: he abandons the role of the tyrannical patriarch assumed by fathers in Ozon's films and blames Frantz's and other young men's deaths on their fathers' misplaced patriotism and militarism:[7] 'Und wer hat eure Söhne umgebracht? Wer hat sie an die

HOMOEROTIC OVERTONES 59

Front geschickt? Wer hat ihnen Bajonette und Munition geliefert? Wir. Ihre Väter . . . Wir sind verantwortlich.' ('And who killed your boys? Who sent them to the front? Who supplied them with bayonets and munitions? We did: their fathers . . . We are responsible.') By simultaneously identifying himself as an Oedipal father and as part of a wider community, Hoffmeister spells out the commensurability of family and society, and of father and Fatherland.

Implicit in the repeated invocation of Manet's painting, the imbrication of death and queerness becomes explicit in the scene of Frantz's death (Figure 3.1).[8] Narrated from the vantage point of a cemetery and, equally appropriately, set inside a rectum-like trench, the flashback opens with French soldiers marching towards a battle before a sudden explosion disperses them. The camera cuts to Adrien jumping into a trench and then vacillates between his face and that of the enemy soldier the Frenchman has unexpectedly encountered. The two men are wide-eyed and breathing heavily, their lips parted in an expression that could as easily be taken for bewilderment as for sexual excitement. If Ozon largely follows Lubitsch's representation of this episode, he supresses Anna's presence, which the American director brought in metonymically through the German soldier's letter to his fiancée. By guiding the dying man's hand so that he may sign the letter, Paul becomes symbolically anointed as Elsa's husband and the Horderlins' (renamed Hoffmeisters) surrogate son. In *Frantz*, however, the heteronormative tale is queered. After Adrien fires a shot at the German, an explosion projects him on top of his victim and the screen goes momentarily dark. The position of the two men, one lying on top of the other, and the angle of the camera that films the two men's heads from above and in close-up, connotes sexual intercourse. But, contrary to the visual narrative, Adrien's monologue once again complies with heteronormative standards. While his description of the two bodies' position is ambiguous – 'Nos deux corps, l'un contre l'autre, lui mort et moi vivant' ('Our bodies lying together,

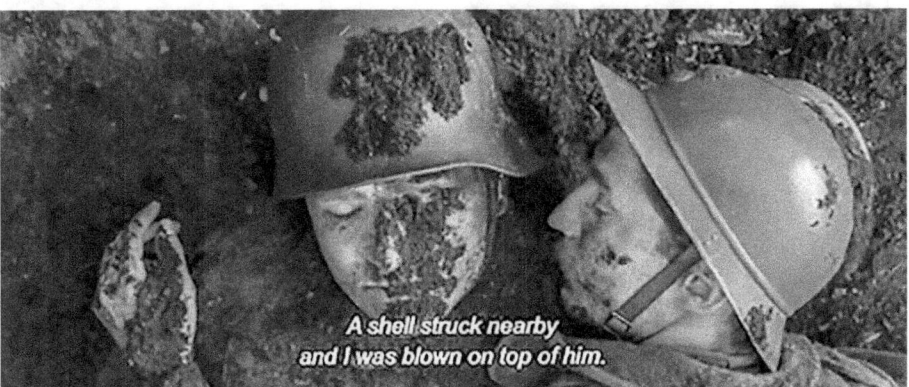

Figure 3.1 Frantz and Adrien in the trenches

him dead, and me alive') – he never mentions the dirt that covers him and Frantz, and that potentially symbolises the defilement attached to homosexuality by the conservative societies the two men belong to. Its speculative symbolism aside, the dirt occasions Adrien's caressing gesture with which he cleans Frantz's face. Adrien's hand then proceeds to stroke the dead man's lips, and his head edges slightly forward as if he wants to kiss him. Finally, the camera zooms out into a medium and then long shot, showing Adrien's entire body gently twitching before slowly dropping away from Frantz's corpse.

The coincidence of Frantz's death with the culmination of the two men's retrospectively imagined relationship brings to mind the French expression 'la petite mort', which nowadays tends to designate an orgasm and which Ozon himself has used as the title of a short film narrating the liberating effect of a father's death on a gay photographer.[9] Even if it is not the death of the father but of a patriarch in waiting around which *Frantz* revolves, this death has a similarly cathartic effect on the film's protagonists. While it enables Anna's escape from the life of a wife and mother that she seems predestined for, Adrien channels his mourning into a fantasy of a homosexual relationship which provides a welcome counterweight to the loveless marriage he is about to enter. 'Grâce à ce mensonge', he confesses, 'j'ai découvert qui était Frantz, sa famille, sa maison, sa fiancée. Chaque jour, je l'ai aimé un peu plus.' ('Thanks to my lie, I discovered who Frantz was, his family, his house, his fiancée. Every day, I loved him a little more.') Even before Adrien's confession, death and homosexual desire are enmeshed, as illustrated by the already mentioned riverbank scene, during which Anna prompts Adrien about his scars (Figure 3.2). As the camera slides down to and closes in on Adrien's penis, whose bulging shape is discernible through the wet fabric of his long johns, Adrien admits that 'Ma seule blessure c'est Frantz.' ('My only wound is Frantz.') Ozon's translation of war trauma into (homosexual) desire can be productively structured with Max Cavitch's

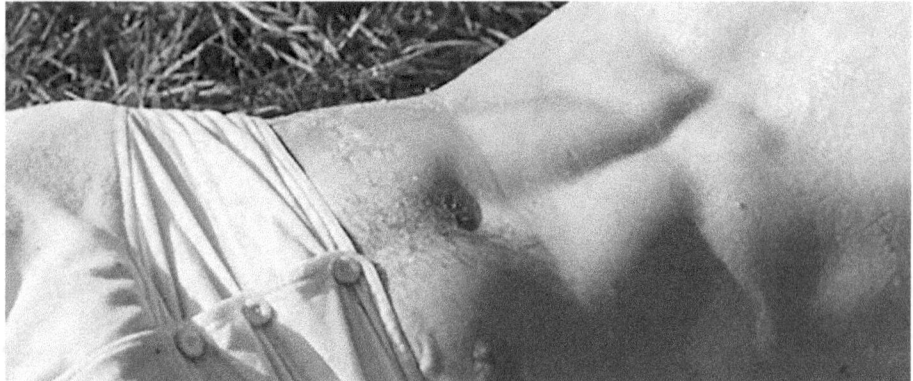

Figure 3.2 Adrien's wet body

elaboration of the mourning strategies developed alongside queer theory. These strategies tie in with what Cavitch, alluding to Edelman's reconceptualisation of gay ethics, calls 'preposthumous resistance to the logics of reproduction', and include 'the overruling [of the] reticent with the antagonistically explicit', 'displacing mortuary and memorial decorum with improvised and impatient performances', or 'freshly embracing the work of anger, ambivalence and melancholy' (Cavitch 2007: 313). If these strategies find some embodiment in Adrien's emotional response to Frantz's death, Ozon's rejection of the consolation of futurity is evident in his choice to dispense with the widow's union with the repentant killer, which concludes Rostand's play and Lubitsch's film.

Yet, even though Ozon replaces Hollywoodian clichés with a queered ending, he stops short of making a straightforward commitment to homosexuality. Adrien's story closes with his reintegration into the *haute bourgeoisie*, as represented by Adrien's authoritarian mother (Cyrielle Clair) and her coterie, through a marriage of convenience. The film's half-hearted effort to queer this conventional denouement can be gleaned, firstly, from the androgyny (and possible bisexuality) of Adrien's fiancée, Fanny (Alice de Lencquesaing). Secondly, as a sister of Adrien's friend, François, who, like Frantz, died at the front and who was Frantz's namesake, Fanny is cast as the next best thing to Frantz. However unsatisfactory, such an ending confirms Edelman's conception of homosexuality as a non-identity confined to the position of negativity in relation to the prevalent social order, from where it must disturb or queer social organisation and our investment in it (Edelman 2004: 17). The conclusion to Anna's story carries a similar resonance. Despite having been jolted by Adrien, Anna continues her relationship with him in the past conditional, the letters she sends to the Hoffmeisters from Paris replicating Adrien's earlier deception. Anna's lies are complete with her visit to the Louvre in the film's closing sequence, which, due to its colour tonality and oneiric quality, may also belong to the imaginary register. In this scene, Anna, like Frantz earlier, contemplates *Le Suicidé* in the company of a young man, which suggests that her future lies in a heterosexual relationship, even if her partner may not be a model of normative masculinity. Indeed, echoing Fanny's androgyny, the stranger's effeminate appearance subverts strict gender stereotypes. To read the film's closure more positively, one needs to focus on Anna's uncharacteristic radiance and confidence. Consequently, the ending can be reframed with Edelman's theory, that is, as illustrating the link between non-identity and *jouissance*, whose possibility is foreclosed by 'social reality and the futurism on which it relies', but which can be found 'beyond the bounds of identity, meaning and law' (Edelman 2004: 23). Instead of the aforementioned 'good', this *jouissance* offers what Edelman calls 'better' and what he connects to what Lacan calls 'truth', where truth does not assure happiness, but 'names only the insistent particularity of the subject' (Edelman 2004: 5).

THE RETURN OF FRANTZ HOFFMEISTER

Just as traditional cinema is at pains to deny male lack, 'against which it marshals such protective measures as projection, disavowal, and fetishism' (Silverman 1992: 74), it similarly offers little space for the representation of other than heteronormative identities or for questioning the sacred ideas of the nation or the family. These comments pertain in particular to heritage film which, acting as '*ciment identitaire*', 'bind[s] audience members together, creating in them both a shared sense of belonging and a shared sense of loss' (Esposito 2011: 12–14). This is achieved precisely through the exclusion from the nation's body of any marginal identities, and the correlated representation of this body as ethnically and culturally homogenous (Oscherwitz 2010: 42). Put differently, cinematic adaptation of canonical literary texts 'disavows difference in both literary and sexual inheritance: both work to conserve the purity of the national body' (Handyside 2011: 55). Bearing in mind these remarks, I will now discuss how, while observing some rules governing heritage film, *Frantz* subverts its ethos. By queering war-induced trauma, Ozon's film interrogates the dominant narratives on the nation, war and masculinity, which heritage film tends to reinforce. Additionally, by adapting Rostand's play and Lubitsch's film, Ozon connects two texts created in the aftermath of the First World War and intended as an aesthetic warning against future military conflicts, to present socio-political concerns. He thus validates Hutcheon's position that adaptation is a transgenerational phenomenon which often involves a migration towards more favourable conditions and which is always shaped by the moment of its production (Hutcheon 2006: 28–31). Finally, by destabilising the convention of heritage cinema, *Frantz* succeeds in engaging more diverse audiences than those usually targeted by this cinematic genre.

Just as in Thatcher's Britain heritage cinema diverted viewers' attention from the grim economic and social reality (Corner and Harvey 1991: 72; Higson 2003: 49), in France it knew its heyday during a major economic and political crisis (Darnton 1984: 19). The reforms undertaken by François Mitterrand and his culture minister, Jack Lang, were to help the administration 'take control of French history' and, by concentrating on its great moments such as the 1789 Revolution, turn this history into a source of pride for the beleaguered nation (Austin 1996: 144). Daniel Vigne's *Le Retour de Martin Guerre* (1982), Andrzej Wajda's *Danton* (1983), Yves Angelo's *Colonel Chabert* (1994) or Patrice Chéreau's *La Reine Margot* (1994) were expected 'to reestablish and promote an "authentic" national culture that [the Mitterrand government] perceived as disappeared' (Oscherwitz 2010: 37). The 'state-sponsored narratives that constituted a return to the traditional values and to traditional film aesthetics' (Oscherwitz 2010: 37) used the past as a means of 'shoring up notions of national identity in unstable, increasingly global times' (Esposito 2011: 11). Consequently, some see heritage cinema as 'reconstructing myths already mobilised by the nation' (Hayward 1993: 15) and/or as a reaction to the Nouvelle Vague's formal experimentation and concern with the present (Oscherwitz 2010: 37). Others have disparagingly regarded heritage films as aimed at a 'middle-class, middle-brow, middle-aged and largely female audience' (Monk 2002: 180) and have branded them as 'politically conservative bad objects' (Monk 2011: 13). Similarly scathing comments have been directed at the more general category of adaptation, which has been called secondary, derivative, belated, middlebrow or culturally inferior (Hutcheon 2006: 3).

What *Frantz* shares with heritage film is its setting in 'highly resonant periods and spaces of the national past' (Oscherwitz 2010: 33) and its meticulous re-creation of the represented historical reality, as exemplified with the right-hand drive car owned by Adrien and apparently typical of the time (Ozon, 2016). The presence of classical music in *Frantz* is also characteristic. Apart from the original Mahler-inspired soundtrack by Philippe Rombi, viewers hear Chopin's posthumous Nocturne in C sharp minor and easily recognisable pieces by Rimsky-Korsakov and Tchaikovsky. Ozon's selection of music is consistent with his film's Eurocentrism, another standard feature of heritage cinema (Dyer and Vincendeau 1992: 6). Indeed, Frantz draws both explicitly and implicitly on a wealth of texts of European literature and cinema, such as Verlaine's and Rilke's poetry, Manet's painting, or Curtiz's and Hitchcock's films.[10] The focus on the family is yet another hallmark of cinematic adaptation, where 'the nation is reproduced both in terms of the reproduction of the nation's image and the transmission of national memory' (Handyside 2011: 54). The nation 'is mapped onto the figure of the (nuclear) family secure in its place in the landscape as the privileged place of national belonging' (Handyside 2011: 54). Substantiating the idea that heritage film conveys the continuity of both the family and the nation (Handyside 2011: 55), *Frantz* follows the Hoffmeisters and the Rivoires, whose social status reflects the customary preoccupation of heritage cinema with the upper and middle classes. Finally, Ozon's film supports the view that heritage film programmatically features 'historically significant buildings, or culturally resonant landscapes and interiors' as part of its 'tendency to generate heritage space – a nostalgic space of memory – rather than narrative space' (Higson 2003: 177). While the first part of *Frantz* is set in Quedlinburg, which is a UNESCO world heritage site, in the film's second half we are treated to the sight of easily recognisable historical buildings, such as the Musée du Louvre or the Opéra Garnier.

Seemingly in line with this pattern, the film's final scenes are set at a chateau belonging to Adrien's family. However, rather than creating a nostalgic space of memory, the Rivoires's opulent estate provides a stage for Ozon's caustic critique of the *haute bourgeoisie* and its tenacious adherence to a certain way of life. On her arrival at the chateau, Anna finds a community seemingly unaffected by the war: Adrien is out horse riding and in the evening his mother will host an elegant dinner followed by a private recital. By renouncing his musical career in Paris to entertain the local coterie, and by marrying Fanny only to please his mother, Adrien has embraced the ideals of continuity and futurity, or, in other words, has chosen to secure the perpetuity of the family, the nation and the status quo. Yet, at a dinner party, during which guests gleefully reminisce about the celebrations accompanying the armistice, Adrien undermines the master narrative by corrosively invoking his memory of the mental asylum where he spent the momentous day. In the same vein, Adrien completes a guest's comment about people dancing with a remark 'sur les cadavres' ('on people's graves'). In this way *Frantz* refocuses our attention on the war's long-lasting fallout obfuscated by the 'dominant fiction' and consisting in the veterans' physical and mental wounds, the losses endured by the fallen soldiers' families and the rise of nationalism on both sides of the border, which, as Ozon anachronistically reminds us, foreshadows the unbridled ferocity of the Second World War. To put it in another way, untypically for heritage cinema, *Frantz* favours critical engagement with the past instead of its glorification and, in so doing, it undermines the pre-established conception of Europe's twentieth-century history.

What further distinguishes *Frantz* and, more broadly, Ozon's oeuvre from cinematic adaptations which, mainly for financial reasons, rely on culturally prestigious literary works (Hutcheon 2006: 29) is its dialogue with 'relatively obscure or relatively unsuccessful texts' (Handyside 2011: 57). And so *Frantz* draws on Rostand's now forgotten play and on Lubitsch's *Broken Lullaby* that, although eventually successful, flopped upon its release.[11] The French auteur's iconoclastic approach to adaptation is additionally apparent in his film's cast: unlike French heritage cinema that ensures large audiences by engaging stars such as Gérard Depardieu or Catherine Deneuve (Austin 1996: 142), with the exception of Pierre Niney, Ozon has selected little-known actors.[12] *Frantz*'s principal difference from heritage cinema lies, however, in the fact that it does not share the perspective on the First World War promulgated by mainstream French cinema. Although some filmmakers have assumed anti-conformist, transgressive or anti-militaristic positions, while more recent productions have focused on the individual's experience,[13] Ozon additionally adopts the German perspective and perhaps even invites us to emulate Anna's and the Hoffmeisters' generosity of spirit in relation to the former enemy. By focusing on the war's losers, Ozon also forestalls the sense of national pride and unity usually incited by heritage film in the home audience. Finally, *Frantz* provocatively equates German and French militarism and nationalism, which it does, firstly, by investing 'La Marseillaise' with a meaning different to that which it carries in *Casablanca* and, secondly, by showing Adrien's hostile reception in Germany to be echoed by the resentment Anna meets with in France. Consequently, *Frantz* precludes an easy identification with the national past or even with the French victims of the war, for, notwithstanding his trauma and guilty conscience, Adrien remains responsible for killing an unarmed man. He is also portrayed as a liar and coward, who ultimately lets himself be reclaimed by the prevalent social order.

In line with the view that taking interest in the 'losers of history' is 'the most reliable guide to a hopeful future' (Wesseling 1991: 111, 113), Ozon's cinematic retelling of a story set in the wake of the First World War unquestionably accounts for present and future reality. *Frantz* thereby once again defies the spirit of heritage film, where the past is shown as 'detached from the present [. . .] rather than as an assertion of continuity between the two' (Oscherwitz 2010: 34) or, put differently, as 'discursively stable and clearly separated from the present by . . . the markers of period reconstruction' (Vidal 2012: 53). This means that viewers of cinematic adaptations 'are invited to understand the plot of the film as though [they] were *contemporary* with the characters, while at the same time indulging [their] pleasure in a world that is visually compelling precisely because of its *pastness*' (Craig 1991: 12). Conversely, Ozon has spoken openly of his film's intended resonances with today's Europe, where some politicians are calling for the return of borders as a buffer against much-feared immigration (Ozon, 2016).[14] His film's emphasis on the mutual animosity between France and Germany, represented as each other's mirror-images, indicates both Ozon's understanding of the European project as a mechanism capable of thwarting future military conflicts and fear for the stability of the political structures that are being undermined by the widespread rise of populism or by Brexit. For, even if the 2016 referendum took place only shortly before the film's release, Ozon presents *Frantz* as his response to the xenophobic climate that had determined its outcome (Abraham and Ozon 2017). By reworking a film by a German-Jewish immigrant to America or by focusing on the hostility with which Adrien and Anna meet in Germany and France respectively, Ozon connects the story he is retelling to the wider, topical and closely inter-related questions of immigration and nationalism. His film relates to more present concerns also through its engagement with homosexuality and depression, whereby it unsilences Rostand's sexuality and his ailing mental health that culminated in the playwright's suicide (Simon 2013). Finally, giving credence to the opinion that it is with the future in view that '[t]he queer present negotiates with the past' (Rich 2005: 58, quoted in Kelly and Pugh 2016: 1), Ozon stresses that our understanding of history invariably hinges on the concerns of the present and that, correlatedly, our contemporary anxieties inflect our readings of the past.

Another way in which *Frantz* manifests its 'presentification' of history, as Hutcheon calls postmodern art's 'dialogue with the past in the light of the present' (Hutcheon 1988: 19–20), are the flashbacks which can be construed as a double-coded metatextual comment on Ozon's self-contradictory engagement with heritage film. In other words Adrien's imaginary relationship with Frantz can be deciphered as a *mise-en-abyme* of the film itself that strives to create a mimetic illusion despite being a work of fiction and which undermines the very ideology that conventional heritage cinema reaffirms. Although confabulated, Adrien's – and later Anna's – narrative responds to the Hoffmeisters' conservative *Weltanschauung* and has the power to appease their grief and enable their mourning for Frantz. Conversely, the revelation of Adrien's reason for visiting Quedlinburg has a devastating effect on Anna's mental health, while one does not even dare to imagine the shattering impact of the truth on Frantz's parents. Adrien's tales thus become a vector for Ozon's critique of a cinematic convention that offers a highly stylised, not to say distorted, image of history and that, coincidentally, has been dubbed 'quintessential flashback' (Oscherwitz 2010: 41). Considering that Adrien – and later Anna – create deceitful versions of reality, be it past or present, with a view to satisfying society's expectations of conventional heteronormative relationships, I read the flashbacks as Ozon's attempt to undermine our faith in historical narratives conveyed by heritage film. At the same time, however, projected in the backdrop of Adrien's and Anna's narratives, the colour images communicate the subversive potential of cinematic adaptations. To rephrase, whereas Adrien's monologue and Anna's letters set out to arrest and prevent change, and to offer a reassuring version of reality as a remedy against present uncertainties, the silent images become a site for the reconstruction of historical events through a critical and contemporary lens, and for the enactment of marginal identities, including sexual ones.

CONCLUSION

By simultaneously using and abusing the genre of heritage cinema (Hutcheon 1988: 20), *Frantz* endorses its sympathetic evaluations, as instantiated by Hutcheon's re-examination of adaptation. Repositing the Romantic obsession with originality as an aberration rather than a rule, and noting that storytelling has traditionally been about repeating existing narratives (Hutcheon 2006: 2, 4, 21), the Canadian theorist redefines adaptation as a 'a repetition without replication' which satisfies our need for both familiarity and novelty (Hutcheon 2006: 176). This means that adaptation 'involves both memory and change, persistence and variations' (Hutcheon 2006: 176), and is capable of 'engaging in a larger social or cultural critique' (Hutcheon 2006: 94). Referring specifically to Ozon's earlier reworkings of cultural texts, Fiona Handyside reframes adaptation as 'potentially queer, as it . . . offers the possibility of subversion precisely through its play between the "original" and the "copy"' (Handyside 2011: 56). While *Frantz* is no exception in this respect, Ozon's modification of Rostand's play should also be contextualised with Hutcheon's conception of adaptation as a stage for articulating political positions and personal agendas that radically differ from those behind the source text (Hutcheon 2006: 106). Reviving the recently unfashionable concept of authorial intentionality, Hutcheon sees adaptation as a process of taking possession of another's story and 'filtering it through one's own sensibility, interests and talents' (Hutcheon 2006: 18). In *Frantz*'s case, this is illustrated by Ozon's choice to title his film with the German version of his own name, and to stamp Adrien's and Frantz's posthumously imagined encounter with his own sexuality. Ozon's wish to mark the story he is appropriating with his personal and distinctive fingerprint is also palpable in the themes of suicide and struggle against authoritarian paternity, which are absent from *L'Homme que j'ai tué / The Man I Killed* or *Broken Lullaby*, but which abundantly feature in Ozon's oeuvre. Finally, while maintaining Rostand's and Lubitsch's pacifist message, Ozon retells Europe's tragic twentieth-century history with reference to our present complacency before the resurgence of nationalism and intolerance towards the Other, which the French director locates at the root of the two world wars that his film respectively memorialises and anticipates.

In all this, *Frantz*'s queering of the past plays a vital role, supporting the belief that '*queer* is used most energetically as a disruptive mode of enquiry, one that destabilises expectations of normativity', whether these are directed at gender identities or historical master narratives (Kelly and Pugh 2016: 3). In Ozon's film, normative sexualities and dominant ideologies not only dovetail, but are also challenged with equal vehemence. Notably, Ozon offsets hegemonic masculinity fleshed out by Herr Kreutz and generally thought to be crystallised by the experience of combat with war trauma that his film links to pacifism and subsequently queers. Rather than showing the experience of the trenches to be instrumental in turning young men into 'protectors and providers', as propagandic discourse had it before and during the First World War (Meyer 2009: 2), Ozon reimagines these young men as victims of Oedipal violence and anticipates their struggle to re-join postwar society should they survive. Pursuing the Oedipal trope, the French director sets up a synonymy between the patriarch and society, which he reinforces through the phonological relationship between the repeatedly used German terms 'der Vater' ('the father') and 'das Vaterland' ('the Fatherland'). Whereas patriarchal society is shown to be behind the 'dominant fiction' that, for Edelman, entails the belief in the linearity of history and the possibility of reaching meaning through signification, Ozon insists on the cyclicality of the past and the inability of nationalistic and militaristic narratives to signify the reality of the trenches with their tragic and lasting fallout. As a result, although constrained by its heteronormative *transtext*, that is by the intertextual web of narratives that come into conversation within an adaptation (Stam 2005: 85), *Frantz* endows homosexuality with '[t]he corrosive force of irony' capable of undermining the dominant discourse of power (Edelman 2004: 23), even if it is unsuccessful in rescuing it from the position of oppositionality to which society relegates it. This is illustrated, for instance, by Adrien's afore-analysed undoing of the totalising narrative on the armistice, which excludes the loss of life and physical and/or mental health. As well as the failure of normative discourses to convey the experience of the front, the queering of Adrien's mourning for the man he killed exposes the inadequacy of canonical genres, such as heritage film, when it comes to articulating traumata or indeed to making these traumata intelligible and compelling to audiences other than the habitual viewers of cinematic adaptations. One way to remedy this inadequacy is to queer conventional narrative strategies and normative storylines, as Ozon does when he subversively mobilises a cinematic genre associated with conservatism, elitism and nostalgia to foster change, be it political, sexual or aesthetic.

I wish to thank Professor Marianne Liljeström (University of Turku) for taking the time to comment on an early draft of this chapter.

NOTES

1. The term 'heritage film' was first coined to designate costume dramas made in Thatcher's Britain. Although Andrew Higson's study concentrates on films made in the 1980s and 1990s, and depicting aspects of English past, it acknowledges that the label of 'heritage cinema' can encompass films made outside this scope (Higson, p. 10).
2. Adrien (literally) mirrors himself in Frantz, and Frantz himself is a reflection of François, Adrien's friend. Anna and Adrien, whose first names begin with the same vowel, are also depicted as each other's reflections.
3. It is possible that Ozon is alluding to Jean-Jacques Annaud's use of black-and-white photographs that have been painted in *La Victoire en chantant / Black and White in Colour* (1976). For an analysis of this and other films that challenge the received image of the First World War, see Blanc-Hoàng (2016).
4. Ozon explicitly identifies the final scene as a happy ending (Ozon 2017).
5. Suicide features in *8 Femmes / 8 Women* (2002), *Gouttes d'eau sur pierres brûlantes / Water Drops on Burning Rocks* (2000), *Dans la maison / In the House* (2012), *Sous le sable / Under the Sand* (2000) and *Ricky* (2009).
6. For example, in Balzac's contemporaneous novel, *La Peau de chagrin* (1831) / *The Skin of Sorrow*, suicide is described as an act of 'tragic grandeur and heroic greatness' (Ilg 2002: 181).
7. These films include *8 femmes / 8 Women*, *Potiche*, *Sitcom*, *La Petite Mort / Little Death* (1995) and *Les amants criminels / Criminal Lovers* (1999). One of the figures consistently cast by Ozon's oeuvre is that of the dominant and abusive father (Lalanne 2002: 82–3).
8. In French, trenches can be referred to as 'les boyaux' ('the bowels').
9. *La Petite mort / Little Death* (1995) tells the story of Paul, who specialises in taking pictures of men as they climax. The triangulation of photography, *jouissance* and the death of Paul's estranged father brings to mind Roland Barthes's meditation on the photographic image's both mortifying power and ability to channel bliss (*jouissance*), as opposed to pleasure (*plaisir*) (Barthes 1980). Ozon's short film works with both these notions by

rooting Paul's trauma and consequent frigidity in his father's early rejection of him in response to a photograph of Paul as a baby. As if to undo the trauma through reciprocating the castrating Oedipal gesture, Paul photographs his father's unconscious and naked body before gauging out the eyes in one of the photos he has taken. This symbolic patricide has a cathartic effect not only on Paul, who now gives himself fully to his lover, Martial, but also on Paul's sister, Camille, whose personal growth has been stifled by her closeness to her father. Similarly, in *Sitcom* and *8 femmes / 8 Women* the patriarch's death liberates (homosexual) desire from the shackles of social convention.

10. Although he made *Casablanca* during his Hollywood period, Curtiz, who was of Jewish-Hungarian origin, had been an established film director in Budapest before emigrating to the United States.
11. Likewise, *8 femmes / 8 Women* is based on Robert Thomas's little-known *Boulevard* play and *Gouttes d'eau sur pierres brûlantes / Water Drops on Burning Rocks* on Fassbinder's obscure play.
12. Niney may be known to viewers through his role in the biopic of Yves Saint Laurent and as a member of the national Comédie Française theatre.
13. Among those productions are Raymond Bernard's *Les Croix de bois / Wooden Crosses* (1932) or Jean Renoir's *La Grande Illusion / The Grand Illusion* (1937), which both foreground the plight of disabled soldiers. More recent examples of pacifist approaches to the Great War include Jean-Pierre Jeunet's *Un long dimanche de fiançailles / A Very Long Engagement* (2002), which addresses the predicament of the working classes who were used as cannon fodder and whose stories were subsequently suppressed (Blanc-Hoàng 2016).
14. In another interview, Ozon stated: 'I had the feeling that speaking about that time, it was a way to speak about today too, with the rise of nationalism in Europe, some politicians asking for a return to borders' (Abraham and Ozon, 2017).

WORKS CITED

Abraham, Raphael and François Ozon (2017), 'François Ozon on Nationalism, Avoiding Sex and His Film *Frantz*', *Financial Times*, 28 April, <https://www.ft.com/content/411c91de-29c0-11e7-9ec8-168383da43b7> (last accessed 12 December 2019).
Arnaud, Claude (2016), *Jean Cocteau: A Life*, trans. Lauren Elkin and Charlotte Mandel, New Haven, CT: Yale University Press.
Austin, Guy (1996), *Contemporary French Cinema: An Introduction*, Manchester: Manchester University Press.
Barrett, Frank J. (2001), 'The Organisational Construction of Hegemonic Masculinities: The Case of the US Navy', in Stephen M. Whitehead and Frank J. Barrett (eds), *The Masculinities Reader*, Cambridge: Polity Press, pp. 77–99.
Barthes, Roland (1980), *La Chambre claire*, Paris: Gallimard/Seuil.
Blanc-Hoàng, Henri-Simon (2016), 'Expressing Pacifist Views through the Recovery of World War I's Silenced Voices in Jean-Jacques Annaud's *La victoire en chantant* (1976), Bertrand Tavernier's *Capitaine Conan* (1996), and Jean-Pierre Jeunet's *Un long dimanche de fiançailles* (2004)', in Marcelline Block and Barry Nevin (eds), *French Cinema and the Great War: Remembrance and Representation*, Lanham, MD: Rowman and Littlefield, pp. 35–55.
Block, Marcelline and Barry Nevin (eds) (2016), *French Cinema and the Great War*, London: Rowman and Littlefield.
Butler, Judith (1993), *Bodies that Matter: On the Discursive Limits of 'Sex'*, London: Routledge.
Cavitch, Max (2007), 'Sex after Death: François Ozon's Libidinal Invasions', *Screen*, 48: 3, 313–26.

Christensen, Ann-Dorte and Palle Rasmussen (2015), 'War, Violence and Masculinities: Introduction and Perspectives', *NORMA*, 10: 3–4, 189–202.
Connell, R. W. (2001), *Masculinities*, Cambridge, MA: Polity Press.
Corner, John and Sylvia Harvey (1991), 'Mediating Tradition and Modernity: The Heritage/Enterprise Couplet', in John Corner and Sylvia Harvey, *Enterprise and Heritage: Crosscurrents of National Culture*, London: Routledge, pp. 45–74.
Craig, Cairns (1991), 'Rooms without a View', *Sight and Sound*, 1: 6, 10–13.
Darnton, Robert (1984), *The Great Cat Massacre: And Other Episodes in French Cultural History*, London: Basic Books.
Domeier, Norman (2014), 'The Homosexual Scare and the Masculinisation of German Politics before World War I', *Central European History*, 47: 4, 737–59.
Dyer, Richard and Ginette Vincendeau (1992), 'Introduction', in Richard Dyer and Ginette Vincendeau (eds), *Popular European Cinema*, London: Routledge, pp. 1–14.
Edelman, Lee (2004), *No Future: Queer Theory and the Death Drive*, Durham, NC: Duke University Press.
Esposito, Maria (2011), '*Jean de Florette*: Patrimoine, the Rural Idyll and the 1980s', in Lucy Mazdon (ed.), *France on Film: Reflections on Popular French Cinema*, London: Wallflower Press, pp. 11–26.
Handyside, Fiona (2011), 'Queer Filiations: Adaptation in the Films of François Ozon', *Sexualities*, 15: 1, 53–67.
Hayward, Susan (1993), *French National Cinema*, London: Routledge.
Higson, Andrew (1996), 'The Heritage and British Cinema', in Andrew Higson (ed.), *Dissolving Views: Key Writing on British Cinema*, London: Bloomsbury, pp. 232–49.
Higson, Andrew (2003), *English Heritage, English Cinema*, Oxford: Oxford University Press.
Hutcheon, Linda (1988), *A Poetics of Postmodernism: History, Theory Fiction*, New York: Routledge.
Hutcheon, Linda (2006), *A Theory of Adaptation*, New York: Routledge.
Hutchings, Kimberly (2008), 'Making Sense of Masculinity and War', *Men and Masculinities*, 10: 4, 389–404.
Ilg, Ulrike (2002), 'Painted Theory of Art: "Le Suicidé" (1977) by Édouard Manet and the Disappearance of Narration', *Artibus et Historiae*, 23: 45, 179–90.
Kelly, Kathleen Coyne and Tison Pugh (2016), 'Introduction: Queer History, Cinematic Medievalism, and the Impossibility of Sexuality', in Kathleen Coyne Kelly and Tison Pugh (eds), *Queer Movie Medievalisms*, London: Routledge, pp. 1–18.
Lalanne, Jean-Marc (2002), 'Les Actrices: *8 femmes* de François Ozon', *Cahiers du cinéma*, 556, 82–3.
Le Vay, Lou (2019), *Surrogacy and the Reproduction of Normative Family on TV*, London: Palgrave.
Meyer, Jessica (2009), *Men of War: Masculinity and the First World War*, London: Palgrave.
Misek, Richard (2010), *Chromatic Cinema: A History of Screen Colour*, Oxford: Blackwell.
Monk, Claire (2002), 'The British Heritage-Film Debate Revisited', in Claire Monk and Amy Sargeant (eds), *British Historical Cinema*, London: Routledge, pp. 176–88.
Monk, Claire (2011), *Heritage Film Audiences: Period Films and Contemporary Audiences in the UK*, Edinburgh: Edinburgh University Press.
Oscherwitz, Dayna (2010), *Past Forward: French Cinema and the Post-Colonial Heritage*, Carbondale, IL: Southern Illinois University Press.
Ozon, François (2016), Interview at the British Film Institute (BFI), <https://www.youtube.com/watch?v=XNHG9Vt-5M0> (last accessed 12 December 2019).
Ozon, François (2017), Interview, Rendez-vous with French cinema, '*Franz* Q&A', <https://www.youtube.com/watch?v=vfXgAaozYi4> (last accessed 12 December 2019).

Powrie, Phil (1997), *French Cinema in the 1980s: Nostalgia and the Crisis of Masculinity*, London: Clarendon Press.
Rich, B. Ruby (2004), 'The New Queer Cinema', in Harry M. Benshoff and Sean Griffin (eds), *Queer Cinema*, New York: Routledge, pp. 53–59.
Rubin, James H. (2012), 'Manet's Heroic Corpses and the Politics of Their Time', in Therese Dolan (ed.), *Perspectives on Manet*, New York: Routledge, pp. 119–38.
Sainderichin, Guy-Patrick (1982), 'La Rupture', *Cahiers du cinéma*, 336, p. 18.
Silverman, Kaja (1992), *Male Subjectivity at the Margins*, New York: Routledge.
Simon, Denis (2013), 'Twentieth-Century Dramatizations of the Trials of Oscar Wilde', in Gesche Ipsen, Timothy Mathews and Dragana Obramović (eds), *Provocation and Negotiation: Essays in Comparative Criticism*, Amsterdam: Rodopi, pp. 195–218.
Stam, Robert (2005), *François Truffaut and Friends: Modernism, Sexuality, and Film Adaptation*, New Brunswick, NJ: Rutgers University Press.
Vidal, Bélen (2012), *Heritage Film: Nation, Genre and Representation*, London: Wallflower.
Waldron, Darren (2010), 'Une mine d'or inépuisable: The Queer Pleasures of François Ozon in *8 femmes / 8 Women* (2002)', *Studies in French Cinema*, 10:1, 69–87.
Wesseling, Elisabeth (1991), *Writing History as a Prophet: Postmodernist Innovations in a Historical Novel*, Amsterdam: John Benjamins Publishing Company.

CHAPTER 4

The Crystal-image and Queer Ambiguity in *Sous le sable*

Peadar Kearney

Sous le sable / *Under the Sand* (2000) was Francois Ozon's fourth feature-length film and, in retrospect, proved to be a turning point in his career in many respects. His three previous feature films – *Sitcom* (1998), *Les Amants criminels* / *Criminal Lovers* (1999) and *Gouttes d'eau sur pierres brûlantes* / *Water Drops on Burning Rocks* (2000) – were highly camp, satirical and experimental, yet were all coolly received by critics and film-going audiences alike, frustrating those who had eagerly anticipated his debut after the short films from the previous decade. With *Sous le sable* Ozon experimented with what have since become typical characteristics of his work – unpredictable aesthetic, narrative and production choices – to make the first widely acclaimed film of his career. The film's synopsis is deceptively simple. Marie (Charlotte Rampling) and Jean (Bruno Cremer) leave their Parisian home to go on holiday to the *les Landes* region, in the southwest of France. While there, they go to the beach. Jean goes swimming as Marie sunbathes, but he never comes back. After a police search, Marie is obliged to go back to Paris without him. Months pass and her life continues. She seems to be living her life by going about her usual routine, forgetting what occurred with Jean. She speaks of him as if he is still alive and thinks she is being visited by him (or his ghost?) in their home. Her friends attempt to gently make her aware of what has happened and encourage her to face reality. At times she seems to be on the verge of dealing with Jean's disappearance while simultaneously upholding the fantasy of his ongoing existence. It is not so much the events of the film's narrative that draw the spectator in, but rather the subtle treatment of the distinction between fantasy and reality, and how Ozon blurs the boundary between them. He chose well-known but unfashionable actors to play the lead roles as the film proved difficult to finance and, after an initial hiatus, could only recommence after receiving more financial backing. These all proved, however, to be risks worth taking as it is often credited as the film that established Ozon both in France and abroad. As with many of his films, Ozon examines the humdrum nature of French upper-middle class existence going through tumultuous change. Ginette Vincendeau (2001) describes *Sous le sable* thus: 'François Ozon suffuses the everyday life of the Parisian middle classes (those classic clothes, those elegant apartments) with a sense of dread.'

The importance of *Sous le sable* in Ozon's filmography is reflected in the reactions to the film by some of his most prominent scholars. Thibaut Schilt (2011) addresses the recurring notion of mourning in the film, alongside *Swimming Pool* (2003) and *Le Temps qui reste / Time to Leave* (2005). He pays particular attention to the film's nuanced treatment of Marie's subjective experience of losing Jean: 'It is a work where fantasy merges with actuality; a work deeply anchored in social reality that nonetheless manages, in a virtually seamless fashion, to flirt with the fantastic' (Schilt 2011: 82). Fiona Handyside (2013) comments in detail on the film as being indicative of Ozon's widespread usage of beaches, a key trope in his work: 'His beaches assert queer disruptions of time and space as part of modernity, not other to it' (Handyside 2013: 674). Andrew Asibong (2008) also identifies the profound sense of ambiguity and ambivalence throughout the film, commenting on several key moments where the border between the truth/fiction of reality/imagination is left indistinct (Asibong 2008: 85). Similarly, I am interested in the film's singular treatment of subjectivity, the blurring of the distinction between diegetic reality and fiction, and the sense of ambiguity that pervades the narrative. It is this omnipresence of ambiguity, especially in relation to subjectivity, in *Sous le sable* that will serve as the focal point of my analysis. I aim to add to existing studies of *Sous le sable* by considering these core aspects of the narrative through the combination of the film theory of Gilles Deleuze with queer theory discourse on ambiguity. With my analysis, I aim to demonstrate the extent to which the combination of Deleuzian film theory, particularly the theory of the crystal-image, and Queer theory can be used together to study a film such as *Sous le sable*.

Several critics highlighted the film's ambiguities at the time of release. In *Les Inrocks*, Frédéric Bonnaud (2000) wrote: '*Sous le sable* est tout entier placé sous ce type de fascinantes ambiguïtés' ('*Under the Sand* fully exhibits this type of fascinating ambiguities'). Broadly speaking, this sense of not knowing how to distinguish between what is objectively 'real' and what isn't is present in several Ozon films. In *Swimming Pool* (2003), *Ricky* (2009), *Dans la maison / In the House* (2012) and *Une Nouvelle amie / The New Girlfriend* (2014) there are several ambiguities left open by the films' narratives. In *Sous le sable*, the unanswered questions are limitless. Rather than being a feature of the narrative, as in the previously mentioned examples, *Sous le sable* 'vibrates with ambiguity' (Schwarzbaum 2001: 51). Is Jean actually dead? Is he appearing to Marie as a ghost or is his 'presence' her imagination? Did he intentionally disappear? Did he commit suicide? Does Marie actually not believe that he is gone and is still in contact with him or is she just having trouble coping with the circumstances of his death? These questions are echoed by critical reactions to the film at the time of release (see Bonnaud 2000, Brion 2001, Ebert 2001, Mandelbaum 2001, Scott 2001). Indeed, the soberness of the film's style allows the many ambiguities present to be treated without being subject to any sort of fixed response, as the narrative events flow and remain open-ended. This, in turn, allows us to consider the film's mode of meaning production to be subtlety undefined, avoiding overarching, fixed interpretations, and instead placing an emphasis on evolving notions of self and identity.

SOUS LE SABLE AND THE CRYSTAL-IMAGE

In *Cinema 2* (1989), Gilles Deleuze defines the crystal-image as: 'the uniting of an actual image and a virtual image to the point where they can no longer be distinguished' (Deleuze 1989: 334).' He identifies a crystal-image as one that brings together the 'actual', which is to say 'the real' or what is tangible within the diegesis of the film, and the 'virtual', which may be 'non-real' and includes elements such as subjectivity, dreams or imagination within the same narrative world. Furthermore, the crystal-image fuses these two inherently opposing notions in such a way that one cannot be distinguished from the other. This corresponds to the way in which ambiguity functions in *Sous le sable* and allows us to reconsider the 'reality' of Jean's ontological status, the factual circumstances leading to his death and the extent to which Marie comprehends these events. What makes these types of actual and virtual images particularly interesting in the case of *Sous le sable* is the effort to remove distinguishing features that would usually separate them. Although the film is stylistically sober and realistic, it wilfully blurs the distinction between fantasy and reality. Ozon commented on this aspect of the film:

> there's always a kind of mix between fantasy and reality . . . In *Sous le sable*, I am supportive of Marie, except in the first part where I'm more concerned with offering an objective portrayal of the couple's life. I really wanted to be with her, in a state close to compassion. (Ozon 2010)

The film's perspective closely aligns with Marie's subjective experience, as she deals with the disappearance of Jean. Yet, much more than being a simple treatment of subjectivity, what emerges from the film is the idea that the apparent distinction between one's own perspective and objective reality can be distorted via this 'mix between fantasy and reality'.

After the disappearance of Jean, Marie is forced to return to Paris without him. In the next sequence, we see Marie at a dinner party, speaking lightheatedly about Jean in the present tense, seemingly unaware of the mildly alarmed reactions this is causing in her friends. On returning to her apartment, Jean is there to welcome her as if he has never left. For the viewer, there is an unsettling inconsistency between what we think to be true and the images the film presents us with at this point. Marie speaks about her husband in the present tense and is greeted by him in the most banal fashion, yet up until this point, we have been led to believe that he has disappeared and died. In a truly Ozonian paradox, it is the sheer banality of Jean's 'return' that surprises us most about this sequence; they speak about the evening Marie has had, Jean reads before bed, lying on his side as before, and in the morning they eat breakfast together before Marie leaves. We ask ourselves – has Jean really disappeared? If he has, is this him returning as a ghost? Or is this merely the subjective projection of a woman dealing with grief?

Yet, such questions are unanswered as Marie goes about her daily routine. On the one hand, Jean's return does appear to have been triggered by Marie's outward projection – a close-up shot of her in brief reflection seems to trigger Jean's entry into the scene, with a first shot in particular casting his imposing spectral silhouette from the next room's light (Figure 4.1). The extradiegetic music suggests the entrance of a dissonant tone of tension. Yet, it remains that the sheer banality of her ignoring his disappearance leaves us with the impression that it may not even have happened. All the subsequent sequences with Jean take place in their apartment. The ambivalence of Jean's spectral figure raises several questions concerning the objective reality of his presence. Ozon balances both the real and the imaginary, distorting the line between them in order to offer us what he refers to as a 'mélange du fantasme et de la réalité'. In *Le Monde*, Jacques Mandelbaum (2001) referred to it as 'a troubling mix between real presence and imagiantion'. As Mandelbaum writes, on this level the film is troubling, offering the spectator little sense of the distinction between seemingly antithetical images. Imaginary projection is extended to the spectator's point of view without any prior explanation in order to construct a fluid configuration of perspective. As the film progresses, our understanding of Jean's presence does feel more assured, which is to say we increasingly have the impression that Marie's imaginings function as a coping mechanism, yet this does not prevent us from considering the figurations in terms of ambiguous indiscernibility. At first, the images force us to ask, is this real or not? It is real in the sense that Marie seems to believe that Jean is still alive, yet Marie's entourage appears to understand what has *really* happened. Perhaps the more suitable question is whether or not these images are physical or mental? It is entirely possible that the figure of Jean is purely mental, a subjective projection of Marie's desire to avoid certain aspects of reality, but everything

Figure 4.1 Vincent's presence

that we see is portrayed to be objectively true. The images are in part subjective to the degree that the viewer does not believe that Jean is actually there, yet the images also contain several objectively *true* elements such as the message that Vincent leaves Marie before the second time she 'imagines' Jean, or Vincent's presence in the apartment the last time. There is of course no singular answer to the questions, but rather a teasing out of a complex account of perspective.

Deleuze describes the relationship between the actual and virtual aspects of the crystal-image in terms of 'indiscernibility':

> Distinct, but indiscernible, such are the actual and the virtual which are in continual exchange. When the virtual image becomes actual, it is then visible and limpid, as in the mirror or the solidity of finished crystal. But the actual image becomes virtual in its turn, referred elsewhere, invisible, opaque and shadowy, like a crystal barely dislodged from the earth. (Deleuze 1989: 70)

He explains this in terms of the multi-faceted image that has both 'limpid' and 'opaque' sides that are characterised by degrees of exchange between the two. This can be related to *Sous le sable* in terms of the crystal-image on two counts: it can be understood in terms of the thematic situation represented in the narrative, and it can be understood in relation to visual expressions of opacity. At times the viewer has the impression that they can grasp the reality of the situation being presented, only for this to be undercut by a tangible sense of misunderstanding in a subsequent scene. There are constant shades of clearness and ambiguity at play, reflecting what Deleuze describes as the limpid and opaque side of the crystal-image. Visually, Marie is often seen through or in front of different types of surfaces that present varying degrees of transparency. This is done in an understated fashion that retains the film's dry aesthetic tone, expressing the constantly fluctuating sense of knowing and being unaware. Early in the film Marie passes in front of the opaque window of a service station bathroom as she travels to *les Landes*, totally unaware of her husband's personal struggles and that these are the last days that she will spend with him. Later, we see Marie and her new love-interest, Vincent, through a glass fish tank as they eat together in a restaurant, as she is apparently enjoying the freedom of being a single woman while thinking that her husband is at home waiting for her. Afterwards, we see her through the window of a pharmacy looking through a phonebook as she is starting to learn more about her husband's life, with the window reflecting the indifferent Parisian street-life that is passing by. We see her through a car window that heavily reflects the trees outside as she attempts to find out more information about what has happened. Finally, we see her in front of the opaque window of the morgue waiting room as she is about to deny the all-but conclusive evidence that they have found Jean's body. Schiller (2005) comments on Ozon's choice to repeatedly film Marie (Rampling) in this way: 'It is as if objective and external time continues to flow, but her internal experienced sense of time has stopped' (Schiller 2005: 222). Schiller's description conveys the layered sense of meaning present in these images, a visual tension between the objective/external and the subjective/internal. In this sense, multiple images are contained in one image, and there are competing levels of meaning to be taken into account. Marie's subjectivity is expressed as a gauze-like film that shrouds her perspective and separates her from the world that surrounds her, in comparison to which objectivity exists in harsh contrast.

The film's sense of opacity culminates with the very last shot, when Marie goes off into the distance, running towards a distant figure on the beach (Figure 4.2). Handyside has commented on this image, and the figure that Marie runs towards, in detail:

> His ambiguity profoundly affects how we read the end of the film: is this figure another ghostly hallucination of Jean, born of desperation to deny his death; or is it a different man, who attracts Marie precisely because he is not Jean but rather offers hope of a new relationship? (Handyside 2012: 64)

Figure 4.2 Marie at the beach

Handyside demonstrates how the liminality of the beach as a physical space reflects the liminality of this distant figure seen there, who could either be objectively real or subjective projection. The notion of liminality here is closely linked to what I describe as the film's opacity. Just as the beach is a liminal space between land and sea, our understanding of the film's ending resides in-between possible interpretations. This is the film's ultimate ambiguity and most opaque moment. Has Marie accepted what has happened or is her fantasy continuing? For the purpose of this analysis, I am not interested in the answer to such a question but rather how the question functions in relation to the film's meaning. The question allows the film to avoid any singular sense of interpretation and opens up possibilities as to how the viewer may identify with the narrative. The viewer might be unsure how to interpret the scene due to a lack of clarity, as Marie moves away from our perspective and the film ends. Yet, there is no defined sense of interpretation. Throughout, there are these constant shades of clearness and ambiguity; different situations and different images move through multiple levels of possible meaning.

According to Deleuze, this indiscernibility of the actual and the virtual is often concisely captured in film via the 'mirror-image':

> [. . .] This circuit itself is an exchange: the mirror-image is virtual in relation to the actual character that the mirror catches, but it is actual in the mirror which now leaves the character with only a virtuality and pushes him back out-of-field. (Deleuze 1989: 70)

The mirror-image is an extremely prominent stylistic feature that is linked to the omnipresent sense of ambiguity throughout Ozon's work. Characters are often shown alongside their own reflection or contemplating their own image in a reflective surface. For example, we can find numerous examples throughout *Water Drops* (2000), *Time to Leave* (2005), *Frantz* (2016) and *L'Amant double / Double Lover* (2017). There is a sustained interest in how the subject may relate to its own reflection, with the possible dissonance that may exist between subjective perceptions of the self and how they may be seen by others in reality. *Sous le sable* presents us with a variety of mirror-images. For example, Ozon often uses a mirror to avoid resorting to a shot-counter-shot to film a conversation. The principal subject is established in the foreground, with the opposite angle provided alongside it in a mirror in the background. Rather than a thorough sense of what is happening, embellished by multiple camera angles in the space being filmed, we have one frame containing multiple frames. This mirror-image holds multiple viewpoints, containing multiple acts of looking. This represents the fractured sense of perspective that Ozon is addressing in the film; one's own experience is just one way of seeing and is subject to being contradicted by another. Just as we have seen how there are several levels of meaning, which are expressed in one frame when we see Marie (Rampling) through naturally occurring visual reflections, there are competing perspectives in the film's mirror-images. Ultimately this serves to open up the film's treatment of subjectivity beyond a univocal account of perspective. There are competing levels of meaning amongst multiple ways of seeing.

The most common mirror-image is Marie looking at her reflection in a mirror. She is presented as a character that has a pronounced interest in physical appearance. She is often shown applying make-up or simply checking her appearance. She is also seen eating pasta with no sauce for dinner and when Jean says that he isn't hungry, she responds 'C'est bien, comme ça tu maigriras un peu' ('Good, you'll lose a little weight that way'). In addition to this, she regularly goes to the gym and wishes Jean would do the same. All of this displays a marked concern with appearance that is frequently evoked visually with the recurring mirror-image of Marie. Thinking of this in terms of the Deleuzean mirror-image, we are reminded of the simultaneous presence of the actual and the virtual, what is most directly 'real' and what may not be (Deleuze 1989: 70). The mirror shows us what ought to be considered objectively 'true' – a reflected image of what is being looked at in the mirror. Yet, when we consider that the mirror's reflection is also seen subjectively through one's own experience, we realise that the reflection is just as open to perception as everything else. Following this line of thought, we can see that the mirrors and reflections of *Sous le sable* are just as much an exchange between the real and the non-real, the objective and the subjective, as any of the other images that Marie is seen to be perceiving throughout the film. Marie projects what she wants to see, and this is what she sees reflected, but is this really what is there? Ozon states in an interview:

> The film then follows a different path in the winter. Everything becomes more psychological, facts are less certain: we're inside Marie's head, where the path is ambiguous, less definite, blurrier, more fragile, like quicksands. (Ozon 2010)

Marie clearly wishes to be seen in a certain way, but even what would appear to be the most incorruptibly 'true' is embedded with a sense of indiscernibility that destabilises both individual perspective and an infallible collective 'truth'.

INDISCERNIBILITY, AMBIGUITY AND QUEERNESS

By establishing the extent to which these notions of indiscernibility and ambiguity are omnipresent in *Sous le sable*, we understand that they are key ideas in the film. Rather than build towards a specific narrative goal in a linear fashion, the film is more of an exploration of the ambivalent nature of subjectivity. In the following section, I will demonstrate how the film forges a link between the crystal-image and a sense of queerness through the ambivalent nature of identities and ambiguous notions of perception and meaning that it portrays.

As Thibaut Schilt notes, *Sous le sable* is the first feature of Ozon's that does not treat homosexuality, yet 'there is something queer about *Sous le sable* . . . Ozon's queer sensibilities surface in indirect ways' (Schilt 2011: 88). I agree, as does Fiona Handyside, who, in reference to *Sous le sable*, states: 'His films offer a way of envisaging a queer cinema that is not predicated on individual bodies performing discrete acts but which aims to create a framework for constantly reconfiguring what queer forms and practices might be' (Handyside 2012: 55). Handyside identifies the various aspects of *Sous le sable* that challenge and disrupt fixed notions of time, space and, identity. If we develop the line of thought established here and consider Ozon's work in terms of, to use Handyside's wording, 'a framework for constantly reconfiguring what queer forms and practices might be', we can address the narrative ambiguity that is prominent in the film. I aim to demonstrate further ways in which Ozon's 'queer sensibilities' surface by analysing the ambiguity of the narrative's overall sense of meaning production, and the film's penchant for fluid, porous imagery.

My analysis of *Sous le sable* in this section will be further informed by considering the film in terms of a queer aesthetic, that is, how queerness critiques and deconstructs traditional binarisms. Or as Plana explains, what unites work that corresponds to a queer aesthetic is critiquing, disrupting or subverting the oppositions considered natural and going beyond the dualisms that condition normative ways of thinking (Plana 2015: 10–11). *Sous le sable* addresses similar normative constructs. Handyside (2012) commented on the way the film disrupts certain oppositional constructs characterised as dualisms such as past/present, alive/dead, mental/physical as a 'queering of mourning'. She uses the figure that Marie sees on the beach at the film's conclusion as a queer example, noting how it radically undermines both 'temporal categories (he is a figure from the past, the present and the future) and ontological states (he is a physical presence, a psychotic hallucination and a libidinal fantasy)' (Handyside 2012: 65). Drawing on Handyside's remarks and focus on the last sequence, I propose exploring the film's apparent categorical evasiveness in relation to the distinction between explicitness and ambiguity. Ambiguity in relation to truth and meaning is a prevailing theme throughout Ozon's work; for example, we can think of the 'false' flashbacks of *Sitcom* (1998) and *Frantz* (2016), the alibis and counter-alibis of *8 femmes / 8 Women* (2001) and the ambivalent identities, sexual or otherwise, of *5x2* (2004), *Le Temps qui reste / Time to Leave* (2005) and *Le Refuge / The Refuge* (2009). In *Sous le sable*, there is a constant switching movement between explicitness and ambiguity; it can be read at a surface level as the story of a woman who loses her husband to a suicide and of her struggle to deal with this loss and build a new life for herself, but such an interpretation would ignore all of the stylistic devices used by Ozon to imbue the story with ambiguity. In either case, it is not so much the juxtaposition of explicitness and ambiguity that is of interest, but rather how the film seemingly operates at both ends of such oppositions in a simultaneous fashion. The film's minimal aesthetic is key in relation to this point. Mandelbaum (2001) touches on this in his review of the film:

> The directing, extraordinarily frugal and subtle, does not really allow us to choose between a realistic interpretation (he is living but his wife cannot, for an unknown reason, reveal his disappearance) and the metaphysical variation (the film is the flow of consciousness of a woman who cannot let herself mourn the passing of her beloved). (Mandelbaum 2001)

The film's dry and sober style creates a surface-level sense of explicitness. Few visual or technical effects are used, the majority of the camera work is minimalist, and there is very little extradiegetic music. Yet within this explicitly clear outline, an air of ambiguity is maintained. Marie is constantly filmed in front of and behind visual screens and reflections that are varying degrees of clearness. Jean's ghost is introduced into the story alongside diegetically real elements with no direct narrative explanation. The film's ending, as we have seen, denies a conclusive narrative ending. This, I argue, is another way in which

Ozon's queer sensibilities manifest in the film; with these two types of image being combined with no distinction between them, the narrative is simultaneously explicit and ambiguous, troubling and disrupting any singular interpretation of the film. Just as the distinction between explicitness and ambiguity is challenged, so too is the boundary between subjectivity/objectivity, reality/imagination, truth/fiction and actual/virtual.

The film's treatment of form and linearity also corresponds to this sense of queerness. Michele Aaron (2004) considers these to be core aspects of queer aesthetics in film. In *New Queer Cinema* she describes how queer films 'frequently defy cinematic convention in terms of form, content and genre' and speaks of them in terms of a 'lack of respect for the governing codes of form or content, linearity or coherence' (Aaron 2004: 4). Rather than a specific genre or set of themes, she identifies queer cinema in terms of style and attitude of filmmaking. This reflection informs my analysis of the form, content and treatment of linearity in *Sous le sable*. In one sense, the film is wholly linear with no flashbacks or dream sequences and all of the events are presented in their natural order, unlike in the majority of Ozon's cinematic oeuvre. Yet within this apparently natural notion of time, there lies the subjective experience of the film's protagonist that is marked by various loops and replications that deny any sort of straight passage from one situation to another. There are various points of repetition marked out by frame compositions and shot angles. These occur when Marie goes to the beach for the first and last time and when she has breakfast with Jean and Vincent. In the analogous frames, the fluid nature of time in the film is visible. There are very clear elements of duplication; we see Marie arrive at the same beach, from the same point of view that we did the last time (Figure 4.2). She enters a static frame and camera angle and we see her from behind as she walks towards the sea. Similarly, when she has breakfast with Jean and then with Vincent, we see the same table from the same angle. The table is laid out in the same way and Jean and Vincent wear the same colour. Marie butters 'tartines' and places them on Vincent's plate as she did with Jean before. Yet within these points of repetition, there is also a certain sense of the mundane passage of one thing to another. On the beach, the clear, vivid sky has given way to ominous winter clouds and most of the grass has died away, leaving shrubs. Marie wears a grey overcoat instead of her red summer dress. Similarly, in the breakfast scenes, she wears a grey dressing-gown instead of the bright blue pyjamas of before. The wall in the background is the same colour but seems to be presented in a more decaying light. In both cases the intense, vivid palette of the first frame has given way to more pallid, blander tones. In these examples, we can therefore see time being presented as a fluid notion. In relation to linear time, the film breaks the rigid perception of meaning into multiple possibilities. Within the diegesis, we have both the sense of things happening and non-events, situations repeating themselves and profound change occurring.

A sense of fluidity pervades *Sous le sable*. Writing in *The New* Yorker, Anthony Lane (2001) remarked that 'the film is wonderfully liquid', with the character of Marie being marked by a series of flows: 'she herself flows back and forth between youthfulness and the riptide of age, between what she dreams of and what she knows to be true' (Lane 2001). At the university where she teaches, Marie reads a section of Virgina Woolf's *The Waves* to her class that compares the notion of time to the fluid evasiveness of water; '"And time," said Bernard, "lets fall its drop. The drop that has formed on the roof of the soul falls. On the roof of my mind time, forming, lets fall its drop"' (Woolf 1931: 184). Clearly overcome by the lines, Marie is obliged to end her lecture early. Schiller (2005: 220) comments on the deep resonance these lines take on in the film: 'As she reads this, Marie seems to become aware of the void that the merely habitual nature of her actions covers, aware of the empty place in her life, and of her loss'. Later, at dinner, Marie and Vincent are filmed briefly through the water of a fish tank and she cites a line from Woolf's suicide note to him. Woolf drowned herself by filling her pockets with stones and walking into the River Ouse. Like Jean, her body would not be found until a long of time after the drowning took place.

Water is also visually omnipresent in the film. This is most marked at the different moments of the film where water occupies all of, or the vast majority of, the visual field. The very beginning shows us the Seine with Notre-Dame de Paris in the background. The camera takes a broad movement across the river, allowing it to fill the screen while moving. Then, the shot displays the film's title as the camera shows a stream of traffic along the quays where we will meet the two main characters. The Seine seems static and unmoving, indifferent to all that is happening around it. Next we see the Atlantic Ocean from Jean's perspective from the beach. The waves crash in against the sand. With the benefit of retrospect, we are aware of the toll that the merciless ocean will take on Jean as he disappears. At another point, we are immersed in the swimming pool where Marie exercises, the morning after we see her imagine Jean in their apartment for the first time.

The film's imagery of fluidity evokes the sense of categorical evasiveness, and indeed queerness, that I have described throughout this section. All that is evasive about fixed categories and identities calls into question the extent to which such categories and identities are natural at all. The film flows between objective reality and subjective projection; events, people, and places take on another form, possibly looking similar on a surface level, but becoming radically different in their nature. These differing depths of change mean that perception is destabilised, and one is left wondering what is really there. This is also expressed through ideas of permeability and porousness, as with the film's very title. Underneath the sand at the beach where Jean disappears, what is really there? Broken down matter, disintegrated over time, regardless of what once was. On certain levels the answer is obvious, but in a close-up shot Marie grasps out, reaching for what is there, but everything slips through her fingers as the porous nature of change cannot be stopped, regardless of context. The image evokes her helplessness, as she tries to cope with the disappearance of her husband with no one really there to help. Sand slips through her fingers just as time advances; nothing can be done to change what has already passed. As we have seen, Ozon refers to the film's nature, and the configuration of Marie's perspective, as 'un terrain de sables mouvants' ('field of quicksand') (Ozon 2010). What may seem monotonous is also constantly changing by its very nature. The ontological status of what is happening can be so hard to grasp or 'define' because it is composed of small, complex parts. The image brings us back to the Woolf citation, comparing water to time. Water, like sand, is indifferent to the things to which we attach importance, endlessly reforming and regenerating, all the more evasive the harder we try to grasp it. Whether it is by means of fluidity or porousness, the film's production of meaning is characterised by ambivalent flows. Despite surface-level appearances that may seem marked by a continuous sense of repetition, change and regeneration are constantly taking place, whether positive or negative. What may once have seemed fixed and defined, such as Marie's married life, a perception of the reality, disintegrates like sand, flows away like water in the River Seine or the Atlantic Ocean. This sense of constant flux and undefined states rings true of the disintegration of various identities and categories that are at play throughout the film.

CONCLUSION

Through close analysis of *Sous le sable*, this chapter has established a link between the Deleuzean crystal-image and notional uses of queer theory, by connecting them via indiscernibility and ambiguity. First, for Deleuze and the application of the crystal-image, this refers to the indiscernibility of the actual and the virtual and the manner in which this plays out thematically and visually in the film. This is particularly apt for *Sous le sable*, and Ozon's work in general, because there is so often a sense of the distinction between physical and mental elements being intentionally blurred to the point of not being able to differentiate between the two. The article then considered this same indiscernibility through the lens of queer theory, beyond the depiction of sexuality and instead focusing on how the film destabilises certain fixed and traditional modes of perception, with this being a key component of the narrative's function.

By simultaneously drawing on these two rich theoretical perspectives, the omnipresence of ambiguity in Ozon's work in general and the need to probe it further come to the fore. Across all of the genres and forms that Ozon has worked with, going right back to the shorts, ambiguity has proven to be one of his most consistent tropes. He once referred to this as 'a game with the audience' (Ozon 2017) but I argue that it is key to better understanding his work. As we have seen in this chapter, an appreciation of Ozon's treatment and various uses of ambiguity, ambivalence and indiscernibility are crucial to deciphering his films. Such concepts allow for space, time and identities to be opened up, rather than be closed off. New possibilities are created via the proliferation of multiple meanings and interpretations that come with films such as *Sous le sable* that place the onus on the spectator to find their meaning. Throughout the film, notions of objectivity and subjective experience are constantly engaged in the process of change, despite surface-level continuity. For all the apparent simplicity of the film's narrative and stripped-back style, there lies underneath a depth of flux and unending dynamic movement that has now become an established characteristic of Ozon's cinematic art.

WORKS CITED

Aaron, Michele (2004), 'New Queer Cinema: An Introduction', in Michele Aaron (ed.), *New Queer Cinema: A Critical Reader*, New Brunswick, NJ: Rutgers University Press, pp. 3–14.
Asibong, Andrew (2008), *François Ozon*, Manchester: Manchester University Press.
Bonnaud, Frédéric (2000), 'Sous le sable (review)', *Les Inrockuptibles*, 30 November, <https://www.lesinrocks.com/cinema/films-a-l-affiche/sous-le-sable-3> (last accessed 3 July 2020).
Brion, Patrick (2001), 'Cinéma D'hier, Cinéma D'aujourd'hui', *Revue Des Deux Mondes*, March, pp. 178–82.
Deleuze, Gilles (1989), *Cinema 2*, trans. Hugh Tomlinson and Robert Galeta, Minneapolis, MN: University of Minnesota Press.
Ealy, Nicholas (2017), '"Tu es déjà rentré?" Trauma, Narcissism and Melancholy in François Ozon's *Sous le sable (2000)*', *Studies in French Cinema*, 17: 3, pp. 217–35.
Ebert, Roger (2001), 'Under the Sand (review)', *RogerEbert.com*, 10 August, <https://www.rogerebert.com/reviews/under-the-sand-2001> (last accessed 3 July 2020).
Hain, Mark (2007), 'Explicit Ambiguity: Sexual Identity, Hitchcockian Criticism, and the Films of François Ozon', *Quarterly Review of Film and Video*, 24: 3, pp. 277–88.
Handyside, Fiona (2013), 'Ghosts on the Sand: François Ozon's Haunted Beaches', *Continuum: Journal of Media & Cultural Studies*, 27: 5, pp. 663–75.
Handyside, Fiona (2012), 'Possibilities of a Beach: Queerness and François Ozon's Beaches', *Screen* 53: 1, pp. 54–71.
Ince, Kate (2008), 'François Ozon's Cinema of Desire', in Kate Ince (ed.), *Five Directors: Auteurism from Assayas to Ozon*, Manchester: Manchester University Press, pp. 112–34.
Lane, Anthony (2001), 'Fantasy Land: A Monster in Shrek, a Ghost in Under the Sand', *The New Yorker*, 4 May, <https://www.newyorker.com/magazine/2001/05/21/fantasy-land> (last accessed 3 July 2020).
Mandelbaum, Jacques (2001), 'Charlotte Rampling et l'amour fantôme', *Le Monde*, 7 February, <https://www.lemonde.fr/archives/article/2001/02/07/charlotte-rampling-et-l-amour-fantome_4153004_1819218.html> (last accessed 3 July 2020).

Ozon, François (2010), *Universciné.com* 30 November 2010, <http://www.francois-ozon.com/fr/entretiens-sous-lesable> (last accessed 15 August 2019).

Ozon, François (2017), Interview, Rendez-vous with French cinema, '*Frantz* Q&A', <https://www.youtube.com/watch?v=vfXgAaozYi4&t=1s> (last accessed 15 January 2020).

Plana, Muriel (2015), 'Introduction générale', in Muriel Plana and Frédéric Sounac (eds), *Esthétique(s) queer dans la Littérature et les arts: Sexualités et politiques du trouble*, Dijon: Editions Universitaires de Dijon, pp. 9–30.

Schiller, Britt-Marie (2005), 'A Memorial to Mourning: 'Under The Sand'', *Literature/Film Quarterly*, 33: 3, pp. 217–23.

Schilt, Thibaut (2011), *François Ozon*, Urbana, IL: University of Illinois Press.

Schwarzbaum, Lisa (2001), 'Under the Sand (review)', *Entertainment Weekly*, 595, 5 November, p. 51.

Scott, A. O. (2001), 'The Intoxicating Embrace of Grief Holds Both Pleasure and Distress', review of *Under the Sand*, *The New York Times*, 4 May, <https://www.nytimes.com/2001/05/04/movies/film-review-the-intoxicating-embrace-of-grief-holds-both-pleasure-and-distress.html> (last accessed 3 July 2020).

Vincendeau, Ginette (2001), 'Sous le sable (review)', *Sight & Sound*, 11: 4, p. 59.

Waldron, Darren (2010), '"Une mine d'or inépuisable": the queer pleasures of François Ozon's *8 femmes/8 Women* (2002)', *Studies in French Cinema*, 10: 1, pp. 69–87.

Woolf, Virginia (1931), *The Waves*, New York: Harcourt.

CHAPTER 5

French Ozon / Global Ozon: French Specificity and Globalisation in *Jeune & jolie*

Felicity Chaplin

Following her first encounter with a client, seventeen-year-old Isabelle (Marine Vacth) leaves a luxury hotel room to return to her family home in an affluent Parisian neighbourhood. Between the closing of the hotel room door and the opening of the front door of her family home, the camera tracks Isabelle's journey in three concise shots: a medium close-up of her on an escalator against the cold, reflective surfaces of a non-descript building; a static shot from behind of her walking through an underground metro station; a close-up of her hands as she takes a paperback copy of *Les Liaisons Dangereuses / Dangerous Liaisons* by Pierre Choderlos de Laclos from her bag. In this sequence of fragmentary shots, we see the conjunction of the global and the local: the anonymous 'non-places' of the hotel room, the escalator, the unnamed underground station and the interior of the train carriage situate Isabelle as a global citizen, while the inclusion of the French literary classic establishes a national specificity for the scene (Figure 5.1).

François Ozon's cinema is firmly grounded in France and French culture and traditions. However, the French specificity of *Jeune & jolie / Young & Beautiful* (2013) does not exclude the broader issues raised by globalisation. Indeed, *Jeune & jolie* occupies an interstitial space between French specificity and globalisation. This chapter explores the tension between the specific and the global in *Jeune & jolie* by examining the way in which Ozon uses intertextuality, *mise-en-scène*, music, setting and cinematography to construct both a milieu at once French and global, and an identity for his main character at once French and postmodern.

Figure 5.1 Isabelle on the escalator

THE PLACE OF *JEUNE & JOLIE* IN OZON'S OEUVRE

Jeune & jolie, which follows *Dans la maison / In the House* (2012) and precedes *Une Nouvelle amie / The New Girlfriend* (2014), tells the story of seventeen-year-old Isabelle, a senior student at the prestigious Lycée Henri IV in Paris, who embarks on a life of high-class prostitution. To put the film into context, Kevin Jagernauth in a review for *IndieWire* writes: 'the film brings to mind recent pictures such as *Elles* and '*Sleeping Beauty*' which both focused on young women who slide into selling their bodies' (Jagernauth 2014). In spite of its reference to this growing phenomenon of student prostitution in France, *Jeune & jolie* is, as Nick Roddick argues, 'not really about teenage prostitution . . . it is more about a young woman leaving one life (childhood) and entering another' (Roddick 2013: 48). Thus, it is not the subject matter as such which makes *Jeune & jolie* a typical Ozon film. Indeed, Roddick describes Ozon as a 'unique (and uniquely French) mix of showman and auteur . . . who specialises in immaculately lit, gorgeously framed pictures of a bourgeois world beneath whose glowing surface there is (usually) a lot more going on than is at first apparent' (Roddick 2013: 48). Similarly, Ginette Vincendeau claims that *Jeune & jolie* confirms Ozon's reputation as 'the gifted maker of elegant and entertaining films on risqué subjects' (Vincendeau 2013: 66). While Jonathan Murray referred to the plot of *Jeune & jolie* as 'potentially stupid and salacious in equal measure' (Murray 2014: 51), Fiona Handyside notes that Ozon's films frequently 'oscillate between high camp and subtle chamber pieces, the former usually set in the enclosed space of the home, the latter often featuring a beach' (Handyside 2012: 66).

Jeune & jolie is generally considered to belong to the subtle chamber pieces, finding its place among films like *Le Temps qui reste / Time to Leave* (2005) and *Sous le sable / Under the Sand* (2000); yet as Peter Bradshaw observed in his review, the 'intense seriousness' of *Jeune & jolie* 'can only be appreciated by not taking it too seriously' (Bradshaw 2013).

For Alistair Fox, Ozon is the most recognised director associated with the Young French Cinema internationally due, in part, to the widespread distribution of several of his films and their relative box office achievement (Fox 2014: 216). Nonetheless, as Vincendeau points out, 'the daring and eclecticism that give Ozon's work its high profile also mean that he fits uneasily within established critical paradigms, whether classic European auteur cinema, international queer cinema, "Young French Cinema" or "New French Extremism"' (Vincendeau 2002: 312). One element that unites at least Ozon's most successful films outside France is that they are all in effect examples of genre cinema. Indeed, his two most successful films outside France, *Swimming Pool* (2003) and *8 femmes / 8 Women* (2002), are examples of the murder mystery and the musical, respectively, although Ozon always brings his own peculiar take on genre to his filmmaking. As Thibaut Schilt writes: 'Drawing on familiar cinematic traditions . . . Ozon's cinema simultaneously defamiliarizes those traditions in the eyes of the spectator. His films consistently, even obsessively, venture into uncertain sexual territories, represent human interaction in unanticipated ways, and altogether defy generic categorisation' (Schilt 2011: 2-3). This is certainly true of *Jeune & jolie*.

Unlike other contemporary European auteurs who have an international and transnational reputation (for example, Michael Haneke, Yorgos Lanthimos and Lars von Trier), Ozon is a resolutely 'national' director. Whereas these aforementioned directors often work in different languages, use international casts and shoot in international locations, Ozon's films are all – with the exception of *Angel* (2007) and, in part at least, *Frantz* (2016) – primarily set and produced in France, use almost exclusively French actors, often deal with typically French themes and generally reference French culture. This does not mean that Ozon's cinema does not deal with broader issues beyond their French settings; his preference for the *intimiste* drama means that his films tend to revolve around questions of familial relations and French social mores. *Jeune & jolie* is no exception to this rule; yet its subject matter, setting, and to a certain extent how it is shot suggest more global considerations than are usually associated with an Ozon film, particularly when compared with the work of a director like Haneke, who Kate Ince calls 'a leading example of transnational filmmaking', both in terms of the director's nationality and his films' production' (Ince 2012: 86). Ince further points out that 'despite the wide international distribution of Ozon's films, all his features have been backed by French Fidelité Productions, and increasingly by the cinematic arms of French television companies such as France 2 Cinéma' (Ince 2008: 11). Indeed, *Jeune & jolie* was financed by French companies Mandarin Cinéma, Mars Films, and France 2 Cinéma. Thus, Ozon's films stand in contrast to the usual contemporary European art cinema tradition of the transnational co-production in which the unmarketability of the subject matter means that funding has to be sourced from different national bodies. Ozon's films may in general belong to what some critics have referred to as the return of French cinema, a 'new New Wave' in which films featuring specifically French themes are produced and shot in France for a French and international audience.

CULTURAL EXCEPTION

In order to understand the French specificity of Ozon's cinema in a global context, it is important to link it to the wider socio-cultural phenomenon of 'l'exception française' or 'l'exception culturelle' ('French exception' or 'cultural exception'), which can be loosely defined as a social, political and cultural project which aims to protect the values and mores of French society in an increasingly globalised context. In *Jeune & jolie* this cultural exception is represented through depictions of the French education system (of which Ozon himself is a product) and through the use of archetypal French texts such as the poetry of Rimbaud, the songs of Françoise Hardy, Laclos's *Les Liaisons dangereuses / Dangerous Liaisons* and films such as *Belle de jour* (Luis Buñuel, 1967) and *Vivre sa vie / My Life to Live* (Jean-Luc Godard, 1962). It is also closely tied to Ozon's use of the typically French *intimiste* tradition of filmmaking.

Historically speaking, while French exception can be traced back to Napoléon, it really begins with Jules Ferry's modern French education reform in the late nineteenth century. As part of his nationalisation of the French education system, Ferry insisted on the primacy of French language and culture not only in France but in its territories and colonies as well. While much has changed since decolonisation, in France and many of its territories, French culture is still dominated by Ferry's model. As Susan Collard points out, French schools

> had the task of transmitting a universalist *culture générale* as the necessary grounding for all future citizens. Using state-imposed textbooks, it involved the transmission of a considerable volume of knowledge about French history, art, and literature . . . taught through the medium of the French language. (Collard 2000: 40)

Jeune & jolie offers a brief look inside the French education system. The film is partially shot at the prestigious Lycée Henri IV, the school Ozon himself attended, and which includes among its alumni such important figures of French culture as Jean-Paul Sartre, Guy de Maupassant, Gilles Deleuze,

Andre Gide and Simone Weil. It comes as no surprise, then, that in the scene in which Isabelle and her classmates read a poem by Rimbaud, what follows is what Vincendeau calls a 'highly sophisticated' discussion of the poem's themes (Vincendeau 2013: 66). It would be wrong to assume that this is a typical class of French high school students – a good point of comparison is *Entre les murs / The Class* (Laurent Cantet 2008) – rather, it serves the double function of establishing Isabelle's social situation while at the same time adding a biographical element to the film.

According to Brian Jenkins, 'the idea that France is somehow unique is deeply imbedded in the nation's self-image . . . It reflects the conviction that France has an exemplary, universal role as a civilising force, that its aspirations are those of humanity at large' (Jenkins 2000: 112). French filmmaking is still strongly subsidised by the state, via the Centre national de la cinématographie (CNC). France has also made sure that Paris is the home of the Fondation européenne des métiers de l'image et du son (FEMIS), created in 1986 by the then culture minister Jack Lang and now considered Europe's most important institute for training future professionals in the cinema industry. Ozon trained at FEMIS, alongside other notable French directors such as Louis Malle, Alain Resnais, Claire Denis, Céline Sciamma and Arnaud Desplechin. Indeed, Ozon belongs to what has become known as the 'FEMIS' generation of filmmakers which was founded under the guidance of the Mitterrand presidency. As Vincendeau points out:

> [the] cultural policies of President François Mitterrand and his culture minister Jack Lang in the 1980s ensured even more money was poured into filmmaking, in part to defend the 'cultural exception' (the pledge to treat culture differently to other commercial products) . . . Changes in the French audiovisual landscape equally worked to the newcomers' advantage. One was the reconfiguration of the IDHEC film school in Paris as the Fémis in 1986, with a more overt orientation towards auteur cinema, which led to the 1990s filmmakers sometimes being called the 'Fémis generation'. (Vincendeau 2019)

However, as Jenkins claims, 'some have argued that globalization and "normalization" are putting an end to French exceptionalism' (Jenkins 2000: 113). Ozon's films can be regarded as an example of the persistence of French exceptionalism and part of a greater socio-political push for the reassertion of French identity in the era of globalisation and the European Union.

INTERTEXTUALITY

According to Ince, the bourgeois, French, patriarchal family is the main site of drama, comedy, fantasy and subversion in Ozon's films (Ince 2008: 7). It may seem strange at first to categorise *Jeune & jolie* as a family drama, or even a melodrama, but much of the film is set in the family home (the holiday house in Le Pradet on the Riviera and the apartment in Paris), and the central conflicts in the film are essentially familial. Ozon's focus on family dramas and sexual relationships at first glance appears to continue the French *intimiste* cinematic tradition, a genre specifically associated with French cinema's national identity. Vanderschelden defines *intimiste* as

> subtle introspective and intimate dramas which often draw on the conventions of melodrama, but can also be associated with period film, costume drama and psychological investigation. It is a genre linked to the image of French cinema abroad, often identified by slow narratives and domestic plots involving relationships or family life, a quest for identity or a change of life circumstances. (Vanderschelden 2013: 18)

Ozon's films also subvert this typically French genre, usually by introducing complex, transgressive, or 'queer' sexual and gender relations and fantasy elements. For Handyside, queer 'can be used to describe any sexuality not defined as heterosexual procreative monogamy (usually the presumed goal of most classic Hollywood couplings); queers are people (including heterosexuals) who do not organise their rhetoric according to this rubric' (Handyside 2012: 57). In fact, if one were to remove altogether the teenage prostitution plot from *Jeune & jolie*, one would have a typical coming-of-age melodrama, addressing ordinary heterosexual teenage girl problems such as boyfriends, dating, virginity, mothers, little brothers, stepfathers and school such as would be found in any teenage magazine. Indeed, the title of the film is taken from the French magazine *Jeune & jolie*, a publication linked quite specifically to the melodrama of the heterosexual teenage girl's life. The magazine, which was discontinued in 2010 due to falling sales, was 'dedicated to young women aged between 15 and 24. Launched in June 1987, its aim was to accompany young women through this key stage of their life' (Dormoy 2010). Ozon uses the magazine title to signify the banality of such images of teenage life and juxtaposes the character of Isabelle with that of her school friend Claire (Jeanne Ruff), whose main concerns seem to come straight from the pages of *Jeune & jolie* the magazine. Isabelle's path, on the other hand, is the antithesis of the stereotypical teenage girl drama seen in the magazine. In this way, *Jeune & jolie* demonstrates another common feature of Ozon's cinema: 'protean, unbound characters who scarcely ever choose a predictable path' (Schilt 2011: 9). The poster for the film, showing a half-naked Marine Vacth, is in a way a deconstruction or queering of the typical *Jeune & jolie* magazine cover, which had a policy of no nudity (Figure 5.2).

SPECIFICITY AND GLOBALISATION   93

Figure 5.2 Isabelle on the hotel bed

Intertextuality is an important feature of Ozon's filmmaking and the sources he draws on are generally from French culture, adding to the French specificity of his films. Once considered simply a matter of a text quoting or citing another text, intertextuality became the general form of textuality in postmodernism. As Julia Kristeva remarks: 'Every text takes shape as a mosaic of citations, every text is the absorption and transformation of other texts' (quoted in Culler 1975: 73). Postmodern texts such as Ozon's films are tapestries of different sources; some overt, others more obscure. Theorists of intertextuality argue that textual analysis can reveal the mesh of references which make up a postmodern text. Intertexts for *Jeune & jolie* include those which explicitly belong to the diegesis, like the Rimbaud poem; those which are directly imported to the film, such as the songs of Françoise Hardy; and those which function on a deeper level as cultural reference points. Intertexts with a more subtle presence include Luis Buñuel's *Belle de jour* (1967) and Jean-Luc Godard's *Vivre sa vie / My Life to Live* (1964), which is indirectly referenced when Isabelle tells her mother: 'C'est ma vie' ('It's my life'). Other references function on different levels at the same time: there is a scene in which Isabelle is shown reading Laclos's novel, which, although scandalous at the time of its publication, the author described as a morality tale about the corrupt and squalid nobility, a theme explored in a contemporary context in *Jeune & jolie*. Ozon uses the reference to Laclos not to refer to the liaisons between Isabelle and her clients, but rather to the hypocrisy of the bourgeois family with its own intrigues and duplicities. Late in the film, for example, it is revealed that Isabelle's mother is having an affair; Isabelle uses this knowledge against her mother to secure her confidence. Indeed, Ozon describes Isabelle as 'something of an exterminating angel' – a further reference to Buñuel – and remarks that her family members 'try to do their best in a complex situation, but she confronts them with their hypocrisy and lies' (Ozon 2013). Indeed, Ozon does a similar thing with a literary reference in the earlier *Swimming Pool*, in which reference to the Marquis de Sade's castle provides a framework within which to stage the sadomasochistic fantasies of a proper English crime writer, played by Charlotte Rampling.

The most obvious and significant intertexts in *Jeune & jolie* are the prominent French cultural figures Arthur Rimbaud and Françoise Hardy: Rimbaud signifies youth in revolt and ennui while Hardy's songs capture the melancholy of adolescent estrangement. Both are used to add layers of meaning to Isabelle's seemingly enigmatic behaviour, yet neither provides a wholly satisfactory explanation to the central enigma of the film: Isabelle's decision to turn to prostitution. This is indicative of the way in which, according to Schilt, Ozon 'continually evinces a reticence to fit inside the boundaries of mainstream cinema, engaging in a cat-and-mouse game with critics and often wrong-footing the spectator' (Schilt 2011: 3). Thus, the function of intertextuality in *Jeune & jolie* is twofold: to defer or disrupt meaning making on the one hand, and to establish French specificity on the other.

FRANÇOISE HARDY

Jeune & jolie is structured according to the seasons and is divided into four corresponding episodes or vignettes. Ozon employs the motifs of the seasons in a way reminiscent of archetypal literary criticism in which the imagery of the seasons is linked to dramatic or generic modes – summer (romance), autumn (tragedy), winter (irony or satire) and spring (comedy) – but which also calls to mind the Romantic idea of seasons as standing in for stages or moods of life, particularly as depicted in poems like Rimbaud's later *Une Saison en enfer / A Season in Hell* (1873). The film opens in summertime with Isabelle, on holiday with her family on the French Riviera, celebrating her seventeenth birthday and losing her virginity to Felix (Lucas Prisor), a German boy also holidaying with his parents. The autumn episode begins with the return to Paris and follows Isabelle as she returns to school and embarks on a double life as a call girl, and ends with the death of her regular client, Georges (Johan Leysen). The winter episode begins with the revelation of Isabelle's deception to her mother and ends with her meeting and dating a boy her own age from school. The spring episode begins with a traditional family brunch and ends with Isabelle meeting the widow of her former client Georges.

Each season in *Jeune & jolie* is accompanied by a Hardy song. Hardy is often considered a leading figure of the French yé-yé movement of the early 1960s, but her melancholy and introspective songs did not entirely suit the frequently upbeat, playful and sometimes nonsensical songs associated with the yé-yé phenomenon. While assuming an ostensibly pop sound, Hardy's songs dealt with themes of loneliness, solitude and estrangement. In an interview, Ozon remarked: 'the choice of Françoise Hardy's songs to structure the story came rather naturally. For me, she best sang of the sadness and disillusionment of adolescence' (Ozon 2013). The inclusion of musical numbers is a recurring feature of Ozon's films. Schilt notes that for Ozon 'songs are precious time savers' (Schilt 2011: 6). Adrian Martin writes that something Ozon shares with Hollywood directors of the 1950s like Vincente Minnelli and Douglas Sirk is 'a certain force of stylish displacement. The passions that drive Ozon's characters are rarely expressed directly in violent or passionate acts' (Martin 2019). For Martin, emotions in Ozon's films 'are displaced from the characters' bodies and find expression elsewhere – in décor, and in music, especially bits of musical quotation like pop standards' (Martin 2019). Ozon himself remarks that a 'single song summarizes four pages of dialogue, conveys feelings, and instantaneously reveals something about the characters' psychology. It is extremely convenient' (Schilt 2011: 6).

The first Hardy song used in *Jeune & jolie*, 'L'Amour d'un garcon' ('The Love of a Boy'), plays over a scene which depicts Isabelle's seventeenth birthday party at her family's villa, the day after she lost her virginity to Felix. The song continues to play on the soundtrack as this scene cuts to a series of shots of the family leaving the villa to return to Paris: Isabelle in her room packing her suitcase; the family locking up the villa, packing the car and shutting the gate; the car leaving the driveway; the family in the car with the receding beachscape in the background. Significantly, Ozon plays this song for its entire duration. It is a narrative song, which offers, however tentatively, an internal, emotional or psychological counterpoint to the action. The song's lyrics express how a young woman's first sexual encounter with a boy has irrevocably changed her, and features the lines 'j'ai bien changé' ('I have really changed'), 'l'amour d'un garçon . . . peut tout changer' ('the love of a boy . . . can change everything'), and 'la petite fille que tu as connue, non, je ne suis plus' ('the girl that you've known, I am no longer'). While it is tempting to read this as a direct expression of Isabelle's *innenwelt* or 'inner life', the final shot of the sequence, which precedes a fade to black, is of Isabelle shot from behind the glass of the car window. The window functions as a hermeneutic metaphor, at once transparent and impenetrable (Figure 5.3). Indeed, as Ozon remarks of his heroine, Isabelle is 'une fille qui nous échappe' (Bauman, Tobin and Ozon 2013: 24) (a girl who escapes us).

Figure 5.3 Isabelle in the car

Ozon introduces the second Hardy song, 'À quoi ça sert?' ('Why Even Try?'), during the film's 'Autumn' episode. Just as a scene between Isabelle and her client Georges is coming to a close, the opening lines of Hardy's song commence: 'Comme toi j'ai un cœur qui ne peut rien promettre' ('Like you, I have a heart that can promise nothing'). These lines are sung over a close-up of Georges and Isabelle in an embrace both sexual and paternal. The framing, dialogue, and shot composition suggest a kinship which transcends the prostitute/client relationship, however the following montage sequence, along with Hardy's lyrics, remind us that such kinship is fleeting: Isabelle shot walking down the hotel corridor; a close-up of Isabelle's bare back which pans up to reveal her in the act of fellatio; a mid-shot of Isabelle in a hotel bathroom with an unnamed client; Isabelle walking another hotel corridor; a close-up of Isabelle's face shot from outside a window, the skyline of Paris superimposed in reflection across her face; a shot of Isabelle's reflection in the mirror of a public toilet.

The third Hardy song, 'Première rencontre' ('First Encounter'), is used to draw the following episode, 'Winter', to a close. In this sequence, Isabelle attends a house party with her friend Claire. A shot of Isabelle arriving at the party is overlaid with the 80s synth pads and reverbed snares of 'Midnight City' by French electronica group M83, a song contemporaneous with the action of the film. The music, now established as diegetic, continues as Isabelle weaves her way through the crowd of partygoers. She wanders through the apartment impassively observing the typical teenage party behaviour: expressive dancing, drinking shots, making out, and throwing up in bathroom sinks. She passes through the apartment onto the terrace, where she meets her classmate, Alex (Laurent Delbecque). They make small talk before Isabelle lets him kiss her. As they embrace, 'Midnight City' transitions briefly to 'Baptism' by Canadian electronic music duo Crystal Castles. Isabelle returns inside and dances with Claire, but after only fifteen seconds 'Baptism' morphs into Hardy's 'Première rencontre', accompanied by a slow-motion shot of Isabelle dancing, creating the impression of her as a young woman out of sync with time and place. The lyrics which are at once melancholic and hopeful, reinforce the mood created by the music and the slow-motion sequence. They describe a young woman's first encounter with 'celui qui viendrait/Me sortir un jour de l'enfance/Et avec qui je partirais loin' ('the one who'd come/ And rescue me one day from my childhood/ And with whom I'd go far/Far away'). Although musically quite different, 'Midnight City' and 'Première rencontre' both capture the dual quality of adolescence: mourning and rebirth. If Hardy's songs exalted the experience of adolescence for the 1960s and 1970s, 'Midnight City' was emblematic for Isabelle's generation; indeed, it was considered by *Billboard* magazine as one of the 'Songs that Defined the Decade' for the 2010s and both 'shaped and reflected the music and culture of the period' (Glicksman 2019). 'Première rencontre' continues to play as the film cuts from the party to a shot of Isabelle and Alex on the Pont des Arts as dawn breaks over Paris. The following lyrics are heard accompanying the scene:

Quand je l'ai vu c'était un peu ça
il n'avait rien de plus qu'un autre
mais j'ai su que c'était celui-là
et pas un autre

(When I first saw him
He was like any other
But I knew he was the one
He and no other)

The scene closes with a shot of the many padlocks which once adorned the railing of the Pont des Arts, followed by a fade to black as the song concludes. Both displacement and irony are at work in this sequence: Hardy's lyrics give no clear indication of Isabelle's internal state. As Ariane Allard writes: 'les pourquoi s'estompent, tandis que les pistes explicatives sont évacuées' (Allard 2013: 20–1) ('the why fades, while the explanatory avenues are abandoned'). The same can be said for the final Hardy song, which plays over the end credit sequence: 'Je suis moi'. The tautological nature of the title offers no insight into the mystery of Isabelle's being.

RIMBAUD

Ozon imbeds Rimbaud's poem in the diegesis of *Jeune & jolie* in an ingenious way by having high school students read it aloud in class. According to Vincendeau, the inclusion of the poem is 'a little obvious in its intent but redeemed by the freshness of the performances, including some from non-professional actors' (Vincendeau 2013: 66). Indeed, Ozon deliberately allowed the student extras to respond to the poem in their own way, partly to demonstrate how the line 'No one is serious at 17' functions as 'a kind of motto' in France (Ozon 2013). Ozon wished to highlight the Frenchness of the poem and at the same time deconstruct its axiomatic meaning:

> I wanted to show this young girl who embodies the Rimbaud poem that's read in the film . . . And yet, in a way, Isabelle is still very serious. She thinks very seriously. She's exploring her identity. She just finds a very strange way to do it. (Ozon 2013)

Vincendeau argues that Ozon's 'prettied up vision of teenage prostitution . . . shows none of the economic, social, and physical realities of prostitution' (Vincendeau 2013: 67).

Nonetheless, Ozon's film does depict a contemporary social phenomenon in French, and indeed, European, society: the student prostitute who sells herself for reasons other than money. As Adam Sage notes, *Jeune & jolie* 'reflects the experience of tens of thousands of French students, who are turning to prostitution, a proportion of them for reasons other than avoiding poverty' (Sage 2014: 27). France goes on to provide statistics which suggest that Ozon's film has tapped into a rather widespread issue in French society:

> a survey of 18,831 students at Montpellier University in southern France suggested a high level of tolerance towards prostitution among the country's future elite. Nearly 20 per cent of respondents said prostitution was an acceptable way to earn extra money, and two-thirds said paid sex could not be considered as an act of violence. The results of the survey lend weight to student unions' claims that at least 40,000 students in France are involved in the activity. The survey found that 62 per cent of the female students who prostituted themselves came from middle- or upper-middle-class families. (Sage 2014: 27)

The central enigma of *Jeune & jolie*, then, is why a young girl from a well-to-do bourgeois family turns to prostitution in the first place. The explanation as to why Ozon presents us with this vision of teenage prostitution is perhaps contained in the use of Rimbaud – not so much in the poem itself, which appears to celebrate the carefree nature of teenage life – but in the biography of the poet. Indeed, the most famous portrait of Rimbaud, a photograph taken by Étienne Carjat in 1871, shows the poet at age seventeen.

Rimbaud's life has a kind of mythical significance in French culture. At the age of twenty he announced he was done with poetry and took up arms dealing, among other things. Svetlana Boym sums up Rimbaud's life as follows:

> He abandons poetry for the sake of the drama of life. The poet stops writing at the age of twenty... and undertakes a series of journeys in search of true modern life ('la vraie vie'). He attempts to enlist in the army, then goes to the Orient... where he makes a living as a trader and occasionally as an arms dealer. At his death he leaves a bundle of prosaic letters full of descriptions of... ennui. (Boym 1991: 38)

In a similar way, it might be argued that Isabelle is done with the 'poetry' of youth and takes up life as a prostitute. The driving force behind this move, as with Rimbaud's, is not strictly economic. One of the problems of making sense of Isabelle's decision in the absence of the economic motive is the apparent indifference that lurks behind it. On an existential level, Isabelle's decision may be simply a matter of achieving a kind of agency. As Nicole Wallenbrock points out: student-prostitutes 'have some agency, scheduling their clientele via the internet and text messages' (Wallenbrock 2015: 416). As Wallenbrock goes on to argue, Isabelle does not fit the profile of the student-prostitute as the latter appeared in the media from about 2008 onwards:

> Although most studies show financial need as the motivating factor for student-prostitution, *Jeune et jolie* refuses such a commonplace incentive... Possessing anything she desires, Isabelle saves the cash, not once dipping into the hidden envelope in her wardrobe. In this way, the student becomes an even more ideal prostitute: she sees her clients for sexual experimentation, not to pay bills. (Wallenbrock 2015: 419)

Perhaps the enigma of Isabelle's decision can be addressed through the very French concept of ennui, which translates loosely as boredom, indifference, restlessness or dissatisfaction. As Gerald Macklin points out, paradox and restlessness are the keys to understanding Rimbaud's life and poetry, and modernity as such (Macklin 2011: 379). Indeed, in a certain way, Isabelle fulfills Rimbaud's injunction from *Une saison en enfer / A Season in Hell*: 'Il faut être absolument moderne' ('One must be absolutely modern'). As Macklin argues: 'This is a form of victory but the new era will be something other than a blissful transcendence. Rather it will represent a personal accomplishment as the poet turns his back on false friends and couples' (Macklin 2011: 394). Ennui is a concept central to nineteenth- and early twentieth-century French poetry and is most commonly associated with Charles Baudelaire, who introduced the concept as a motivating force in *Les Fleurs du mal / The Flowers of Evil* (1857). In the first poem of this cycle, 'Au lecteur' / 'To the Reader', Baudelaire identifies ennui both as the motivation behind all the seemingly incomprehensible and often immoral actions of human beings, and as the central affect of modernity. For Baudelaire, dissatisfaction with modern life and values was the primary cause of ennui, an idea taken up by Rimbaud in his poetry and letters. However, Rimbaud, like Hardy and Laclos, functions less as a narrative functor than as another text in the construction of Isabelle's – and the film's – Frenchness, an intertextual rather than an 'authentic' phenomenon.

GLOBALISATION

France has had an uneasy relationship with globalisation, viewing it primarily as impacting on French values and identity. This has not only shaped government action; it has led to the introduction and continual updating of policies to protect and promote culture at home and to stimulate the desire to champion diversity internationally (Walkley 2018: 18–19). For Sarah Walkley, France has also:

> seen some of the most defiant reaction against globalisation from blockades outside Disneyland Paris to a high-profile backlash against McDonald's. It has been one of the most prominent voices against unfettered economic liberalisation, insisting since the foundation of the GATT that three *lignes rouges* [red lines] – defence, agriculture and culture – should be respected and that they should fall outside the boundaries of free trade. (Walkley 2018: 22)

Walkley goes on to argue that France 'rails against globalisation not because of its economic impact, but for more complex and deeply rooted reasons; it is viewed as an attack on its identity' (Walkley 2018: 24). In *Between Republic and Market* (2012), Sarah Waters isolates five main reasons that the French consider globalisation a threat to their identity, the most important being the cultural. Similarly, Walkley argues that cinema 'is considered an important marker of French cultural heritage and identity' (Walkley 2018: 36).

For Fredric Jameson, the concept and process of globalisation can be broken down into the following inter-related levels: the technological, the economic, the social, the political and the cultural (Jameson 2000: 49). In technological terms, Jameson notes new communications technology and the information revolution, which affect the speed at which money and culture moves around the globe; in economic terms, he speaks of globalisation as the era of transnational corporations or multinationals; in social terms, of the ostensible de-industrialisation of the West which brings with it chronic structural unemployment and the creation of a new global underclass; in political terms, Jameson notes the fate of the nation state and its role and the question of nationalism in globalised culture; and in cultural terms, globalisation for Jameson generally means the 'standardization of world culture' (Jameson 2000: 51), which involves the supposed driving out of 'local or traditional' forms of culture to make way for American movies, television, clothes and eating habits, among other things. For Jameson, in the era of globalisation nationalism is primarily a cultural question, which

> usually appeals not to financial self-interest, or the lust for power, or even scientific pride – although these may be side benefits – but rather to something which is not technological, nor really political or economic; and which we therefore, for want of a better word, tend to call 'cultural'. (Jameson 2000: 51)

Jameson's point is that nationalism is not so much opposed to globalisation as it is generated out of it. It is a textual rather than an existential phenomenon. Jameson nonetheless concedes there may be an 'intrinsic European culture, which can never really be Americanised' (Jameson 2000: 52); and it is somewhere at the conjunction between the intrinsic and the textual that *mise-en-scène* is situated. Isabelle's milieu is unmistakably French; however, the *mise-en-scène* (which includes technology and global 'non-places') gestures beyond the national, and the use of archetypical French texts to construct both a milieu and identity intertextually pushes the film out of the grand modernising narratives such as 'nationhood' towards the postmodern dispersal of these narratives. As Jean-François Lyotard points out, in postmodernity the

> narrative function is losing its functors, its great hero, its great dangers, its great voyagers, its great goal. It is being dispersed in clouds of narrative language elements – narrative, but also denotative, prescriptive, descriptive, and so on . . . Each of us lives at the intersection of many of these. (Lyotard 1984: xxiv)

The global or postmodern aspects of *Jeune & jolie* are signified in two main ways: through Ozon's use of non-places and through the construction of Isabelle as a postmodern subject – that is, her 'Frenchness' as a textual construction; her identity as a surface phenomenon rather than a question of depth – who resists interpretation through the usual hermeneutic channels. In terms of social space or setting, *Jeune & jolie* continues the tradition established by Ozon of setting his films in two main locations: the beach, and the family home. There is, in Ozon's films, what Ince calls a 'unity of place' (Ince 2008: 123) which functions in much the same way as a theatre backdrop against which the melodrama is played out. These places also share the quality of being typically or representationally French; in other words, they function as both familiar and familial; they are places of identity and nationhood. There is a third significant location in which the action of *Jeune & jolie* takes place: the hotel room. The hotel room is what Marc Augé would call a non-place, the ambivalent space that, in Ian Buchanan's words, 'has none of the familiar attributes of place' and which 'incites no sense of belonging' (Buchanan 2010: 30). For Augé, non-places, which also include airports, motorways, shopping malls and underground car parks (where Isabelle meets a client), proliferate in the era of postmodernity. They are the opposite of what he calls 'anthropological' place, which is familiar, inhabited, and provides reference points for stabilising identity, the most common of which is the home (Augé 1995: 35–60). In *Jeune & jolie* we can discern a subtle reversal of non- and anthropological place. Isabelle appears alienated, anonymous and alone in those places usually associated with belonging and stable identity (the home, school, parties, holidays) and at home in those places usually associated with alienation, anonymity and loneliness: hotel rooms, public squares, and metro stations. She is also shown riding escalators, hanging around in lobbies and walking down deserted corridors. The rise of non-places is concomitant with what Jameson calls the 'death of the subject' in postmodernity: the 'end of the autonomous bourgeois monad or ego or individual – and the accompanying stress, whether as some new moral ideal or as empirical description, on the decentering of that formerly centered subject or psyche' (Jameson 1991: 15). This goes some way to explaining the central enigma of the film: Isabelle's 'decision' to pursue a life as a prostitute. Isabelle can be understood not so much as a bourgeois individual with a clearly demarcated *umwelt* and *innenwelt*; rather, like the film itself, she must be read as a postmodern phenomenon as defined by David Harvey: 'a series of texts intersective with other texts, producing more texts' (Harvey 1990: 49).

Postmodern intertextuality, or what Jameson calls 'pastiche' (Jameson 1991: 16), can help make sense of the final scene, in which Isabelle confronts the wife of Georges, who died during one of their liaisons. Indeed, as Vincendeau points out, Ozon's films are stylistically 'united by cinephilia, pastiche and theatricality and above all uncertainty of tone, oscillating between seriousness and frivolity, irony and emotion, reality and fantasy' (Vincendeau 2012: 312). For some critics, this final scene was an afterthought and appeared 'tacked on'. Ozon was even criticised for using it as a vehicle to introduce Charlotte Rampling, an actress he has used twice before, into the film. In fact, according to Ozon, he had initially considered casting Catherine Deneuve as the bereaved wife but considered the reference to Buñuel's *Belle de jour* 'too obvious' (2014). Rampling provides Ozon with a subtler intertextual reference, the 1974 Italian film, *The Night Porter* (Liliana Cavani), an oblique psychological drama in which Rampling plays a Holocaust survivor who embarked on a sadomasochistic affair with a Nazi doctor. Ozon is reluctant to commit to the more obvious psychoanalytic reading of this final scene as an Oedipal fantasy, with the Rampling character in the role of Isabelle's ideal mother and the dead Georges as her ideal father. That Ozon has Isabelle visit a psychoanalyst (played in the film by a real-life psychoanalyst, who Ozon consulted on the psychology of the teenage prostitute) is a narrative red herring; it is indicative of how postmodernity signals, according to Jameson, 'the end of the bourgeois ego' which 'no doubt brings with it the end of the psychopathologies of that ego – what I have been calling the waning of affect' (Jameson 1991: 15). This absence of psychopathology or 'waning of affect' is evident in Ozon's refusal to offer any explanation for Isabelle's actions. As Murray points out, *Jeune & jolie* eludes 'easy comprehension and explanation alike' and ends on 'a studiedly ambiguous note' (Murray 2014: 51).

CONCLUSION

Vincendeau summarises the plot of *Jeune & jolie* as follows: the 'tale of a gorgeous adolescent girl from a well-off family . . . decides to try being a prostitute' (2013: 67). Further, Vincendeau points out that the film 'stubbornly refuses to supply any conventional explanation for Isabelle's decision', adding that Isabelle is a 'completely impenetrable heroine; that is, we have no access to her inner life, her emotions or thought processes, which might have made her decision comprehensible' (Vincendeau 2013: 67). This incomprehensibility is less the desire to keep these motivations hidden than the tacit acceptance both of the 'end of grand narratives' and the 'death of the subject' theses; of Isabelle not as an individual but a 'text'. *Jeune & jolie* might best be called, following Jameson's definition of pastiche, a 'blank parody': a 'neutral practice . . . without any of parody's ulterior motives, amputated of the satiric impulse, devoid of laughter and of any conviction' (Jameson 1991: 17). The same can be said of Isabelle: she is the 'statue with blind eyeballs' (Jameson 1991: 17) which for Jameson is the figure of pastiche.

WORKS CITED

Allard, Ariane (2013), 'Jeune et Jolie', *Positif*, 631, pp. 20–1.
Augé, Marc (1995), *Non-Places: Introduction to an Anthropology of Supermodernity*, London and New York: Verso.
Baumann, Fabien and Yann Tobin (2013), 'Entretien Avec François Ozon: "Je Voulais Une Fille Qui Nous échappe"', *Positif*, 631, pp. 22–6.

'Blu-ray Review: *Jeune & jolie*' (2014), <https://eurodrama.wordpress.com/2014/03/23/blu-ray-review-jeune-jolie> (last accessed 23 July 2019).

Bradshaw, Peter (2013), '*Jeune & jolie* – Review', *The Guardian*, 29 November, <https://www.theguardian.com/film/2013/nov/28/jeune-et-jolie-review> (last accessed 14 June 2019).

Boym, Svetlana (1991), *Death in Quotation Marks*, Cambridge, MA: Harvard University Press.

Buchanan, Ian (2010), *A Dictionary of Critical Theory*, New York: Oxford University Press.

Collard, Susan, (2000), 'French Cultural Policy: The Special Role of the State', in William Kidd and Sian Reynolds (eds), *Contemporary French Cultural Studies*, London: Arnold, pp. 38–50.

Culler, Jonathan (1975), *Structuralist Poetics*, London and New York: Routledge.

Dormoy, Géraldine (2010), 'Le magazine Jeune & Jolie s'arrête', *L'Express*, 6 January, <https://www.lexpress.fr/styles/mode/le-magazine-jeune-jolie-s-arrete_840280.html> (last accessed 23 August 2019).

Fox, Alistair (2014), 'Auteurism, Personal Cinema, and the Fémis Generation: The Case of François Ozon', in Alistair Fox, Michel Marie, Raphaëlle Moine and Hilary Radner (eds), *A Companion to Contemporary French Cinema*, Malden, MA: Wiley Blackwell, pp. 205–29.

Glicksman, Josh (2019), 'Songs that Defined the Decade: M83's "Midnight City"', <https://www.billboard.com/articles/columns/rock/8544126/m83-midnight-city-songs-that-defined-the-decade> (last accessed 4 September 2019).

Handyside, Fiona (2012), 'The Possibilities of a Beach: Queerness and François Ozon's Beaches', *Screen*, 53: 1, pp. 54–71.

Handyside, Fiona (2012), 'Queer Filiations: Adaptation in the Films of François Ozon', *Sexualities*, 15: 1, pp. 53–67.

Harvey, David (1990), *The Condition of Postmodernity: An Enquiry into the Origins of Cultural Change*, Cambridge, MA: Blackwell.

Ince, Kate (2008), 'François Ozon's Cinema of Desire', in Kate Ince (ed.), *Five Directors: Auteurism from Assayas to Ozon*, Manchester: Manchester University Press, pp. 112–34.

Ince, Kate (2012), 'Glocal Gloom: Existential Space in Haneke's French-Language Films', in Ben McCann and David Sorfa (eds), *The Cinema of Michael Haneke: Europe Utopia*, New York: Wallflower Press, pp. 85–93.

Jagernauth, Kevin (2014), 'Review: Francois Ozon's "Young and Beautiful": A Missed Opportunity', *IndieWire*, 26 April, <https://www.indiewire.com/2014/04/review-francois-ozons-young-and-beautiful-a-missed-opportunity-86686> (last accessed 29 June 2019).

Jameson, Fredric (1991), *Postmodernism, Or, The Cultural Logic of Late Capitalism*, Durham, NC: Duke University Press.

Jameson, Fredric (2000), 'Globalization and Political Strategy', *New Left Review*, 4, pp. 49–68.

Jenkins, Brian (2000), 'French Political Culture: Homogeneous or Fragmented?', in William Kidd and Sîan Reynolds (eds), *Contemporary French Cultural Studies*, London: Arnold, pp. 111–25.

Lyotard, Jean-François (1984), *The Postmodern Condition: A Report on Knowledge*, Minneapolis, MN: University of Minnesota Press.

Macklin, Gerard (2011), 'Madness and Modernity in Rimbaud's *Une Saison en enfer*', *Neophilologus*, 95: 3, pp. 379–94.

Martin, Adrian (2019), 'Bedrooms and Bathrooms', August 2004, <http://www.filmcritic.com.au/reviews/s/short_films_ozon.html> (last accessed 11 November 2019).

Murray, Jonathan (2014), 'Young and Beautiful', *Cinéaste*, 39: 3, pp. 50–2.

Osenlund, R. Kurt (2014), 'Interview: François Ozon Talks *Young and Beautiful*', *Slant Magazine*, 25 April, <https://www.slantmagazine.com/film/interview-francois-ozon> (last accessed 17 July 2019).
Ozon, François (2013), 'Adolescence is the Birth of Disillusion', Cineuropa, <https://cineuropa.org/en/interview/238484> (last accessed 17 July 2019).
Roddick, Nick (2013), 'Love for Sale', *Sight and Sound*, 23: 12, pp. 48–51.
Sage, Adam (2014), 'The French Students Selling their Bodies to Pay for College', *The Times*, 4 August, <https://www.thetimes.co.uk/article/the-french-students-selling-their-bodies-to-pay-for-school-30tkspwtgbm> (last accessed 12 October 2019).
Schilt, Thibaut (2011), *François Ozon: Contemporary Film Directors*, Urbana, IL: University of Illinois Press.
Vanderschelden, Isabelle (2013), *Studying French Cinema*, Auteur: Leighton Buzzard.
Vincendeau, Ginette (2002), 'François Ozon', in Yvonne Tasker (ed.), *Fifty Contemporary Filmmakers*, London: Routledge, pp. 311–19.
Vincendeau, Ginette (2013), '*Jeune & Jolie*', *Sight & Sound*, 23: 12, pp. 66–7.
Vincendeau, Ginette (2019), 'After Pialat: The Young Realists of 1990s French Cinema', BFI, <https://www.bfi.org.uk/news-opinion/sight-sound-magazine/features/1990s-young-french-cinema-post-pialat-realists-assayas-kahn-klapisch-kassovitz-desplechin-ozon-breillat-denis> (last accessed 2 January 2020).
Walkley, Sarah (2018), *Cultural Diversity in the French Film Industry: Defending the Cultural Exception in a Digital Age*, London: Palgrave Macmillan.
Wallenbrock, Nicole Beth (2015), 'The Screen Student-prostitute, a Twenty-first-century Discourse: *Mes Chères études* (2010), *Elles* (2011), *Jeune et Jolie* (2013)', *French Cultural Studies*, 26: 4, pp. 415–25.
Waters, Sarah (2012), *Between Republic and Market: Globalisation and Identity in Contemporary France*, New York: Continuum.

PART II

(In)Formal Politics

CHAPTER 6

'The Scent of a Middle-class Woman': Desire, Family and the Adolescent Imagination in François Ozon's *Dans la maison*

Jamie Steele

The films of François Ozon have consistently been the subject of critical and academic debate, with a considerable output that offers sheer variety. A prolific and wide-ranging filmmaker, Ozon's films articulate themes that concern representations of queerness and male sexuality. It is, however, reductive to just consider Ozon's films precisely through the representation of homosexuality in contemporary French cinema. Major scholarly debate concerns the 'queer aesthetic' and temporalities of his filmmaking, whether that is through the challenge to patriarchy and patriarchal culture, 'fluidity of orientation' (Ince 2008: 117), hauntings, and the subversion of the representation of the nuclear family, landscape, setting, and narrative structure. As Schilt contends, 'Ozon's oeuvre is decidedly consistent in its desire to blur the traditional frontiers between the masculine and the feminine, gay and straight, reality and fantasy' (Schilt 2011: 5). As this book chapter argues, Ozon's filmmaking style and approach to institutions at the centre of the French national imaginary articulate a *remise en question* (a reassessment or questioning) of the aforementioned structures and a subversion of the heteronormative assumptions of Western European society and culture (Stanley 2010: 13). This is primarily considered through the analysis of desire and how it permeates the depiction of the school and the family as institutions. In fact, Rees-Roberts provides a neat distillation of the term 'queer' in a French context, arguing that 'Queer, as it is currently understood in the French translation, is resumed as "political self-representation" . . . "a mode of visual expression that interferes with filmic modes of representation in general" (Bourcier 1998: 15)' (Rees-Roberts 2008: 6). Beyond this, the 'queer aesthetic' resonates with broader approaches, in which Ozon's films are generally situated as part of a queer community of filmmaking (Dawson 2015).

Ozon's *Dans la maison* / *In the House* follows Claude Garcia – a schoolboy in France – as he begins to realise his talent for writing. After first submitting his work as school assignments, Claude is actively encouraged to pursue his writing by his tutor, the tautologically titled Germain Germain. His work opens as an exploration of the so-called 'normal family', who live a seemingly tranquil life in an unnamed suburban French city. It sheds light on how Claude interprets the 'normal' family life of his schoolfriend Rapha Artole, his father Rapha Senior, and, quite importantly, Rapha's mother, Esther. Claude gradually becomes a fixture in the Artole household, working informally as a mathematics tutor to help Rapha improve his schoolwork. His desire for Esther rises to the surface through his work, articulated as a *mise-en-abyme*, blurring the adolescent's imagination with his frequent visits to Rapha's house. The teacher, Germain, is captivated by Claude's writing about the inner workings of the 'normal family', enabling, guiding and advising the student to probe further and explore the adolescent's latent desires and fantasies.

Dans la maison coheres with a move by François Ozon to develop his work through 'transtextual adaptation' (Handyside 2012: 57). Handyside contends that '[p]rocesses of adaptation and interpretation can be explored via many of Ozon's films', such as *8 femmes / 8 Women* (2002), *Gouttes d'eau sur pierres brûlantes / Water Drops on Burning Rocks* (2000), *Sous le sable / Under the Sand* (2000), and through pastiche as in *Swimming Pool* (2003) (Handyside 2012: 57). *Dans la maison* is no exception, since it is inspired by the play, *El chico de la última fila / The Boy in the Last Row* by Spanish playwright Juan Mayorga (2006). It attests to the film's theatricality, which operates as a further point of intersection with Ozon's style. The film is also predicated on a literary citation system, pastiching both great French and great European writers, who are frequently cited throughout. The most evident example is the school, which is named after the French writer Gustave Flaubert, whose most famous French text, *Madame Bovary*, makes an appearance alongside *Un Coeur simple / A Simple Heart* as literary recommendations from Germain to Claude. As evidenced by research conducted by the French newspaper *Le Monde*, the names of French schools are primarily male figures from French history (Bronner and Vaudano 2015). Considering the data set, Bronner and Vaudano (2015) reveal that Flaubert is not one of the most frequently cited names from French literature. This, therefore, suggests that the school's name in *Dans la maison* and the reference to *Madame Bovary* in the conversation between Germain and Claude is a deliberate evocation of the film's themes of desire. As a cited influence for Claude to consider and engage with – as he explores his own story – the reference to *Madame Bovary* is peculiar, since it encourages a link to delusions. It raises further questions with regard to Claude's fiction, as the culmination of his own desire and delusions when visiting the Artole household. Ozon recites how the references to literature and 'high culture' are also articulated self-consciously through the film's casting of Fabrice Luchini as the teacher, Germain Germain. Ozon observes that '[i]n France, he's identified as a promoter of French literature – he regularly performs one-man shows based on the texts of La Fontaine and Céline for example, which is known by heart' (Godet 2013). While noting the cinematic references, Jonas Grethlein also addresses the narrative techniques borrowed from classical storytelling, such as '[t]he intricate entanglement of absorption and reflection across various levels of representation aligns *Dans la maison* with the *Ethiopica* [*Aethiopica*]' (Grethlein 2017: 134). The sequences of *mise-en-abyme*, in particular, add layers to the narrative, with Germain entering into Claude's story on two occasions.[1]

IN/OUT OF SCHOOL?: 'QUEERING' EDUCATION IN FRANCE

Ozon's film 'queers' the French school as a core French institution. Dawson argues that 'queer temporalities' have 'a focus on non-normative life schedules either alongside or rather than queer gender or sexuality' (Dawson 2015: 185). In the case of *Dans la maison*, Ozon adopts a technique which 'relies on a good deal of *talk*' and coheres with 'Ozon's dialogue-driven cinema' (Gerstner and Nahmias 2015: 27–8). In this sense, Ozon 'relays a narrative in which communicating ideas aesthetically requires *talking through* these very ideas' (Gerstner and Nahmias 2015: 28). Ozon's film creates a *mise-en-abyme* structure that is predicated on the dialogue between the teacher and the student, and how the writings of the adolescent character are imagined and filtered through Germain and and his wife Jeanne as well as through Claude's voiceover. The spectator is charged with the responsibility of deciphering Claude's imaginative writings or Germain's and Jeanne's feedback. The narrative framework of Claude's active learning is not engendered through the conventional and traditional forms of education, disseminated from teacher to student, but through the learning from within the household through observation and Germain's feedback outside the classroom, in liminal spaces such as the school corridors, and, on two occasions, within the house. The imparting of knowledge and feedback is provided through sequences of intervention that draw attention to the film as medium and act of writing as fantasy.

Gerstner and Nahmias (2015) posit the development of a critical dynamic in *Dans la maison*, which creates an active dialogue between the spectator and the filmmaker. For these scholars, Jeanne Germain operates 'as the spectator's surrogate', 'suggesting possible areas for character and story development' (Gerstner and Nahmias 2015: 27), whereas 'as M. Germain (Ozon?) sees it [the postmodern art in Jeanne's gallery], distinct form must follow strategically aestheticised content' (Gerstner and Nahmias 2015: 27). As Sotinel neatly argues, 'Ozon constructs a hall of mirrors: the sequences in Rapha's house are subjected to criticism by Germain Germain, whose admiration at times borders on love for his student' (Sotinel 2012).² Germain intervenes in Rapha's bedroom, appearing from behind Rapha and Claude, in an act that appears similar to crawling out from beneath the desk. The moment at which Germain appears is significant, since it is at the point when Rapha states that he felt 'undressed' and humiliated when asked to read his story about Claude aloud in class. The conversation that unfolds between Claude and Germain occurs in Rapha's presence, and they discuss how to flesh out the character of Rapha within Claude's *mise-en-abyme* story. The ideas about how to develop the character of Rapha are 'talked through' (to adopt Gerstner and Nahmias's terms [2015]) between Germain and Claude, in a self-reflexive and referential mode that is akin to the filmmaker's provocations for nuancing each character. The inclusion of Germain at the same eye-level as the two students is telling, as he crouches behind them, removing the conventional power relations between teacher and student. The act of writing and developing characters is formed through exchange and dialogue, as an equitable partnership between Germain and Claude. The choice of language also highlights the public/private subversion, with Rapha stating that he is 'undressed' publicly while Germain and Claude are both present in his bedroom. It also 'queers' and subverts the traditional notion of education, by providing entrance for the teacher into the student's domestic life, and, in particular, placing a public interaction into a very private sphere, heightened by the fact that the conversation is taking place in Rapha's bedroom (Figure 6.1).

Figure 6.1 In Rapha's bedroom

Sotinel's 'hall of mirrors' (Sotinel 2012) reverberates through Claude's first kiss with Rapha's mother. In the film's press pack, Ozon interprets this as a crucial moment for Germain's 'intrusions' into Claude's writing, with Ozon arguing that '[t]here comes a point when Germain has to penetrate the fiction, become an active participant. When Claude kisses Esther, Germain steps out of the pantry because the desire is too intense for him' (Wildbunch 2012). Claude writes a poem for Esther, leading to a passionate embrace between the mother and the surrogate son, who has been helping Rapha with his tutoring (as she notes in the dialogue). The use of repetitive non-diegetic music and Germain's introduction again to this sequence from the larder highlights that we have entered into Claude's story. The sequence is predicated on questions of desire, emanating from both Claude (in terms of his writing) and Germain (through his encouragement and intervention). As Claude notes, he is 'following his desire' as Germain provides feedback on the sequence, the passionate kiss and embrace between Claude and Esther, and the glance from Rapha as he sees Claude 'taking his place' in an Oedipal narrative. Germain strolls into intimate areas and moments, conflating the private/public life, where he 'witnesses' the student's passions and desires. The feedback and comments that he directs towards the story unfold in the private setting, as Claude notes that he has taken the advice on board. The glances and looks at this point become crucial, with Germain stepping closer to intimately observe the embrace between Claude and Esther, as if he has now become an implicit voyeur, piquing his own interest in Claude. Rapha's glance towards Esther and Claude is interpreted by Germain as 'farce', since it reaffirms convention in narratives of voyeuristic young desire. Since the sequence and the glance are laced with ambiguity, the notion of desire operates either by pitting the students as rivals or placing a hurdle in front of Rapha and his queer desire for Claude. The tautology of the voyeur position is reaffirmed in the final sequence, as Germain takes the place of voyeur. The voiceover at the conclusion of this sequence evinces this turn, since Germain rather than Claude articulates the repetitious line of 'à suivre' ('to be continued') for the first and only time in the film (Figure 6.2).

In terms of an analysis of the school in *Dans la maison*, pedagogy and the teacher–student relationship could easily lend itself to socio-political comment; a search for a contextual depth, political commitment and social consciousness whereby the film is offering a critique of the system, society and politics. Such an interpretation is tempting given that Ozon is a contemporary of *le jeune cinéma*, as Stanley crucially notes (Stanley 2010: 42–3). As Stanley contends in the context of Ozon's *Les Amants criminels / Criminal Lovers* (1999), 'this is not the last time that Ozon will allude to a hotly debated topic only then to fail to engage with the issue in a politically committed . . . or "realist" manner' (Stanley 2010: 43). In essence, there is some latency to the social and political comment and critique in Ozon's films, but it is not as explicit or front and

Figure 6.2 Germain emerges from the pantry

centre as with the filmmakers of the aforementioned *le jeune cinéma*. This is particularly intriguing to consider, since the socio-politics of *Dans la maison* appear at the forefront of Brody's (2013) film review in *The New York Times*.

The representation of the school falls into this interpretation through the forms of education between the student and the teacher that take place outside the classroom, through advice and discussions that take place in an empty classroom for private tutoring, and through the corridors, as well as through the brief moments after the conclusion of a lesson. It is also through the use of language, as noted by Germain with his antiquated views on pedagogy and education, such as with the references to 'educator' and 'learner' – a use of language that pertains to a knowledge exchange – rather than 'teacher/professor' and 'pupil'. This implies a top-down and systematic transmission of knowledge. Brody refers to the film's discussion of '"this whole stupefying new pedagogical discourse", meaning a gentler, more human mode of education than the one Germain has been trained to deliver' (Brody 2013). Brody further historicises the use of this pedagogical language as derivative of Lionel Jospin's period as Minister of Education in France when he outlines that:

> the student is at the centre of the educational system – a remark that proved controversial, because, to that point, it was more or less a given that education itself, the transmission of knowledge, was at the centre of a famously rigid system. (Brody 2013)

The alignment between Ozon and Jospin is also contextually salient, since, in the nascent period of Ozon's film career, he 'made a sympathetic documentary

(*Jospin s'éclaire*) about the French socialist presidential candidate Lionel Jospin' (Asibong 2008: 8). The comment on pedagogy and the French education system appears more than just serendipitous, operating rather as a political point regarding a call for change within rigid systems. There is reciprocity between the teacher and the learner/student, which is breaking down traditional boundaries and relationships. As Ozon contends, 'Usually students learn from their teachers, but here, the learning goes both ways. And the back-and-forth between reality and writing lends itself to a playful reflection on storytelling and the imagination' (Ozon n.d.).

The film's opening sequence offers a non-traditional representation of the school through its decision to adopt a school uniform for all students, unusual for schools in France. In *Le Monde*, Sotinel observed that the uniform employed in *Dans la maison* is 'vaguement britannique' ('vaguely British') (Sotinel 2012), and is set against the diegetic backdrop of a time in which 'national education has given way to the old fantasy of a school uniform, supposedly designed to remove any social differences [between the students]' (Sotinel 2012).³ These two points dialectically contrast in *Dans la maison*, setting new forms of pedagogy alongside the implementation of structure and organisation. This dynamic also emerges in Germain's teaching style. He is seemingly against this form of pedagogy, seen in his disdain during conversations with the headteacher, but, as French contends in *The Guardian*, 'Germain despises most of his fellow teachers for their conventional thinking and despairs of his pupils for their uniformity and lack of imagination' (French 2013). This leads to Germain's interventions with Claude in settings reserved more for the student to experience, such as corridors, empty classrooms, playgrounds and within Rapha's house (in the sequences of Claude's act of writing and story). The students also stay in their uniforms in the private context, often within Rapha's house and at key moments, such as Claude's embrace of Esther. Both Claude and Rapha are still wearing their uniforms in this story within Rapha's house as Germain intervenes, highlighting how the form of teaching and education has persisted in the private sphere. This also queers the students' day-to-day interactions.

'NORMAL FAMILIES': THE BOURGEOIS SCENT

Kate Ince's study of Ozon's filmmaking from its nascent stage contends that 'the family has been central to Ozon's cinema' (Ince 2008: 118). The notion of the so-called 'queering of the family' has been adopted frequently in the context of contemporary French cinema and Ozon's films. Ince (2002) highlights the emergence of a 'queer cinema aesthetic' (i.e., the *mise-en-scène*) and the multiplicity of sexual relations in France in the late 1990s and early 2000s.

Returning to Ozon, both Chilcoat (2008) and Kooijman (2005) suggest that Ozon 'queers the nuclear family' in his earlier film, *Sitcom* (1997). One of the primary distinctions between Ozon's *Sitcom* and the later *Dans la maison* is that the father figure does not turn into an example of the so-called 'paternal monster' (Schilt 2011: 49). Kooijman argues that Ozon's earlier film *Sitcom* 'reworks the image of the normative family, from the destruction of the bourgeois family to its replacement by an alternative "queer" family' (Kooijman 2005: 73). While the reference to *Sitcom* is appropriate through the depiction of the bourgeois family, the approach to the nuclear family in *Dans la maison* is much softer. Ozon posits that:

> [m]y view has changed with time. In *Sitcom*, I tried to rebuild the family by killing the patriarch. Now with *In the House*, the family is stronger than the young boy, I see the need for family in society. At the same time it is a neurotic place. (Gilbey 2013)

The framing of the family is, therefore, interpreted through the lens of neurosis, youth and desire. It is less critical of the patriarchal structure of the family; instead it is shaped by the introduction of a stranger in the form of Claude. As Ozon further notes in the film's press pack:

> Claude believes he can infiltrate the family and destroy it from the inside but, as it turns out, the family's love is stronger and Claude can't find his place, he is excluded [. . . and] the family unit possesses a centrifugal force which bonds them together and expulses outsiders. (Wildbunch 2012)

This changes the dynamics of the family for Claude, as he interprets it as a source of desire through his own writing.

In *Dans la maison*, Ozon is clearly offering a comment on the family. Claude's imaginative writing on the nuclear family provides a glimpse into what Claude sees as a 'normal family'. Dialogically throughout his writing, he refers to the family as 'normal', that is to say it is predicated on a heteronormative assumption of the workings of contemporary nuclear family life. It is also in contrast to Claude's own family life, in which his mother has left, leaving him alone to support his unemployed father who lives on disability allowance. The Artole home offers Claude an escape from his single-parent household into one that conforms to heteronormative assumptions of the family. However, since the *mise-en-abyme* narrative is revealed as within the adolescent's imagination – as evidenced by Claude's voiceover and the sequences in which Germain intervenes in the narrative – the image of the 'normal' family is one that is predicated on fantasy and desire. In terms of film criticism, Blondeau interprets a rather 'archetypal' representation of the 'bourgeois family' (although the mother is frequently referred to in the film in the context of *la classe moyenne*) in its depiction of the mother, father and son (Blondeau 2012). However, Eisenstat views the outsider's perception of the nuclear family in his story as means of 'tak[ing] aim at this normal family, dismissing Rapha Artole Senior [. . .] as a vulgar galoot, and objectifying Rapha's comely yet passive mother Esther' (Eisenstat 2013). The use of *mise-en-abyme* is crucial within the objectification of Esther by Claude through his imaginative writing while 'at the epicentre of the family'. He sneaks into Esther and Rapha Senior's bedroom, navigating the dark corridors, before caressing Esther's foot as a synecdoche of his repressed desire for the mother. The shot objectifies Esther's foot as a representation of the act of copulation between the father and mother. The figurative relationship of Claude as outsider and surrogate son is communicated at the close of the sequence. Seated in a chair behind the parents as they copulate, the character of Wong Lee – a Chinese businessman with whom Rapha Senior works – appears in the couple's bedroom. The frequent references to China and the Orient throughout Ozon's film resonate with film noir's use of such references as a way of defamiliarising the setting. In this instance, it is clear that the spectator is witnessing a fantasy. After the act of coitus, Claude imagines himself positioned between the mother and the father, in the place of the child who is secure and safe in-between his parents. In essence, the Freudian desire for the mother from the position of the child is clearly articulated, culminating in acts of voyeurism. In this instance, the bedroom operates as a nurturing space for Claude, providing the teenager with a symbolic sense of safety and security beside the figurative mother and father. For Claude, it marks a desire to return to a childlike state in the household and bedroom, which contrasts with the school that is less of a nurturing space due to its adoption of a male name and patriarchal reference in Gustave Flaubert. It is perhaps more in line with the qualities of early schooling, which has feminine connotations, as seen in the name 'l'école maternelle'. However, the family is 'queered' through Claude's position between the parents as an outsider, and this poses a threat to the heteronormative family.

Claude, the agent of desire or – to borrow Asibong's (2008: 35) terms when analysing *Teorema / Theorem* (Pier Paolo Pasolini, 1968) – 'sexual angel', is not only active in 'defamiliarising' (Schilt 2011: 3) and destabilising the 'normal family' as it is presented to the spectator through Ozon's narrative structure. Claude also penetrates Germain's marriage through his adolescent imagination, as well as through his essays, which Germain must grade. In turn this affects the relationship between Germain and Jeanne. Jeanne also reads Claude's essays and initially seems disgusted by the desire that Claude expresses for his friend's mother. Ozon contends in the film's press pack that the intertextual relationship with *Theorem* pertains to Claude's 'contamination' of the marriage (Wildbunch 2012). Claude is also introduced to Jeanne and Germain's bed through his essays. Asibong's interpretation of *Sitcom* is illuminating at this point, since '[t]he effect the rat [in Ozon's *Sitcom*] appears to have on his wife and children never threatens Jean's place as father within the family home, despite the spectator's reasonable expectation that, inevitably, it will' (Asibong 2008: 37). In a similar way, Claude's essays do not - at first - appear to destabilise Germain's marriage and relationship with his wife. However, upon Claude's physical penetration of Germain's apartment, the marriage is placed in doubt and questioned through his intervention, leading to its inevitable breakdown. This is indicated by the film's final scene as Germain sits alone (until the arrival of Claude) on a park bench, longingly gazing through the windows of a nearby apartment block. Gerstner and Nahmias contend that this final sequence shows that:

> we see that what lie[s] before Claude and M. Germain are a series of stages, or *Rear Window*-like projections, in which numerous scenarios are displayed. For Ozon, every window tells a story, but the telling of the story demands precision on the part of the artist. (Gerstner and Nahmias 2015: 26)

As such, the scene comments on Claude's story so far, in which 'numerous scenarios' have been considered by him with which to end his story. As we have seen, Claude adopts the position of the outsider and the voyeur to project his own desire onto the family. This is also captured through these reflections that highlight how Germain has imparted his own desires into Claude's story by also adopting a voyeuristic position in 'Claude's story as mise-en-abîme' (Grethlein 2017: 135).

The presence of the outsider (Claude) in the Artole household 'queers' the family, by offering a challenge to its stability. Through Claude's imagination of the family in his writing, it is uncertain what is 'reality' and what is fiction in the film's set pieces in the household. The outsider character destabilises the family through his friendship with Rapha Junior and his desire for Esther. The film's denouement also lends this theme of 'defamiliarising' (Schilt 2011: 3) to Germain, with the presence of the student and his writing leading to the breakdown of Germain and Jeanne's marriage. It is also too simplistic to pair this 'queering' to just two sequences in the film; the first when Germain's wife Jeanne asks him whether the lack of sex and his impotency in their relationship is due to an interest in his student Claude, and the second when Rapha Junior kisses Claude in the family's guest room. Instead, these moments pertain to a homoeroticism that sits within the more complex and nuanced relationships between the characters. While it is important not to be dismissive of these important themes, they are situated within an interplay between the characters in which power dynamics regularly shift, predicated on desire, fantasy and escapism.

The nuclear middle-class family remains a key continuity for Ozon, since, in his previous films *Sitcom* and *8 femmes / 8 Women*, there is a presence of 'a classically patriarchal family, in which gender roles and generational differences function according to the highly familiar dynamics of the bourgeoisie' (Ince 2008: 120). There is a difference to note between these representations of the French middle-class, with the aforementioned films pertaining to a more upper-middle class stratification, while the family in *Dans la maison* is more middle-class or 'moyenne' (if we are to consider that these class stratifications and distinctions exist within white, suburban middle-class French society). However, these images are presented critically. For example, in the case of *Dans la maison*, these class representations are viewed through the lens of the adolescent imagination, which is nurtured by the teacher. The vision and interpretation of the family is 'susceptible to fantasy sparked by [. . .] Claude's own tale (or fantasies)' (Brody 2013). However, the 'normal' and 'archetypal' French family is further 'defamiliarised' (Schilt 2011: 3) through a process of Americanisation (resonating with Ozon's *Sitcom*) and frequent references to China. These references emerge through the use of music in Jeanne's art gallery, the exotic objects displayed on furniture in the Artole household, the discussion of an LA-based artist, and the businessman, Wong Lee. As Ozon notes in *Les Inrocks*, Rapha's father recalls Burt Reynolds (rather than Tom Selleck) through his facial hair and that '[t]his French family [. . .] is very stylised, and Americanised'.[4] As such, the family does not cohere with the image of a stereotypical 'French family', because of their appearance, predilection for glossy interior design magazines and the father's and son's love of basketball, whether watching or playing the sport together. It is certainly a presentation of father-son relations that goes against the grain in a European context, with the major team sports being football and rugby in France.

In *Sitcom*, Kooijman also posits that the film includes 'the destruction of the bourgeois nuclear family, which immediately suggests a comparison to Pier Paolo Pasolini's classic *Teorema / Theorem* (1968)' (Kooijman 2005: 76). Pasolini also gets a mention in *Dans la maison*. As Gerstner and Nahmias argue, '[a]t one point when reiterating the importance of narrative conflict and problem solving in writing, he [Germain] scolds Claude for turning his sociological experiment into a Pasolini film [*Teorema*, one presumes]' (Gerstner and Nahmias 2015: 27). In fact, Gerstner and Nahmias contend that '*Dans la maison* is not Pasolini's queer cinema' (Gerstner and Nahmias 2015: 27). However, Viano's textual analysis of Pasolini's *Theorem* posits that '[t]he mysterious guest is like an acid test revealing the identity of the signs-in-crisis' (Viano 1993: 202). Viano considers Pasolini's film through the lens of 'epistemological crisis' and a questioning of whether 'we know anything after the traditional terms of knowledge have been upset' (Viano 1993: 200–1). In Ozon's film, Claude – as the stranger – 'upsets' the established relationships and narratives between the family members, reconfiguring the balance between father and son as they watch the basketball games, and as an agent of desire with Rapha's mother. The so-called 'normal family' is evidently destabilised.

In addition to this reference point from outside Ozon's oeuvre, Kooijman's work on *Sitcom* also includes analysis of the nuclear family that resonates with *Dans la maison*. Kooijman argues that – in *Sitcom* – '[t]he gay son functions as the family's "soft" spot, a point of entrance for the outside that enables the exposure of the family from within' (Kooijman 2005: 77). There is evidence of a certain thematic continuity between *Sitcom* and *Dans la maison* in this regard, since the son (Rapha, in *Dans la maison*) functions as the 'soft spot' and the 'point of entrance' for Claude as he penetrates the nuclear family. Drawing from *Theorem*, Claude is the 'stranger' who enters into the household, queering and subverting its dynamic. On the evidence of the references in the narrative, it is too simplistic to posit that Rapha represents the gay son, since the binaries of gay/straight are left ambiguous. It is equally appropriate to posit bisexuality or non-binary approaches to relationships, sex and sexual desire. That is to say that Rapha does not 'come out of the closet', so to speak. Ozon's films are more concerned with the 'ability to lift his narrative out of the banal circumscriptions of everyday discourses around sexuality, and onto a more radical place of ethical inquiry' (Asibong 2008: 18). As Johnston argues in his analysis of '(post-)queer citizenship' in France:

> what may be regarded by some as the positive process of 'coming out', is in fact an expression of Foucauldian power relations forcing the individual into processes of confession, thus placing the individual in the position of dominated, rather than dominating. (Martel 1996 quoted in Johnston 2008: 90–1)

Rapha's embrace of Claude could be more appropriately considered as an expression of 'queer youth's desire' (Gerstner and Nahmias 2015: 25) in which adolescent desire becomes more significant and discernible. Gerstner and Nahmias contend that 'Ozon's queer cinema [most of all *Dans la maison*] . . . makes use of the New Wave tradition' in which there are stylistic and aesthetic references to François Truffaut and later Maurice Pialat, culminating in 'the realm of unsettled queer youth and the search to satisfy desire' (Gerstner and Nahmias 2015: 24–5). Desire is presented in the film through the relationships between the two adolescent characters, particularly from Rapha's perspective, and through Claude's writing, which articulates his desire for the mother figure. However, desire is not just represented through the writing and the relationships between the characters, since the references to voyeurism also articulate the spectator's own desires and power through watching. In the French magazine *Positif*, Royer highlights this articulation of desire by contending that 'Claude's prose satisfies our desire in fiction, the voyeuristic desire to penetrate the intimate lives of others more than our own' (Royer 2012: 41).[5]

In *Dans la maison*, this is bound up with questions of power, particularly when considered in the context of the family. The sequence of this embrace between Rapha and Claude occurs in the guest room. It is described in voiceover by Claude as 'strange' and 'at the epicentre of Rapha's family's private life'. The non-diegetic background music, and the switching on of dimmed lights in a room creates an uncanny and subversive atmosphere, charged with emotion. This is heightened by the claps of thunder that follow as Claude lies on the bed, having glanced over to see Rapha's mother's dolls, lying 'mutilated' around the old doll house. The space of the guest room – populated by Claude as the outsider – is a transgressive space, where homoerotic desires unfold in the private sphere. Rapha gives Claude a red basketball shirt to wear, and is excited by him undressing. This culminates in their kiss, instigated by Rapha. For Rapha, the guest room is a revelatory space that is laced with Ozon's doublings, Rapha felt 'undressed' in front of the classroom in the school when discussing his friendship with Claude, and Claude – after helping him feel less humiliated by writing an exposé for the school magazine *Le Flambeau* – is now partially undressed (literally) in front of Rapha. This is the moment when Rapha is at his most vulnerable in expressing his emotion and physical love for Claude, a letting-go that is followed by him punching the wall, which attests to the difficulty he has in experiencing his feelings and same-sex desire. For both characters – Claude and Rapha – this is the initiating moment of sexual awakening; Rapha squirms and fits while he sleeps, as Claude gazes voyeuristically in the darkness. Claude is revealed to be a voyeur through *mise-en-abyme*. He sits in the corner of Rapha Junior's dark room, wearing Rapha's basketball shirt, imagining watching Rapha's father and mother copulate in their bedroom, as in the 'peeping tom' psychoanalytical narratives of David Lynch. In both cases, Claude adopts a position of power through his desire for Esther. He is a voyeur of the parents in the act of sex, and he has knowledge of Rapha's desire for him.

The desire is still bound up with questions of power, as evinced by Johnston (2008), resulting in acts of violence between the two young male characters. The denouement of the friendship between Claude and Rapha is articulated through the aforementioned 'Foucauldian power relations' (Johnston 2008: 91). The fight between Rapha and Claude is first discussed through the dialogue of team sports, that is, through a sense of collective and solidarity between 'teammates'. However, the use of the loaded terminology by Claude pertaining to Rapha's sexuality highlights the presence of these intrinsic power relations for individuals who do not conform to heteronormativity, with Rapha fighting Claude in order to maintain control of his own sense of identity. In this way, Ozon's film clearly articulates the remaining power relations that are bound up with desire and sexuality in twenty-first-century (Western and Western European) culture.

As noted, Claude's infiltration into the relationship between Germain and Jeanne affects both individuals. For instance, Claude becomes an object of fantasy for Jeanne in place of her husband, whose impotence was previously foregrounded. The acts of physical contact, of posited sex, and sexual encounters between the characters are reconfigured into the body of the adolescent, who becomes a fantasy for middle-class women. The act of youth's desire is, therefore, seen as transgressive. The Oedipal-style narrative and notions of desire by Claude for older women in the film (Jeanne and Rapha's mother) are heightened by the absence of a mother figure within his own family. The lack of a strong father figure (Claude plays basketball with Rapha and his father) and mother in his family leads Claude to create his own sense of unity through desire for the mother in the Artole and Germain marriages. With the absence of his own mother, Claude's imaginative writings and sequences of embrace and suggested copulation with older women highlight the lack of Freudian-like resolution for the adolescent. Even though the film's denouement suggests that 'He [Claude] claims to have learnt from Germain that her [Jeanne's] infertility is the reason why they are childless' (Grethlein 2017: 135), the association of family is posited (problematically) in relation to the female body. However, the evidence presented to the spectator attests to the opposite. It is as if Claude represents their forbidden fruit, supplanting and replacing the figure of the father in the 'normal family' (in terms of the desire between the mother and Claude) and the surrogate father (teacher) Germain. It recalls a transgressive Oedipal narrative of replacing father figures in search for sex with mothers.

Drawing on the hermeneutics of adolescent desire and imagination, Ozon's *Dans la maison* 'queers' the presentation of two French institutions in the school and the middle-class, suburban family. The school is 'defamiliarised' (Schilt 2011: 3) through subtle nuances, such as the uniform, and how the act of learning and feedback imbricates the public and private sphere. The two sequences in which the teacher, Germain, enters both the house and Claude's imagination highlight how the act of teaching and learning has penetrated the private sphere, in a way that is ultimately condemned by Germain losing his job at the film's denouement. Ozon's sequences of feedback and intervention break conventional temporalities in cinema, presenting a 'queer temporality' (Dawson 2015) that foregrounds the intricacies of adolescent fantasy and desire, articulated through *mise-en-abyme*. Although the family is not destabilised permanently by the outsider (Claude), Ozon's film highlights how the so-called 'normal' family is laced with dark and uncertain corridors of desire that are traditionally closed off the to the outside. The presence of Claude reveals these youthful desires and allows them to be exposed through his act of storytelling, challenging the status quo and assumptions that lie beneath the nuclear family.

NOTES

1. Grethlein also observes that 'Claude's story serves as a mise-en-abîme' (Grethlein 2017: 135).
2. 'Ozon construit ainsi un labyrinthe de miroirs: les séquences dans la maison de Rapha sont soumises à la critique de Germain Germain, qui oscille entre l'admiration quasi amoureuse pour son élève' (Sotinel 2012). Unless otherwise noted, all translations are my own.
3. '[c]ette année-là, l'éducation nationale a cédé au vieux fantasme de l'uniforme, censé effacer les différences sociales' (Sotinel 2012).
4. 'Cette famille française dans le film est très stylisée, américanisée' (Kaganski 2012).
5. 'La prose de Claude satisfait notre désir de fiction, désir voyeuriste de pénétrer l'intimité d'autres vies que la nôtre' (Rouyer 2012: 41)

WORKS CITED

Asibong, Andrew (2008), *François Ozon*, Manchester: Manchester University Press.
Blondeau, Romain (2012), '"Dans la maison", un thriller drôle et enlevé', *Les Inrocks*, 9 October 2012, <https://www.lesinrocks.com/cinema/films-a-l-affiche/dans-la-maison> (last accessed 16 May 2020).
Brody, Richard (2013), 'In Class with "In the House"', *The New Yorker*, <https://www.newyorker.com/culture/richard-brody/in-class-with-in-the-house> (last accessed 2 July 2020).
Bronner, Luc and Maxime Vaudano (2015), 'De Jules Ferry à Pierre Perret, l'étonnant palmarès des noms d'écoles, de collèges et de lycées en France', *Le Monde*, 18 April 2015, <https://www.lemonde.fr/les-decodeurs/article/2015/04/18/de-jules-ferry-a-pierre-perret-l-etonnant-palmares-des-noms-d-ecoles-de-colleges-et-de-lycees-en-france_4613091_4355770.html> (last accessed 22 August 2020).
Chilcoat, Michelle (2008), 'Queering the Family in François Ozon's *Sitcom*', in Robin Griffiths (ed.), *Queer Cinema in Europe*, Bristol: Intellect, pp. 23–33.
Dawson, Leanne (2015), 'Queer European Cinema: Queering Cinematic Time and Space', *Studies in European Cinema*, 12: 3, pp. 185–204.
Eisenstat, Jared (2013), 'Review: In the House', *Film Comment*, 17 April, <https://www.filmcomment.com/blog/review-in-the-house-francois-ozon> (last accessed 21 June 2020).
French, Phillip (2013), 'In the House – Review', *The Guardian*, 31 March, <https://www.theguardian.com/film/2013/mar/31/in-the-house-review> (last accessed 1 July 2020).
Gerstner, David A. and Julien Nahmias (2015), *Christophe Honoré: A Critical Introduction*, Detroit, MI: Wayne State University Press.
Gilbey, Ryan (2013), 'François Ozon: "I'll admit I'm a little bit twisted"', *The Guardian*, 28 March, <https://www.theguardian.com/film/2013/mar/28/francois-ozon-interview-in-the-house> (last accessed 29 June 2020).
Godet, Aurelie (2013), 'Interview/ François Ozon: In the House', *Home*, 26 March, <https://homemcr.org/article/interview-francois-ozon-in-the-house> (last accessed 22 May 2020).
Grethlein, Jonas (2017), *Aesthetic Experiences and Classical Antiquity: The Significance of Form in Narratives and Pictures*, Cambridge: Cambridge University Press.
Handyside, Fiona (2011), 'Queer Filiations: Adaptations in the Films of François Ozon', *Sexualities*, 15: 1, pp. 53–67.

Ince, Kate (2002), 'Queering the Family? Fantasy and the Performance of Sexuality and Gay Relations in French Cinema 1995–2000', *Studies in French Cinema*, 2: 2, pp. 90–7.

Ince, Kate (2008), 'François Ozon's Cinema of Desire', in Kate Ince (ed.), *Five Directors: Auteurism from Assayas to Ozon*, Manchester: Manchester University Press, pp. 112–34.

Johnston, Cristina (2008), '(Post-)queer citizenship in contemporary Republican France', *Contemporary French and Francophone Studies*, 12: 1, pp. 89–97.

Kaganski, Serge (2012), 'François Ozon: visite guidée de son oeuvre', *Les Inrockuptibles*, 10 October, <https://www.lesinrocks.com/2012/10/10/cinema/actualite-cinema/verbation-ozon> (last accessed 1 July 2020).

Kooijman, Jaap (2005), 'Family Portrait: Queering the Nuclear Family in François Ozon's *Sitcom*', in Patricia Pisters and Wim Straat (eds), *Shooting the Family: Transnational Media and Intercultural Values*, Amsterdam: Amsterdam University Press, pp. 73–88.

Ozon, François (n.d.), 'Interview with François Ozon', Françoisozon.com, <http://www.francois-ozon.com/en/interviews-in-the-house/335-entretien-avec-francois-ozon> (last accessed 14 December 2019).

Rees-Roberts, Nick (2008), *French Queer Cinema*, Edinburgh: Edinburgh University Press.

Rouyer, Philippe (2012), '"Dans la maison": Portrait de l'artiste en lycéen', *Positif*, October 2012, pp. 40–1.

Schilt, Thibaut (2011), *François Ozon*, Urbana, IL: University of Illinois Press.

Sotinel, Thomas (2012), '"Dans la maison" intime de François Ozon', *Le Monde*, October 10 2012, <https://www.lemonde.fr/culture/article/2012/10/09/un-maitre-des-jeux-de-miroirs-dans-le-labyrinthe-de-la-fiction_1772368_3246.html> (last accessed 2 July 2020).

Stanley, Alice (2009), *Representations of Sexuality in the Films of François Ozon*, Unpublished PhD thesis, University of Warwick.

Teorema / Theorem, film, directed by Pier Paolo Pasolini. Italy: Aetos Produzioni Cinematografiche, 1968.

Viano, Maurizio (1993), *A Certain Realism: Making Use of Pasolini's Film Theory and Practice*, Berkeley, CA: University of California Press.

Wildbunch (2012), 'In the House Press Pack', *Unifrance.org*, <https://medias.unifrance.org/medias/121/73/84345/presse/dans-la-maison-dossier-de-presse-anglais.pdf> (last accessed 2 September 2020).

CHAPTER 7

Bringing Up Baby in the Twenty-first Century: *Le Refuge* and the Ozonian Family

Thibaut Schilt

François Ozon's eleventh feature film *Le Refuge* is at once unmistakably Ozonian and a new horizon for the prolific French director. Released internationally under the English title *The Refuge* and as *Hideaway* in the US, the film opened at festivals in late 2009, won the special jury prize at the San Sebastián international film festival and was shown in theatres in France and abroad the following year. Shot on a shoestring budget and with strict time constraints due to its main actress's real-life pregnancy, this 88-minute contemporary drama came out on the heels of the director's flying baby fantasy film *Ricky* (2009), a box office failure, and in the shadow of the big-budget, Catherine Deneuve-starring, and commercially successful feminist comedy *Potiche* (2010).[1] *Le Refuge* chronicles the developing rapport between two grieving characters: Mousse, a recovering addict who withdraws from the world to mourn the recent loss of her partner Louis and come to terms with an unexpected pregnancy; and Louis's gay brother Paul, who joins Mousse in her seaside refuge and offers his emotional support. The director's touch is apparent in the story's unhurried pacing, waterfront location and ongoing exploration of mourning, motherhood and complex human interactions, recalling his entire past filmography, both short and feature-length, and most notably *Une Robe d'été* / *A Summer Dress* (1996), *Regarde la mer* / *See the Sea* (1997), *Sous le sable* / *Under the Sand* (2000), *Swimming Pool* (2003), *5x2* (2004), *Le Temps qui reste* / *Time to Leave* (2005) and *Ricky*.

Although Ozon has stated that he did not intentionally make this film as part of a trilogy on death and mourning following *Sous le sable* and *Le Temps qui reste* (Schilt 2011: 155), *Le Refuge* has much in common with these two predecessors, on thematic and stylistic levels, as well as with *Swimming Pool*, another drama about loss in which a solitary heroine seeks refuge in a country home in southern France and bonds with an initially unwelcome guest. Additionally, Fiona Handyside has eloquently demonstrated a connection between Ozon's seaside films in the way they use beachscapes as timeless, queer spaces that serve a 'metaphorical function as [sites] of liquidity, fluidity and change' and as liminal places that both 'un[do] heteronormativity's insistence on a linear march towards the future and [queer] affective relations' (Handyside 2012: 55–6). She specifically analyses films featuring ostensibly heterosexual women, and identifies a particularly strong bond between Ozon's medium-length film *Regarde la mer* and *Le Refuge* in their atemporal depiction of babies (the first already born, the other in gestation) and in the way both films queer 'the normative frameworks of reproductivity, and in doing so transform them' (2012: 58–9). Interestingly, *Le Refuge* closes a chapter in Ozon's filmography as the last 'beach film' he has directed, as the seven full-length films released between 2010 and 2019 no longer include this familiar location (though his *Été 85*, which was released in summer 2020, is set on the coast of Normandy).

In this chapter, I first situate the understudied *Le Refuge* as a film that pursues Ozon's signature style and thematic preoccupations yet innovates on a number of fronts. Secondly, I focus on the ways in which the film continues to complicate visions of motherhood and kinship structures articulated elsewhere in the director's career, all the while engaging in contemporary debates around the definition of the family. Lastly, I discuss the film's portrayal of queer fatherhood through the figure of the openly gay Paul, a caring surrogate father to his deceased brother's child and a contrasting alternative to the monstrous or absent paternal figures in Ozon's previous films *Sitcom* (1998), *Les amants criminels / Criminal Lovers* (1999), *Gouttes d'eau sur pierres brûlantes / Water Drops on Burning Rocks* (2000) and *8 femmes / 8 Women* (2002). The timing and socio-political context of the film's release are also crucial to its full appreciation. Even though Ozon has declared that he does not seek to change viewers' mentalities with his cinema (Schilt 2011: 167), *Le Refuge* seems to be intervening in contemporary debates over LGBTQ rights in France. It came out ten years after France authorised civil partnerships for gay couples (the 'Pacte Civil de Solidarité' or PACS) and three and a half years before the legalisation of same-sex marriage (2013's Taubira law). It also anticipates debates still ongoing in the country around reproductive rights, including adoption for same-sex couples (now legal since 2013); access to reproductive technology (*procréation médicalement assistée*, or PMA), on track to be finally legalised for all women in summer 2020; and gestational surrogacy (*gestation par autrui*, or GPA), which remains illegal for everyone in France today.[2]

In similar fashion as the first two instalments in Ozon's unofficial trilogy about mourning, *Le Refuge* travels back and forth between France's capital and the Atlantic coast and emphasises the presence of the liquid element in both locales. The film opens with consecutive images of Paris's river Seine, the busy traffic along its banks, and an elevated metro train darting across the water, a series of establishing shots that are essentially a night-time version of *Sous le sable*'s prologue. A dealer (Émile Berling) visits the nearly empty apartment that Louis (Melvil Poupaud) and Mousse (Isabelle Carré) temporarily occupy and provides the lovers with their next heroin fix. The extra dose Louis injects into his neck vein in the early morning hours proves fatal. Louis's mother (Claire Vernet) finds her lifeless son and sends a comatose Mousse to the hospital, where the young woman learns of her pregnancy. Mousse attends Louis's funeral in the presence of his grand-bourgeois family, including his brother Paul (Louis-Ronan Choisy), his father (Jean-Pierre Andréani) and his mother. The haughty woman announces that the family does not want any heir given the circumstances, and suggests that Mousse visit their family doctor in order to 'settle this matter very quickly'.[3] Mousse initially agrees to the abortion, but instead takes refuge in a country house in a coastal village in southwestern France.

Paul visits Mousse there the following summer and is happy to see her still pregnant. She lives alone in the house, which belongs to an absent and much older former lover, and Serge (Pierre Louis-Calixte), a local resident, regularly brings her groceries. Paul befriends Mousse and also becomes romantically involved with Serge. Over the course of conversations with her new houseguest as well as a prying woman on the beach (Marie Rivière), it transpires that the pregnant (and still mourning) Mousse never thinks of the baby growing inside her (Figure 7.1). Mousse, who is in recovery, is increasingly forced to confront reality and first deliberately touches her pregnant belly while taking a bath. Paul helps her around the house and provides musical comfort by playing the piano and singing Louis's favourite childhood song.

Figure 7.1 Mousse and an inquisitive beachgoer

After picking up methadone at the local pharmacy, Mousse meets a man who confesses his sexual preference for pregnant women. Mousse follows him to his room but refuses sexual intimacy, instead asking the seducer to rock her. After a night out with Paul and Serge, Mousse learns that Paul was adopted, unlike Louis. Later still, an inebriated Paul initiates a sexual encounter with Mousse, who consents. Paul leaves for Spain the following day. A few weeks later, he visits Mousse at a Paris hospital, where she has just delivered a girl, Louise. Mousse leaves Paul with the baby while she smokes a cigarette outside and subsequently flees the hospital. As Mousse looks straight into the camera, we hear in voiceover a letter she has written to Paul asking him to take care of Louise in her absence and promising to return when she is ready to become a mother. The final scene shows Paul holding Louise in the hospital room as the camera zooms in on his smiling face.

SOMETHING OLD, SOMETHING NEW

Le Refuge is a clearly recognisable product of the director's output, and one can detect in this film common Ozonian features that critics have identified before and after its release: the 'centrality of queer desire to his cinema, and the continual performative transformations of identity worked within it' (Ince 2008: 114); a tendency to construct narratives that 'ceaselessly revolve around the question of dynamic movement, shift, progress and change' (Asibong 2008: 1); and a notorious 'nonconformity to pre-established generic conventions' (Reis 2018: 2). Intertextual references, famously common in the work of this ardent cinephile, are also present here and stem from both within and outside the auteur's production. Ozon himself has pointed out a narrative parallel between the early deaths of Bruno Cremer's character Jean in *Sous le sable* and that of Poupaud's character Louis in *Le Refuge*. He also acknowledges a dialogue between *Le Temps qui reste* and *Le Refuge* via Poupaud's presence (and demise) in both stories (Le Pacte 2009: 7–8). Actress Marie Rivière, who played Poupaud's mother in *Le Temps qui reste / Time to Leave*, reappears on the beach – presumably as a different character, though we cannot be sure – to give unsolicited advice to Mousse about the delights and despairs of motherhood. The appearance of Poupaud and Rivière in both of these beachside films in turn pays tribute to the cinema of Éric Rohmer, Ozon's former university teacher, particularly the Poupaud-starring *Conte d'été / A Summer's Tale* (1996) and *Le Rayon vert / The Green Ray* (1986), in which Rivière's character travels to the Basque Country in search of love just a few kilometres from Mousse's hideaway.[4]

Despite these familiarities, *Le Refuge* also marks a series of 'firsts' in the director's career, starting with the urgency with which it had to be written and shot as well as the actress he ended up choosing for the main part. As Ozon explained shortly after the film was completed:

> *Le Refuge* is quite an unusual film that I made very instinctively. Three weeks before shooting I didn't really have a scenario. I didn't have an actress to play the lead role either . . . Then my casting director told me [about the pregnancy of] Isabelle Carré. I'd never worked with her, but I called her to ask if she would accept the role, indicating that I had an idea of the story but strictly speaking no script. She said yes and we went from there . . . We shot the film very quickly – we had to – because she was about to give birth. (Schilt 2011: 156)

In the same conversation, Ozon asserted that he did not conceive of *Le Refuge* as part of a larger, multi-film project because 'there really wasn't time to say to myself, "I've already told several similar stories before this film" . . . but inevitably there are certain themes that come back on their own' (Schilt 2011: 155–6). When asked in a different interview about his choice of making yet another beachside film, Ozon again denied any prior calculations on his part:

> This time it was not my choice! When Isabelle Carré agreed to do the film, she asked whether we could shoot in the southwest of France, where she was going to be on holiday . . . At first I actually said that, for once, I wouldn't film by the sea and would do something in the countryside, but I had no choice! (Calhoun 2010a)

I suspect that Ozon slightly exaggerates the fortuitous elements that surrounded the making of this film. Anyone familiar with his work – and the auteurist approach taught at the Fémis and so crucial to an understanding of independent French cinema – knows that Ozon regularly uses terms like 'instinct' to discuss his approach to filmmaking and routinely conceives of his films (like Jean-Luc Godard before him) as experimental 'attempts' rather than carefully crafted products. And though the risk is certainly calculated, it is undeniable that Carré's six-month pregnancy at the time of the project's inception required even more spontaneity and improvisation than usual. Besides his decision to work for the first time with Carré because she was both available and willing – unlike his more familiar muse Ludivine Sagnier, with whom he had already collaborated three times, but who refused the role – Ozon chose first-time actor Louis-Ronan Choisy for the film's second biggest role. Ozon hired the singer-songwriter because he felt that his real-life gentle character, 'tormented soul' sensitivity and fragility perfectly matched Paul's (Le Pacte 2009: 7). This casting decision, which implies that Choisy would play a character close to himself and would therefore not need much direction, drove Ozon to also hire Choisy to compose the original music and theme song for the film. The resulting piece, also called 'Le Refuge', was written on set 'with the idea that it should be like a lingering perfume, a reminder of [Louis's] presence' (Le Pacte 2009: 7). Variations of the song are heard throughout the film, in musical and sung form, on the piano and on the guitar, within and outside the diegesis, including in a duet between Carré and Choisy during the end credits. Choisy's musical credit also meant that Ozon did not need to hire his long-time composer Philippe Rombi, with whom he collaborated six times prior to *Le Refuge* (starting with *Les Amants criminels* and including *Sous le sable* and *Swimming Pool*) and another six times since then, most recently on the psychological thriller *L'Amant double / Double Lover* (2017). Choisy's simple compositions in *Le Refuge* give the film score (and therefore the film) a different complexion from those featuring the more elaborate and dramatic orchestral work of Ozon's usual collaborator.

In addition to his first collaboration with Carré in the lead role and Choisy as both lead actor and composer, another notable 'first' in *Le Refuge* concerns Ozon's choice to hire a man, Mathieu Hippeau, to assist him with the writing of the script. This decision marks a departure from his past recurring collaborations with three women screenwriters, Marcia Romano and Marina de Van in the 1990s, and Emmanuèle Bernheim since 2000. Ozon justified this choice to hire Hippeau, a friend of his who had already worked in an uncredited capacity on his first (and only) English-language film *Angel* (2007), by stating that the urgency of the situation meant that he could not tackle the screenplay by himself. Knowing that Hippeau was familiar with the theme of maternity, Ozon entrusted the writing of certain scenes to him prior to filming. Later on, during the coastal shoot, Hippeau stayed in Paris and wrote last-minute dialogues for scenes that Ozon had recently added to the original script (Schilt 2011: 161–2). This improvisational style, though unusual even for a filmmaker with self-proclaimed 'instinctual' directing methods, is not unprecedented in Ozon's career and recalls the conditions under which his early featurette *Regarde la mer* was filmed.

The last innovation associated with the making of *Le Refuge* concerns Ozon's forced decision to shoot the film using a high-definition digital camera. This represents a major break from tradition for this lover of celluloid who had always proclaimed his aversion to digital technology and had previously refused to use it to shoot the second part of *Sous le sable*, even after funding had been considerably reduced (Schilt 2011: 81). This time, there was no money to film in 35mm or even 16mm and Ozon had no choice but to become familiar with this technology – he uses the term 'apprivoiser' (literally, to tame) to describe his relationship with the new medium. As he explains, this decision led to other choices:

As I wanted to capture the beauty of the landscape, the light, the natural surroundings and the actors, I chose cinemascope and long lenses to counteract the flatness of digital images, restore focus options and create depth of field. The biggest advantage of these cameras is their ability to shoot in very low light, with little or no artificial lighting. This allowed me to shoot at magic hours: dawn, dusk, nighttime on a beach. (Le Pacte 2009: 8)

The film's skeletal budget did not allow for tracking shots either, and Ozon resorted to using a zoom, which influenced the actors' spatial movements. Ozon summarises: 'We had to keep things simple, always, and move fast, which was actually consistent with the story we were telling. The film's economy was in harmony with the film itself' (Le Pacte 2009: 8). The choice of shooting in widescreen further connects *Le Refuge* with *Le Temps qui reste / Time to Leave* and, while this wider aspect ratio allows the possibility of filming dramatic outdoor beach sequences, it renders difficult the framing of conventional close-ups, creating a distance between the spectator and Mousse that suits the protagonist's own misanthropy.

MOTHERHOOD REIMAGINED

The unique set of circumstances surrounding the making of *Le Refuge*, Ozon's collaboration with new people on the project, and the timing of its release have undoubtedly had an effect on the content of the film itself. This section focuses on the story's depiction of motherhood and its attempt to propose, through the relationship between Mousse and Paul, a new model of kinship for the twenty-first century.

'I don't want to repeat myself', Ozon announced to a critic as he was promoting *Le Refuge* in the United States (Martin 2010). Even though the director concedes that there are thematic bonds between this film and others in his oeuvre in their preoccupation with both mourning and motherhood, he sees Mousse as altogether distinct from previous mothers, including those portrayed in *Regarde la mer* and *Ricky*. For him, Mousse

> keep[s] the child as a way of mourning for her loved one, but without necessarily developing a maternal instinct . . . She has something in her stomach, but it is more an extension of the man she loved than a full-fledged person (Schilt 2011: 156, 158).

Reviewers of the film have often commented on Carré's real-life pregnancy, most of them framing it in positive terms and arguing that it contributes to the film's authenticity (Calhoun 2010b; Dargis 2010; Sotinel 2010).[5] Catherine Wheatley marvels at the aesthetic beauty of Mousse's (half-)naked body in several scenes, and posits that

> the casting of the pregnant Carré allows for some beautifully observed shots of her swollen breasts and tightly stretched stomach, used to stunning effect in scenes of her waddling along the beach half-hippo, half-goddess, or lying in the bath, submerged entirely [except] for the perfectly smooth protuberance of her belly. (Wheatley 2010: 73)

The materiality of Mousse's stomach that Wheatley experiences so viscerally as a spectator contrasts with the character's own perception of her body, as the growing child 'is not experienced by Mousse as an emblem of the future but as a spectral presence from the past' (Handyside 2012: 67). To this end, it is worth pointing out that although mirrors and other reflective surfaces abound in the film – as they do in all of Ozon's 'mourning films' featuring lonely, narcissistic characters – *Le Refuge* notably deprives the spectator of a cliched sequence during which the pregnant character gazes at her belly in the mirror and observes it from different angles with an enraptured smile. Instead of this familiar image of exhilaration, we see a close-up of Mousse drinking methadone in the mirror of the half-opened bathroom cabinet, the angle of which creates a double image of her face that further dramatises her self-absorbed state of mind (Figure 7.2).[6] Even as Mousse progressively accepts her impending motherhood through the probing presence of others – Paul, the woman at the beach, the fetishist seducer – the film continues to deprive the spectator of any scenes of anticipation that present Mousse as outwardly looking forward to her life post-pregnancy. The aforementioned bath scene signals the end of Mousse's denial but fails to confirm any nascent maternal

Figure 7.2 Mousse's double reflection

instinct. It is also unrepeated, and subsequent moments featuring physical contact with her belly mainly involve other people's hands. When Paul brings up her pregnancy in a scene subsequent to the bathtub sequence, Mousse explains that she kept the child so that Louis would 'continue to live inside [her]', ventriloquising Ozon's direct thoughts on the character's choice. When Paul asks whether she ever thinks about the baby's future physical features, Mousse changes the subject and asks him to sing what she calls 'Louis's song', a tune she knows Paul and his brother listened to as children, and one that extends her grief over Louis's loss.

It is then that Paul offers a full diegetic rendition of the song, a musical interlude that temporarily suspends the narrative and that those familiar with Ozon have grown to expect and recognise. This time, we are far from the campy performance of the opening of *Une Robe d'été*, the synchronised dance sequence of *Gouttes d'eau sur pierres brûlantes / Water Drops on Burning Rocks*, or the stylised playbacks in *8 femmes / 8 Women*. The scene is instead much closer in spirit and significance to a subdued musical moment in *Sous le sable* during which the grief-stricken protagonist Marie (Charlotte Rampling) walks around a supermarket with the melancholy song 'Septembre (Quel joli temps)' ('September, Such a Lovely Time of Year') by French chanteuse Barbara playing in the background. In *Sous le sable / Under the Sand*, that episode signals a shift for the character from a melancholic state during which she has denied her husband's death to one that enables the beginning of her mourning process. Paul's soothing ballad in *Le Refuge* alludes to two people attempting to connect with each other in a remote place near the sea. Although the plot connects the song itself with Louis's childhood and in this sequence illustrates Mousse's remaining connection with her deceased partner, the lyrics, in contrast, tell the story not of Louis but of Paul and Mousse and anticipate their subsequent sexual encounter. The song thus arguably plays a dual role as one that initially tethers Mousse to the past but eventually propels her towards the future.

In the meantime, Mousse's present at her seaside hideaway altogether resists dominant discourses around both womanhood and motherhood, and it becomes increasingly evident that her refuge from the outside world also shields her from the constraints of patriarchy. Nothing in Mousse's behaviour, speech or eventual decision to surrender the baby to Paul resembles what Andrea O'Reilly has termed 'the eight interrelated "rules" of "good" motherhood imposed by contemporary patriarchal ideology', which include the presumption that only the biological mother can properly care for her child (rule 1); that the child's needs always come before the mother's (rule 3); and that 'mothers must be fully satisfied, fulfilled, completed, and composed in motherhood' (rule 5) (O'Reilly 2008: 10). It is therefore not accidental that Mousse ends up violently rejecting the film's lone spokesperson for the responsibilities of heteronormative reproductivity (Rivière's character), and that the only two characters who gain entrance to Mousse's shelter (Paul and Serge) turn out to be queer. Paul's questions to Mousse about the baby's appearance and sex betray his own excitement about the future birth and confirm Mousse's lack of interest in motherhood. This displacement of 'maternal instinct' from the figure of the expectant mother to that of the (soon-to-be) surrogate (queer) father is the film's most fascinating attribute, and one that unfolds as a secret hidden in plain sight. Mousse arguably senses Paul's keen interest in the child before he realises it himself. The young man unwittingly begins to seduce her – with his singing, by wearing Louis's perfume, and by simply being physically present and caring – long before their culminating moment of sexual intimacy. As Mousse's trust in Paul grows, she dares to ask him about his preoccupation with her pregnancy: 'Is it because you're gay and you'll never have children?' Paul shrugs off the question but confirms his concern for the child's well-being by inquiring whether the methadone she ingests is harmful to the baby (and Mousse reassures him that it is not).

It should be clear by now that the figure of the future child in *Le Refuge* functions not predictably as 'the key emblem of heterosexual reproductive futurity' (Handyside 2012: 67) but as a symbol for the possibility of queer fatherhood and non-normative mechanisms of kinship. Ozon announces in an interview appearing in the film's press kit: 'It is through this [pregnant woman's] belly that a rebirth occurs. It is also around [her belly] that the relationship between Mousse and Paul takes shape. It is at the centre of their encounter' (Le Pacte 2009: 5). This 'rebirth' casts Mousse and Paul as individuals newly liberated from familial and patriarchal limitations as much as it refers to Louis's symbolic re-emergence as Louise at the film's close. Despite all the baby talk, Paul touches Mousse's belly for the first time very late into the film: 69 minutes into the 88-minute narrative. He does so with both excitement and apprehension as he applies sunscreen to her stomach in a series of close-ups; during this process, he feels the baby moving. This scene follows two crucial moments in the pair's relationship: a blissful bathing session in the ocean at sunset (a visually stunning image of an ostensibly heterosexual couple recalling the last scene of *5x2*); and a conversation on the beach when Mousse states her desire to purchase the seaside house from its ageing proprietor and to ask Serge to check on it in her absence. By asking for Paul's opinion on the potential home purchase, and by including Paul's current lover as an actor in her own life, Mousse also involves Paul in her fantasised scenario of a future freed from heteronormative obligations.

Mousse's stance and ultimate decision to involve Paul in Louise's rearing recalls that of feminist 'empowered mothers' who 'do not regard children as the sole responsibility of the biological mothers' and count on '*co-mothers* or *othermothers*' to assist them (O'Reilly 2008: 7). It is thus essential to keep in mind both Mousse's imagined domestic future and Paul's increasingly conscious desire to have a role in the child's life in order to interpret their lovemaking near the end of the film. As Mousse helps an inebriated Paul undress after a night out with Serge, he asks her whether she loves him (she says yes) and whether she will ever leave him (she says no). He then kisses her hand, caresses her shoulder and, after a cut, we see the two in bed with the lights off. Their sexual encounter happens in a conservatively shot sequence that is atypical in Ozon's cinema: they make love under the covers in almost complete darkness as the camera pans from their panting faces to their entwined arms and legs, which appear in close-ups and extreme close-ups.[7] The scene ends as Paul reaches for Mousse's belly immediately after they orgasm. The next morning, Paul departs for Spain after a tender embrace and a promise to visit Mousse after the baby's birth.

Given the centrality of the future child in their sexual encounter, which begins shortly after Paul attempts to touch Mousse's stomach and concludes with him actually doing so, this sequence must be understood neither as the formation of a future couple nor as a fling triggered by alcohol consumption. Instead, their lovemaking constitutes nothing less than a symbolic impregnation of Mousse by a substitute father figure as well as a symbolic transfer of parental authority that foreshadows Mousse's actual surrendering of Louise to Paul at the film's conclusion. This process of 'transmission' through sex recalls the lovemaking scene near the end of *Le Temps qui reste / Time to Leave* during which the dying gay protagonist Romain (Poupaud) agrees to impregnate a woman in a tender threesome that includes her sterile husband. In the latter scene, which Emma Wilson describes as 'experimental' in its unpredictable portrayal of human interaction and affect (Wilson 2006: 22), Romain literally inseminates the wife and simultaneously forsakes his parental authority over the future child by immediately transferring it to the infertile husband – during foreplay, the two men take turns kissing the woman as well as each other. While the scene of transfer in *Le Refuge* only involves two (grown) individuals (though Louis's spectral presence is possibly on both of their minds), it is also experimental in the way it repurposes the sexual act between a man and a woman and queers it by allowing it to operate outside the framework of heteronormative reproduction.

QUEERING FATHERHOOD

In addition to offering a reimagined vision of motherhood and kinship, *Le Refuge* proposes an empowering model of queer fatherhood rarely seen in Ozon's cinema, French cinema, or French society at large. When *Le Refuge* first screened in late 2009, debates over the legalisation of gay marriage as well as equal access to adoption and alternative means of reproduction had been brewing across Europe since the beginning of the new millennium. The Netherlands was the first country to legalise gay marriage in 2001, followed by Belgium in 2003 and Spain, a nation perceived by the French as more conservative than themselves, in 2005. The next wave of marriage equality came the same year as the film's production, with Sweden and Norway passing a law in 2009, and Portugal and Iceland doing the same the following year. France eventually legalised same-sex marriage in 2013 after months of vocal protests from a well-organised group of mostly Catholic-identified, anti-abortion, right-wing citizens, 'La Manif pour tous'. Participants in these nationwide street protests insisted that they were only fighting for the rights of children and thus supposedly opposed not gay marriage per se but *homoparentalité* (same-sex parenthood), including the rights for same-sex couples to adopt children together and gain access to reproductive technology and surrogacy.[8] The group's main slogan 'un papa, une maman' ('one daddy, one mummy'), coupled with signs that read 'pas de fiction pour la filiation' ('no fiction for filiation') and 'nos ventres ne sont pas des caddies' ('our bellies are not shopping carts'), made clear their opposition to any kind of procreation or kinship structure outside of what they deemed to be 'the natural way'. Although this ideology did not necessarily reflect the views of a majority of the French at the time, the group and its eccentric spokeswoman Frigide Bardot dominated the conversation in the French media during the months leading up to the passing of the Taubira law.

During the same period, the documentary *Naître père / Father's Birth* (2013) by Delphine Lanson was released in French theatres with the tagline 'Une famille pas comme les autres' ('A family unlike any other'). This quietly militant film recounts the journey of a French same-sex couple in a long-term domestic partnership who both become biological fathers to twins thanks to reproductive technology and a surrogate mother in the United States. The crossed-out word in the tagline, which gives it a double meaning, underscores the film's attempt to present the couple's story as both banal, because many gay couples want children, and exceptional, because surrogacy was (and remains) illegal in France. *Naître père* was deemed controversial enough to be rejected by the public national broadcaster France Télévisions, which expressed interest in airing it but ultimately decided against it, and was later shown on France's more seldom watched parliamentary channel (LCP) despite threats aimed at the network from a right-wing member of parliament (Coffin 2013). The (future) fathers' journey to the United States in the documentary also underscores how far behind France was in granting same-sex couples access to reproductive rights. Although seen by relatively few French spectators, the film provides a rare counterpoint (at least within French cultural productions) to the hysteria displayed by members of 'La Manif pour tous'.

The sympathetic depiction of queer parenthood in *Naître père* and its deliberate choice to present its protagonists as a 'regular couple' recall Lynda Goldstein's study of the booming presence (from the mid-2000s onwards) of prime-time television shows in the United States that portray gay fathers in an increasingly nuanced but ultimately (in Goldstein's words) 'normalized' or 'homonormative' fashion (Goldstein 2016: 213). The normalisation process at play in these US shows and in the much scarcer French films that tackle the same subject – in addition to *Naître père*, Vincent Garenq's 2008 dramedy *Comme les autres* comes to mind – does not exactly apply to *Le Refuge*. Indeed, the film's *raison d'être* lies in the developing friendship between Mousse and Paul and in the transfer of custodial responsibilities from a widowed heterosexual mother to a single gay father. However, there is a parallel plot in *Le Refuge* that unfolds more discreetly, in a series of fleeting instants that emphasise the meaningfulness of the relationship between Paul and Serge. After Serge's initial introduction as Mousse's only contact with the outside world before Paul's arrival, the spectator's second encounter with the local man is a surreptitious point-of-view shot from Mousse's perspective of his feet entwined with Paul's a few mornings later. The sight triggers a jealous (and possibly homophobic) reaction from Mousse, who tells Serge at breakfast that his services are no longer needed. Despite this dismissal, Paul pursues a relationship with him, much of which develops off screen, and which Mousse eventually accepts. Because of Mousse's central position in the story, Serge reappears on screen mainly in her presence. While the three of them visit a nightclub together, Mousse witnesses an ardent kiss between the two men, the red lighting and pulsating music further emphasising their passion. She is moved to tears by their love (perhaps also envious of it), and walks away unnoticed.

There is only one scene in which Paul and Serge appear alone, without Mousse bearing witness to their budding romance. While she visits the pharmacy, the two men walk to the beach together and appear in two successive shots, one with Serge gently stroking Paul's hair, the other showing them sitting on a ledge and sharing a laugh with stunning ocean vistas behind them and the strains of a piano playing in the background. This wordless sequence, while brief, leaves the spectator with the impression that their connection is genuine and potentially long-lasting. This picture-perfect image of queer bliss is unusual in Ozon's cinema, whose portrayals of couples of all sexual dispositions notoriously tend to end unhappily, in divorce or in death. In *Le Refuge*, however, there seems to be a deliberate desire to legitimise Paul's partnership with Serge at a time when all of Western Europe was grappling with legitimising same-sex relationships and the rights of these couples to become parents. The rapport that Paul develops with both Mousse and Serge confirm his status as a caring, trustworthy friend and lover who would, if given the opportunity, become an equally caring and responsible father.

In a previous discussion of *Le Refuge*'s predecessor *Ricky*, the fantastical story of a flying baby whose working-class parents and half-sister must deal with his birth and mysterious disappearance, I pointed out a shift in the way fatherhood was portrayed in Ozon's cinema. *Ricky*'s father Paco (Sergi López), although initially accused of child abuse, is eventually cleared of all allegations and emerges as an attentive husband and (step) father at the film's close (Schilt 2011: 140–53). This spousal and paternal legitimacy contrasts with Rose Tremain's original short story 'Moth', *Ricky*'s literary source, in which the father Chester is depicted as absent and inadequate. Besides bucking the model in the film's original inspiration, Paco's character also stands out from the monstrous paternal figures in most of Ozon's filmography, who, according to Jean-Marc Lalanne in his 2002 review of *8 femmes / 8 Women*, are either physically or emotionally abusive (as in *Les Amants criminels* and *Gouttes d'eau sur pierres brûlantes*) or whose absence becomes a source of madness and chaos (as in *Regarde la mer*, *Sitcom*, *Sous le sable*, and *8 femmes*) (Lalanne 2002: 83). The figure of the incompetent or absent father extends beyond 2002, as the characters of John in *Swimming Pool* and Gilles in *5x2* attest. Besides their confirmed parental competence, a further connection exists between Paul in *Le Refuge* and Paco in *Ricky* in that they both become fathers with no biological link to a child.

Because of Melvil Poupaud's presence in both films and the thematic similarities between them, a discussion of fatherhood in *Le Refuge* should also be linked to *Le Temps qui reste / Time to Leave*. In the latter story, the gay protagonist Romain (Poupaud) donates his sperm (in the most natural way possible) to an infertile couple and eventually bequeaths all his possessions to the unborn child shortly before his demise. In *Le Refuge*, Ozon 'kills the (biological) father' Louis (Poupaud) at the very beginning of the story, and while his spectral presence lingers during much of the film, he is eventually replaced by a queer father character (Paul) at the film's end. These permutations demonstrate Ozon's ongoing resolve to experiment with alternative models of kinship and contest fixed paradigms of parenthood.

I have already contended that a displacement of so-called 'maternal instinct' occurs between the two protagonists in *Le Refuge*, a displacement that informs Mousse's final decision to renounce the baby's guardianship. In the letter heard in voiceover that Mousse writes to Paul following her escape from the hospital, she states that she acted on an impulse after she saw the loving way Paul first gazed at Louise. Despite this claim, evidence suggests that she had considered, whether consciously or not, Paul's possible role in her future child's life long before then. Indeed, the film's self-contained universe creates a space that progressively enables Mousse, and the spectator along with her, to envisage Paul's future fatherhood as something both 'natural' and inevitable. This inevitability transpires not only in the interactions between Mousse and Paul, but also in the ways in which the film implicitly compares Paul with other paternal models who all prove to be deficient for different reasons. In the conversation that Mousse overhears the day of the funeral, Louis's father all but admits that he would have preferred it if Paul had died

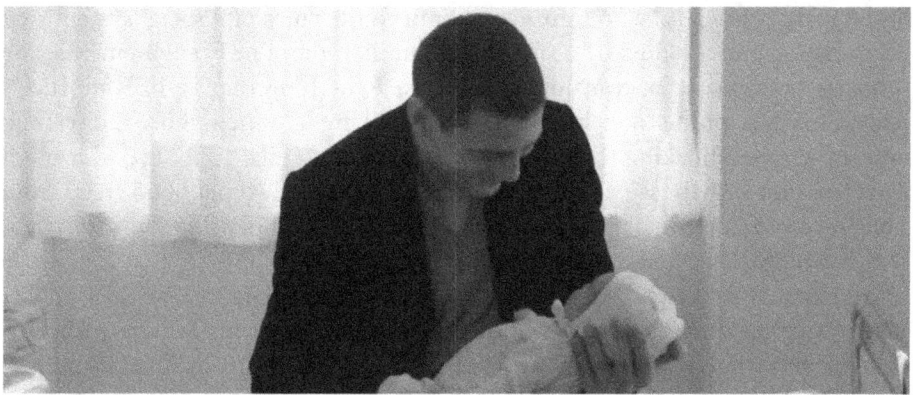

Figure 7.3 Paul and baby Louise

instead of Louis, a vile statement that betrays either his extreme homophobia or his utter inability to love a non-biological child (or both). Mousse in turn mocks the older man whose house she occupies and with whom she had a sexual relationship when she was sixteen and describes him as an unobservant, 'half-blind' man who 'thinks that he is [Mousse's] dad'. Lastly, the tourist who seduces Mousse reveals his problematic relationship with fatherhood as he unabashedly admits that while pregnant women arouse him, he was incapable of making love to his wife when she was pregnant with his own children.

In contrast, Paul selflessly puts his own life on hold to visit Mousse and exhibits nothing but solicitude towards her. He reveals, over an hour into the film, that he was adopted and did not know it until he turned eighteen. He also confesses, as if to reinforce the film's position on the triviality of blood ties, that he is not interested in his own biological origins. At that point, the spectator understands that his affection for the unborn child may stem not only from his love for his brother but also from a desire to challenge his current position within his family and legitimise his status as an adopted, queer member. Far from surrendering to his parents' traditionalistic values (indeed, the very existence of Mousse's child, which Paul encouraged, goes against their wishes), Paul seeks to reconfigure, on his own terms, the boundaries of the family. When the camera slowly zooms in on Paul's smiling face as he holds Louise who has just stopped crying, the film presents, as its final image, a vision of queer fatherhood that is as beautiful as it is indisputable (Figure 7.3).

CONCLUSION

With *Le Refuge*, Ozon continues his career-long examination of human behaviour, challenging traditional kinship structures and introducing defiant queer and female characters who refuse to submit to the rules of a social system that oppresses them. To do so, he subverts a familiar genre in French cinema, the *intimiste* family drama, transforming it into something that is, in Kate Ince's words, neither 'polite [nor] hide-bound' and taking it 'to new, more interesting, and sometimes shocking territory – queer territory' (Ince 2008: 133). Through the character of Mousse, the film proposes a model of womanhood freed from obligations of heteronormative reproduction. With Paul's willingness to father, it correspondingly 'open[s] up the family to new connections' that include 'a more expansive network of individuals' (Handyside 2012: 70). Paul's affable nature further enables him to improve his rapport with his father and maintain an enduring relationship with Serge, as we learn in his final conversation with Mousse at the hospital. Paul's positive depiction as a successful son, lover, friend and (in all likelihood) queer father makes his character stand out in Ozon's filmography and comes at a crucial time in France's LGBTQ history.

Le Refuge was released after a number of European countries had already legalised gay marriage and adoption for same-sex couples (but not France), and during the year following the 2008 'E.B. v. France' case, in which the European Court of Human Rights ruled that France had violated the European Convention on Human Rights by discriminating against a woman in a same-sex relationship seeking to adopt a child (Wanchap and Sykes 2008). Even if Ozon did not actively intend to engage with debates coinciding with the film's production, *Le Refuge* provocatively approaches questions regarding the relationship between reproduction and kinship and the decision to become a parent or to renounce parental responsibility. It argues for the rightful place of queer subjects within the family and the Republic with a quiet simplicity that makes it a powerful manifesto on inclusivity and against heteronormativity. As it does for its two protagonists, *Le Refuge* provides a temporary shelter from a society that notoriously resists queer practices and shames women who reject their predetermined fates.

NOTES

1. The total budget for *Le Refuge* was €3.1m, and the film only made a little over $500,000 at the box office. In comparison, *Swimming Pool*, released six years earlier and one of Ozon's biggest hits, had a budget of €6.1m, and grossed over $22m. The budget for *Ricky*, released immediately before *Le Refuge*, was €6.3m and the film earned a meager $2.1m. *Potiche*, released immediately after *Le Refuge*, cost €11m and made $28m (source: <http://www.jpbox-office.com>).
2. After the French marriage equality law passed in 2013, married same-sex partners gained access to adoption as a couple. Six years later, in September 2019, the French National Assembly provisionally voted to extend access to reproductive technology (*procréation médicalement assistée*, or PMA) to all women, including single women and those in same-sex marriages. The Senate endorsed the bill in February 2020 and a final vote is planned

for summer 2020 (Cordier 2020). It was previously only accessible to married heterosexual couples, and the final law, which remains controversial and reignited protests from same-sex marriage opponents, is expected to be voted on in summer 2020. There are currently no plans to legalise surrogacy in France (Melo Moreira 2019).
3. Unless otherwise noted, all translations from the original French are my own.
4. See Handyside (2009) for a discussion of Rohmer's own beach films, including *Le Rayon vert*. In her later article on Ozon's beach films, Handyside proposes further connections between Rivière's characters in *Le Rayon vert* and *Le Refuge* (2012: 67).
5. In contrast to these positive reviews, Ryan Gilbey dismisses *Le Refuge* as a film 'drowning in self-reference' and lacking verisimilitude (2010: 42).
6. See Ealy (2017) for a discussion of narcissism in *Sous le sable*, Ozon's original 'mourning film'.
7. Ozon claims in an interview that shooting the lovemaking scene under the covers was not his original intention: 'I actually had some strange positions in mind . . . I knew it would be very surprising to see a pregnant woman having sex . . . For me, as a peeping tom, it was more interesting to see her having sex with her big belly, in a strange position.' Ozon says that Carré refused to do the scene and concludes: 'It wasn't the story . . . There are good accidents for films sometimes' (Martin 2010).
8. In the impassioned speech of 29 January 2013 in favour of same-sex marriage that she gave in front of the National Assembly, Justice Minister Christiane Taubira acknowledges that the main source of protest came from those who were fighting for 'the right of the child'. She points out that adoptions by (single) same-sex parents had been legal in France and that many children were already growing up in same-sex families but were legally unprotected if anything happened to the official guardian (Guerrier 2014).

WORKS CITED

Asibong, Andrew (2008), *François Ozon*, Manchester: Manchester University Press.
Calhoun, Dave (2010a), 'François Ozon Discusses *Le Refuge*', *Time Out*, 10 August, <https://www.timeout.com/london/film/francois-ozon-discusses-le-refuge> (last accessed 13 January 2020).
Calhoun, Dave (2010b), '*Le Refuge*', *Time Out*, 10 August, <https://www.timeout.com/london/film/le-refuge> (last accessed 13 January 2020).
Coffin, Alice (2013), 'Delphine Lanson, réalisatrice de *Naître Père*: "LCP a été menacée par un député UMP"', *20 minutes*, 29 July, <https://www.20minutes.fr/television/1193785-20130729-20130729-gpa-interview-realisatrice-naitre-pere-delphine-lanson-lcp-ete-menacee-depute-um> (last accessed 15 July 2020).
Cordier, Solène (2020), 'Le projet de loi de bioéthique et l'ouverture de la PMA adoptés de justesse au Sénat', *Le Monde*, 4 February, <https://www.lemonde.fr/societe/article/2020/02/04/le-senat-adopte-le-projet-de-loi-bioethique-de-justesse_6028404_3224.html> (last accessed 1 July 2020).
Dargis, Manohla (2010), 'Pregnant, But Not What She Expected: *Hideaway*', *The New York Times*, 9 September, <https://www.nytimes.com/2010/09/10/movies/10hideaway.html> (last accessed 13 January 2020).
Ealy, Nicholas (2017), '"Tu es déjà rentré?" Trauma, Narcissism and Melancholy in François Ozon's *Sous le sable* (2000)', *Studies in French Cinema*, 17: 3, pp. 217–35.
Gilbey, Ryan (2010), 'Playing It Safe', *New Statesmen*, 16 August, p. 42, <https://www.newstatesman.com/film/2010/08/ozon-mousse-louis-self-paul> (last accessed 15 July 2020).

Goldstein, Lynda (2016), 'Queering Daddy or Adopting Homonormative Fatherhood?', in *Deconstructing Dads: Changing Images of Fathers in Popular Culture*, Laura Tropp and Janice Kelly (eds), Lanham, MD: Lexington Books, pp. 213–45.

Guerrier, Sophie (2014), 'Le discours de Christiane Taubira pour le mariage pour tous', *Le Figaro*, 27 March, <https://www.lefigaro.fr/politique/le-scan/2014/03/27/25001-20140327ARTFIG00079-le-discours-de-christiane-taubira-pour-le-mariage-pour-tous.php> (last accessed 2 March 2020).

Handyside, Fiona (2012), 'The Possibilities of a Beach: Queerness and François Ozon's Beaches', *Screen*, 53: 1, pp. 54–71.

Handyside, Fiona (2009), 'Rohmer à la plage: The Role of the Beach in Three Films by Eric Rohmer', *Studies in French Cinema*, 9: 2, pp. 147–60.

Ince, Kate (2008), 'François Ozon's Cinema of Desire', in Kate Ince (ed.), *Five Directors: Auteurism from Assayas to Ozon*, Manchester: Manchester University Press, pp. 112–34.

Lalanne, Jean-Marc (2002), 'Les actrices: *Huit femmes* de François Ozon', *Cahiers du cinéma*, 565, pp. 82–3.

Le Pacte Distribution (2009), press kit for *Le Refuge*.

Martin, Michael (2010), 'Ozon Layers', *Out*, 13 July, <https://www.out.com/entertainment/2010/07/13/ozon-layers> (last accessed 8 January 2020).

Melo Moreira, Patricia de (2019), 'L'Assemblée nationale vote l'ouverture de la PMA à toutes les femmes', *Le Parisien*, 27 September, <http://www.leparisien.fr/societe/l-assemblee-nationale-vote-l-ouverture-de-la-pma-a-toutes-les-femmes-27-09-2019-8161107.php> (last accessed 2 March 2020).

O'Reilly, Andrea (ed.) (2008), *Feminist Mothering*, Albany, NY: SUNY Press.

Reis, Levilson (2018), 'Goodbye, "Temporary" Transvestites – Hello, New Girlfriend! Ozon's Transgenre and Transgender Crossovers in *Une nouvelle amie* (2014)', *Studies in French Cinema*, 16 November, pp. 1–25.

Schilt, Thibaut (2011), *François Ozon*, Urbana, IL: University of Illinois Press.

Sotinel, Thomas (2010), '*Le Refuge*: Une méditation sereine sur la maternité', *Le Monde*, 26 January, <https://www.lemonde.fr/cinema/article/2010/01/26/le-refuge-une-meditation-sereine-sur-la-maternite_1296872_3476.html> (last accessed 8 January 2020).

Wanchap, Emma and Emily Sykes (2008), 'Discrimination on the Basis of Sexuality a Violation of the Rights to Privacy and Equality', *Human Rights Law Centre*, 25 January, <https://www.hrlc.org.au/human-rights-case-summaries/eb-v-france-2008-echr-4354602-22-january-2008> (last accessed 2 March 2020).

Wheatley, Catherine (2010), '*Le Refuge*', *Sight & Sound*, 20: 9, pp. 73–4.

Wilson, Emma (2006), '*Time to Leave* (*Le temps qui reste*)', *Film Quarterly*, 60: 2, pp. 18–24.

CHAPTER 8

Transing Dynamics: Ozon's *Une Nouvelle amie* (2014)

Todd W. Reeser

Jean Baudrillard's theoretical essay 'Transsexuel' (1990) ('Transsexuality' (1993)) raises a thorny question about gender in postmodern culture: how to reconcile an understanding of gender as movement-based for cisgender subjects (those who do not identify as transgender), and the experiential reality of gender change or shift from one discrete point to another for those who might identify as transsexual or transgender? On the one hand, the French theorist's overall argument together with the essay's most famous line, 'we are all transsexuals *symbolically*' (Baudrillard 1993: 21) ('Nous sommes tous *symboliquement* des transsexuels') (Baudrillard 1990a: 28),[1] points to the essay's problematic erasure of transgender subjects. Baudrillard mentions 'the artifice of actually changing sex' and includes cases in which 'the operation in question is surgical' (Baudrillard 1990a: 20). Yet, he does not show interest in imagining actual or non-symbolic trans bodies, assuming that 'we' are cisgender and that 'we' can only be symbolically trans, never *actually* trans. 'We' have entered an era based on a 'jeu de l'indifférence sexuelle' ('playing . . . on sexual indifference')[2] (Baudrillard 1990a: 28, his emphasis; 20), in which the supposed poles of gender lack meaning and there is constant play with the signs of clothing, corporality and gesture. For Baudrillard, figures such as Dolly Parton, Kim Kardashian and Michael Jackson would embody this ethos of play as much as Laverne Cox or Caitlin Jenner. As media-centred subjects, 'we' are 'seduced' by images of gender change and movement, and these images necessarily enter into our postmodern psyches because they are so ubiquitous. 'Seduction' in his sense is anti-patriarchal and resists gender stability, a phenomenon that he elsewhere describes as 'the reverse side of sex, meaning and power' (Baudrillard: 1990b: 2). If there is no body or corporeal experience outside signification in Baudrillard's semantic system, then transsexuality or transgender can only contribute to the movement of signification and not be a valid or meaningful human experience on its own embodied terms. Victoria Grace writes:

> Baudrillard's use of the term 'transsexual' is explicitly not intended to invoke the medicalized meaning of 'wrong body' leading to sex reassignment surgery, but . . . to refer to the attraction of 'playing' with the commutability of the signs of sex, with the lack of differentiation between the sexual poles. (Grace 2000: 131)[3]

Is there a way to connect these two approaches to gender, one based on postmodern signification and the other on the real lived experience of transgender not reduced to a play of signs? This chapter does not aim to take a position on Baudrillard's transsexuality per se, but rather it considers how François Ozon's film *Une Nouvelle amie / The New Girlfriend* (2014) bridges the divide between the two approaches, depicting both approaches in the form of the two main characters, one cisgender and one transgender. Ozon's film falls into the French intellectual tradition of signifying play represented by Baudrillard, and whether or not the film responds directly to his theoretical model, it certainly has resonance with it. Ozon's film narrates a story about the phenomenon of the seduction of 'transsexuality' – literally and metaphorically. As one of the two main characters, Claire (Anaïs Demoustier), enters into representational gender movement: she begins as transphobic, stably gendered and heteronormative, but over the course of the film her relation to the lived category of transgender and exposure to new signifying systems of gender lead to a new gender subjectivity on her part. She embodies the Baudrillardian seduction of transsexuality, revealing how sign-shifting and transsexuality can create new forms of subjectivity and human relationality in the moment and over time. Claire's titular transgender 'new friend' (*amie* meaning 'friend' or 'girlfriend'), Virginia (Romain Duris), transes her, suggesting that cisgender bodies can be transed by transgender ones and not simply by a Baudrillardian signifying context that ignores or rejects actual trans bodies. It is not the case, then, that the cultural proliferation of transgender signs, in Baudrillard's system, transes cisgender bodies by itself, for here a transgender subject transes the very category of cisgender. If 'we' are all transsexual symbolically, then it is in part because cisgender symbolism is put into motion by trans bodies. The absent transsexual or transgender subject in Baudrillard's essay is in a sense given presence in the film, but still with a relation to the signifying phenomenon of the theoretical apparatus. Symbolic transsexuality may be a locus of seduction (though not at all in the negative way in which 'vitriolic' Baudrillard sees it), but it is also brought into being by trans experience. As such, the film mirrors other twenty-first-century French trans/cis narratives in which cisgender characters are put into gender motion by trans subjects (see Reeser 2013a; Reeser 2013b).

Ozon's film in a sense corrects the transphobia and trans absence in Baudrillard's infamous essay while at the same time putting into practice its argument about signification.[4] David, who increasingly identifies as Virginia over the course of the film, becomes a woman in part by transforming cisgender signs. Trans subjectivity pertains not only to her own experience of gender, but also to what she *does* to the signifying system of gender itself. The film is not so much about the two main characters' transitions – one more representational and the other more internal and subjective – for the film focuses on the *relation* between the two women and, more specifically, on the ways in which a Baudrillardian seduction of signs and transgender subjectivity are mutually imbricated and cannot be disassociated from each other.

TRANSING RELATIONALITY

On one level, *Une Nouvelle amie* invents a contemporary category of transgender distinct from widespread French cinematic representations of male characters who don women's dress for a period of time and are characterised as 'transvestites', not transgender or transsexual. After the death of his wife Laura, which leaves him to raise his baby Lucie alone, David increasingly dresses as a woman, affirming the gender that he feels inside. One day, Claire, who had been his wife's best friend, accidentally stumbles on David dressed as a woman. The revelation creates an unexpected bond between the two characters who already know each other through Laura, and their relation develops in new ways as the movie continues. When David appears to Claire to go out in public for the first time as Virginia, she is so dressed up that Claire calls her a tall 'travelo', or transvestite. She helps her new friend dress as someone who can pass not as a transvestite but as a woman, and they go shopping at a local mall. Later, in a key scene, the two friends visit an LGBTQ bar named 'Amazone' and watch a drag performance of Nicole Croisille's well-known song 'Une femme avec toi' ('A Woman with You')[5] by a talented queer performer named Eva Carlton (Bruno Pérard). Virginia cries during the performance, realising that she 'is' a woman like the woman of the song. This gender transformation is interrupted when Virginia is hit by a car and falls into a coma. Her feminine clothing and accoutrements are removed by the hospital staff, but Claire brings these to her hospital room and dresses her as a woman while singing Croisille's song. Virginia wakes up as a transwoman, no longer partially a woman, a transvestite, or a cross-dresser. The accident has led to a rebirth by which David has now once and for all transformed into Virginia. In the concluding scene, Virginia and Claire come seven years later to pick Lucie up from school, suggesting that they have become a cisgender woman and a transwoman in a stable relation with a daughter and a baby on the way (Claire is visibly pregnant).

With this gender transformation on Virginia's part, melodramatic as it may be, the film makes an intervention in the history of gender representation in mainstream French cinema. Levilson Reis makes the following argument about the film: 'by showing that David's cross-dressing does not stem from a diegetic necessity but from an intra-psychic desire to become woman, Ozon recasts the "necessity of disguise" of the "temporary transvestite" film narrative' (Reis 2019: 18–19). Previous films that Ozon responds to in this way for Reis include: *La Cage aux folles / The Bird Cage* (Édouard Molinaro, 1978), *Pédale douce / Softcore Queer* (Gabriel Aghion, 1996) and *Le Derrière / From Behind* (Valérie Lemercier, 1999). The film also marks a transition from understanding David's identity as 'homosexual' to understanding it as transgender. To cover up her developing relation with Virginia, Claire tells her husband that David is gay. But as the film continues, any possibility that he is homosexual is easily rejected in favour of the category of transgender.

Reis positions Ozon's film in the cultural context of debates on 'marriage for all' and on gender theory taking place in France around the time that the film was being made. Reis analyses 'four key scenes that stage David's transition in terms of gender performances and modes of becoming' (Reis 2019: 8), all scenes that are 'thresholds of experiences that David goes through to assume a new position in relation to Claire as a transgender subject and not as a "pervert", as she initially brands him' (Reis 2019: 8). At times, Claire stands in for the anti-queer side of the gender debates and her growing acceptance of Virginia parallels Ozon's cinematic call for a cultural acceptance of multiple ways to be a gendered subject. The final scene with Claire and Virginia as a couple, then, functions as a kind of coupling of French cultural context with the category of transgender itself, opening up a new cultural way to form a long-term relationship.

Relying on Reis's excellent analysis, I consider Ozon's film as inventing not only the category of transgender out of transvestite, but also as inventing a transed form of cisgender. Evoking Deleuze as a theoretical model, Reis notes that 'Claire undergoes her own becoming-woman' in the film (Reis 2019: 17) and that 'Claire's process of becoming a woman mirrors Virginia's, and progresses gradually to the point of her accepting herself as a woman' (Reis 2019: 17). The signs of femininity that she appropriates (more feminine dress, more makeup, more of her body revealed) are taken by her husband Gilles (Raphaël Personnaz) as a transformation on her part, which he appreciates because it renders her more like the feminine, normative woman that he would like her to present as. I extend Reis's argument here by focusing on how the process that Virginia and Claire go through is a dynamic one. Each transition is bound up with the other and the ultimate transition does not belong to one character, but *is* the dynamic between the two. In addition, Claire does not so much become a woman but, in a sense, she is transed – in Baudrillard's sense – as she becomes the 'locus of seduction'. In the French theorist's language, she becomes a transsexual symbolically over the course of the film, not simply by virtue of living as a cisgender woman in postmodern culture, but by developing as one part of a cis/trans dynamic. The transformations in the two characters cannot be separated and, ultimately, I read the film as a narrative about the mutual transformation of Claire and Virginia, or about transgender as a dialogic relation itself.

During this transformational process, Claire begins to see non-normative images or simulacra that are not taking place in reality, for she has entered into the realm of playful seduction. In two cases those images are about sexuality: alone in bed while on a weekend trip with Virginia in the countryside, Claire imagines someone coming into her room, kissing her passionately, and making love with her. That person might be Virginia, the only other person in the house, but it turns out to be Laura (David's deceased wife). Claire wakes up to see that this scene is not happening. She is beginning to imagine non-heteronormative ways to have sex as signs of gender are being transformed. In a second scene at a tennis club, Claire enters the men's locker room for no obvious reason and she sees David and Gilles standing under the shower together having anal sex before realising that this act is a mirage. David is penetrating Gilles in the same way that symbolic transsexuality is penetrating Claire's experience of gender normativity (Figure 8.1).

In the rubric of film history, Ozon's relational approach moves in a very different direction from cisgender–transgender relational narratives in which cis characters 'accept' a MTF (male-to-female) trans character, what I might call cisgender narratives of tolerance. In Pierre-Alain Meier's *Thelma* (2001), the titular character hires a taxi driver named Vincent to drive her from France to

Figure 8.1 David and Gilles in the shower

Crete, he becomes attracted to her during the trip, and then he discovers that she is trans. Slowly, he comes to accept her as trans and as an object of erotic desire and love. The transition in this road movie is Vincent's, not Thelma's, and for the two of them to be a couple, he is the one that has to – and does – change. In Jérôme Foulon's *Une Autre femme / Another Woman* (2000), Léa returns to her wife and two children that she left behind to transition. The narrative centres on the cisgender characters' tolerance (or lack thereof) for Léa's gender subjectivity. Alain Berliner's classic film *Ma vie en rose* (1997) treats familial reactions to a girl assigned male at birth and treated as a boy by members of his family and neighbourhood community. The reactions to his gender are complex, but the film's narrative centres almost entirely on cisgender relations to the trans child, defined by tolerance or intolerance. A direct influence on Ozon, Xavier Dolan's *Laurence Anyways* (2012), a Quebecois film about gender transition in the context of a heterosexual married couple, makes cisgender acceptance a key narrative element.[6]

While gender confirmation may in the end be accepted in such texts, what is not considered in any substantive way is the very binarism of the sex/gender system that necessitates the narrative of tolerance itself (though it may be implied). True tolerance, following Marcuse, would require not just incorporating the gender minority into the majority, but also 'intolerance toward prevailing . . . attitudes [and] opinions' (Marcuse, Moore and Woolf 1970: 81). To incorporate the non-normative subject via tolerance can have the effect of normalising and reifying the very system that performed the acts of marginalisation in the first place. In Ozon's film, Claire's own gender movement stands in for an intolerance of gender normativity as cisgender is not in the end tolerated and has to be put into movement too, putting the entire sex/gender system into question by destabilising it.[7]

Ozon extends the limits of trans representation in his own earlier film, *Gouttes d'eau sur pierres brûlantes / Water Drops on Burning Rocks* (2000). The transsexual character Véra went to Casablanca for gender confirmation surgery, but did so to please the patriarchal, dominating Léopold who told her to do so if she wanted him to love her. Véra's 'becoming' a woman creates similarities and affinities with the young gay male character Franz, who is feminised as Léopold's toy boy. But their relation is predicated on gender parallels, not dynamic development, as with Virginia and Claire. The final moments of the film centre on Véra who is trapped, literally, as a transwoman who cannot be loved by the man that she loves. Still, as Schilt points out, 'Véra' is a seer since she 'verra' ('will see') what is to come (Schilt 2011: 127–8; see also Asibong 2008: 64–70). Véra's entrapment gestures towards a representational era yet to be seen, the very one in which Virginia will not be trapped by others but enter into gender dialogue with them. While Ozon's Véra went to Casablanca for medical reasons, Ozon's Virginia a decade and a half later ushers in an era

TRANSING DYNAMICS 149

in which medicalised transition is one option among others and stable heterosexuality is not necessarily the end goal of a relation.[8] Virginia, from this point of view, replaces Véra, permitting a dynamic relationality within the director's own corpus.[9]

TRANSING NORMAN BATES'S MOTHER

A beginning point for this relationality can be located in the scene where Claire unexpectedly first sees Virginia dressed as a woman. Claire wanders into Virginia's house, and sees Virginia from the back (Figure 8.2). She seems to believe that she has walked in on a babysitter and begins to excuse herself, but Virginia then turns around in dramatic fashion. The move parallels what may be the famous trans reveal in Western cinema: the scene from Alfred Hitchcock's *Psycho* (1960) in which Norman Bates's dead mother is turned around to reveal that she is nothing but a skeleton. Hitchcock's influence on Ozon is quite clear in this instance, which is also not surprising given that his oeuvre often refers to the master of suspense (see Hain 2007). In Hitchcock, the scene functions as the film's gender reveal since just after the turn of the head, Norman Bates comes into the basement room with a butcher knife to stab Lila, Marion Crane's sister, while dressed as his dead mother. As he is subdued, Bates loses his dress and wig and is revealed as a man. In a following scene, a psychiatrist explains to Lila, to her husband, and to the police what has happened and that Bates was 'not exactly' a transvestite but a partial reincarnation of his dead mother in his own mind. The Hitchcockian suspense built

Figure 8.2 Claire walks in on Virginia

up in the film dissipates with the normative revelation and the official presentation of the psychology of the queer character. Considering Bates 'queer', Doty notes: 'If Norman is "not exactly" a transvestite, maybe he might also be "sort of" transexual or transgendered, particularly in the final scene of the film, where his male body now houses only "the dominant personality" of his mother' (Doty 2000: 168). In the final scene, Bates is alone, but his queerness or 'sort of' transness is explained to be the motivating force behind the film's plot that resolves everything, leaving cisgender heteronormativity firmly and safely in place. Bates's gender might be in movement, but the teleology of the film and the other characters' perception of a stable sex/gender system are definitely not.

In a sense, a dead woman has been internalised in Ozon's film too. The opening revolves around the death and funeral of Laura, Claire's best friend and David/Virginia's wife. On one level, David takes on Laura's gender subjectivity after her death and becomes her with respect to gender.[10] But that similarity between Ozon and Hitchcock turns into a major divergence. Virginia's gender reveal does not end or stabilise normative gender, ending the suspense, but puts transformation into motion. The gender reveal in this case starts the ball rolling on Claire's transformation. David is not a cinematic reincarnation of a man mixed psychotically with a woman's gender subjectivity. Gender hybridity is very much alive, but it will be formed in a new way: Claire will become a different woman, taking on some of Laura's gendered characteristics (including her sexual relation with David). In addition, Claire will enter into a dynamic relation with David/Virginia, taking on elements of Virginia's transness. Claire will be 'sort of' trans, affected by the trans character and not permitting normativity to assert itself over the trans character. Ozon's gender reveal takes place not with a knife in hand but with Lucie in Virginia's lap, a sign of futurity indicating that a new way to be a gendered subject is in its infancy, yet to come.

Ozon's reveal scene could also be taken as in dialogue with Gus Van Sant's remake of *Psycho* (1998). A shot-by-shot remake, the film was often panned as a highly imperfect copy of Hitchcock's masterpiece, but some have interpreted the remake as a rethinking of the original in a new cultural context and a rethinking of cultural context itself. Schneider argues for 'Van Sant's interest in *calling attention to* (rather than covering up), and forcing people to reflect upon (as they surely did), the self-consciously constructed nature of his project' (Schneider 2006, emphasis in original). Donaldson-McHugh and Moore write that the famous shower scene in the remake forces the modern audience to 'rethink their original presupposed phallocentric gaze, an ideological technology that is belatedly brought into focus through the spectral lens of Van Sant's adaptation' (Donaldson-McHugh and Moore 2006: 230). For me, Ozon does something similar to Van Sant's film by evoking Hitchcock: he calls attention to the fact that a transgender reveal in 2014 cannot have the same emotional valence as it did in 1960 and necessarily makes an entirely different statement about gender. Bates, as a pathologised queer character, would be out of place in twenty-first-century film, and it is not the revelation of transgender pathology that is brought to light in Ozon, but the beginning of a transwoman's trajectory. Ozon cites Hitchcock at a key moment to reorient the original as a transphobic, pathologised normative endpoint instead of a cinematic gender beginning. The citation affirms Reis's argument that Virginia is an explicitly non-pathological transgender figure (Reis 2020: 5–8), but it also establishes a new relationality not predicated on the pathologised relation between Bates and his mother or an intra-psychic pathological relationality. The very idea of transgender dynamic is turned into a viable human relation that will not leave Virginia alone in a prison cell (like Bates at the very end of *Psycho*) but in an affective relation with Claire.

SHOPPING FOR GENDER

In a key scene set in an American-style mall, Virginia and Claire go shopping to buy feminine clothing and accessories, including nail polish, jewellery, clothing, purses and perfume. The scene begins in an enclosed parking lot and the two take an elevator up to the mall where a man and his young son display a subtle but clearly transphobic response to Virginia. Afterwards, she tells Claire that she will pass as a woman in the mall, the elevator functioning as a kind of male-dominated closet space out of which she emerges as a confident (trans)woman.[11] Yet, the shopping trip is not only a gendering expedition for her; it is also a dynamic one as Virginia consults Claire on possible purchases. As they take the elevator, Claire tells Virginia that she should change her voice a bit, helping her to mould herself to the gender norms of the public space. Capitalistic exchange at the mall allegorises the gender exchange between the two characters.

In the preceding scene before they leave to go shopping, Virginia decides to wear a very formal dress, but Claire convinces her to change into a less formal one so that she can pass at the mall. But the real issue is not Virginia's over-the-top clothing, for the camera emphasises Claire's own outfit, a dark jacket with a shirt that together make her appear masculine. Her long hair is also up. When Virginia leaves the room in order to iron her less-flashy dress, Claire moves in front of a full-length mirror to examine herself by herself. With Virginia's outfit too extreme, she raises the question whether her outfit is too masculine. Does *she* too need to go shopping to gender herself more fully? Her self-reflection channels the long-standing textual trope of the transgender subject looking at their 'wrong' gender in the mirror, in opposition to the 'felt'

Figure 8.3 Virginia tries on clothes

gender on the inside (see Prosser 1998: 99–134). No such mirror scene exists for Virginia: in fact, later in the same scene Virginia sits in front of a dressing table's three mirrors to look at herself, not to question herself but to admire herself. Claire appropriates this traditional trans figure and transforms it into a cisgender trope about gender split (the gender I display versus the gender I have), becoming transsexual 'symbolically'. As Virginia comes back with her ironed dress, Ozon shoots Claire from the back, her short hair in focus as Virginia enters the bedroom out of focus. Virginia's gendering process is not in fact the narrative's focus, though it may appear to be. Unlike Virginia, Claire has not yet found her dress nor her gender (Figure 8.3).

The entry into the mall begins with the two women coming up an escalator and Virginia appearing first, with Claire further down behind her. It might appear to be the former's show, but in fact Claire is following Virginia in the terms of transformation. Counterposed with Virginia's various purchases is a feminine red dress that Claire hesitates to buy as she observes herself yet again in the mirror. Virginia strongly encourages her to buy it, but she responds that it may not really be her '*genre*', a double-entendre (not her type of clothing but also not her gender). Virginia notes that it matches her hair and that it gives her 'a tiny waist'. Claire is transed as a woman, moving her gender presentation in a more feminine direction. In this way, the definition of transgender is itself displaced away from a binary move from one gender to another, towards the quantity of gender in a cisgender subject. As they stand together in front of the mirror in the boutique, it is Claire who is the subject of the gaze and whose gender is put into question. As if to emphasise this dynamic, Virginia leaves the store with a matching new scarf around her neck, red like Claire's dress. The two of them are connected, both transed by red clothing.

This double movement around gender is predicated on representation, as an element of commodification (purchased objects that stand in for femininity) as well as an actual series of signs. After making some purchases, the two walk along in front of a wall made up of a series of digital screens of swimming fish. The digital scene suggests that Claire's transformation is representational, not so much stable and internal – like Virginia's – as much as it is fluid and on the surface. The shopping scene concludes with the two going to see a movie. As they sit watching the film, an unshaven man sits down next to Virginia and begins to rub her leg. Claire is unhappy with his advance and makes them leave the cinema abruptly. The man hitting on Virginia is Ozon himself, suggesting that the scene comments on the film that we are watching. Ozon's film is officially embracing transgender as a category, recognising it as such, but it is also seducing with respect to transgender symbolically, inventing signs that invite the cisgender viewer to be seduced in Baudrillard's sense and to be transformed by gender movement. The seduction here highlights, as Ozon has stated (2014), that his real interest in making the film was to bring in new publics and to invite them to 'play with gender'.

'FOLLOW ME'

Eva Carlton's drag performance at the 'Amazone' can be read as a dislodging of gender from the idea of an original. The scene epitomises Butler's famous idea that *'in imitating gender, drag implicitly reveals the imitative structure of gender itself – as well as its contingency'* (Butler 1990: 137, emphasis in original). The song to which Carlton performs (Croisille's 'Une femme avec toi') describes how she became a woman, or how she 'finally felt like a woman' with a man (the 'toi' of the title) (1975). The performer in a sense reveals the contingency of gender by becoming the woman of the song in appearance and in discourse at the same time. Virginia cries during the performance because she 'finally' sees proof that gender does not have to remain God-given or stable, but can change over time. The signs of sex or of the sexed body are removed from any natural connection that they might be assumed to have to the sex assigned at birth, and David is freed to 'finally' become Virginia.

The scene conveys – along with contingency – the possibility of becoming a full woman with a discrete and stable gender (the key line of the song being 'je suis enfin devenue femme, femme, une femme avec toi' / 'I finally became a woman, woman, a woman with you'). Linear expressions such as this one were expressed in classic trans texts: for instance, one of the most well-known transsexual figures in France, Coccinelle – in the chapter of her autobiography on her surgery in Casablanca (Coccinelle 1987: 143) – repeats to herself 'Enfin femme, enfin femme' ('a woman, finally a woman') during her surgery. The Butlerian signs of gender in a sense cease to be contingent as David 'finally becomes' Virginia and one gender becomes the other. The song itself conveys a transition from instability to stability: the woman of the song had been with unstable men: 'Je fréquentais alors des hommes un peu bizarres, aussi légers que la cendre de leurs cigares' ('Back then, I used to be spend time with men who were a bit strange, as flaky as the ashes of their cigars'). The men had unfirm foundations: 'Ils donnaient des soirées au Château de Versailles. Ce n'étaient que des châteaux de paille' ('They held parties at Versailles Castle, but they were only castles made of straw'). Previous men functioned in the realm of signification, first by being associated with Louis XIV's Versailles where spectacle was the rule, and second by virtue of their status as empty signifiers or 'straw castles' without a stable referent to hold them up. Her new man, however, is a fully signifying man and as such can help make her a fully signifying woman. The final three lines of the song repeat 'femme' ('woman') six times, as the discrete endpoint of a trajectory.

There is a double gender movement in the scene, with stable gender transition (becoming a woman) expressed at the same time as gender is revealed as contingent via the actual performance. The former movement cannot exist without the latter, of course, but the latter does not exist without the former in this film. What this double movement suggests is that it is not just David that becomes Virginia, but that Claire's gender can be put into motion as well. She too might 'finally' become a woman, a becoming indicative of the contingency of gender. A stable and linear form of gender becoming might be invented for both characters, but it is in light of an understanding of the contingency of gender. It is certainly true that Claire's cisgender gender transformation might be taken as a move from point A to point B, but in my reading, she incarnates far more the Butlerian contingency of gender or the fluidity of Baudrillardian symbolic transsexuality.

The double transing does not, however, pertain only to the two characters separately, but also to their dynamic. Central to the club scene is the very idea of queer coupledom, or gender contingency as relationality. In fact, the song is about becoming a woman 'with you' or about a gender dynamic that produces new gender subjectivities, precisely what is taking place in the club. The song's referent is dual, incorporating the two characters into its fold. The singer addresses her new lover with the lines: 'Ton visage était grave et ton sourire clair. Je marchais tout droit vers ta lumière' ('You looked serious and your smile was bright [*clair*]. I walked straight toward your light'). Virginia is walking straight towards Claire in doing what she is doing in the scene, as the song and the film's narrative both depict their developing relation as well as their relation to come. Her 'smile' – or one source of her happiness – will be Claire. The song refers to Virginia's gender change, but as linked to Claire specifically.

The scene portrays relationality as concept through a series of medium shots of the audience, as Eva is not the only person to be viewed. As the point of view character, Claire looks around at the diverse, queer audience: there seem to be gay men, lesbians, and transwomen whose presence she notes (see also Reis 2020: 16). More importantly, queer couples display public affection to and for each other. The point of the scene is that the performance does not put in motion simply a single person's gender, as much as a heteronormative monopoly on affection and love in two-person relations. Cisgender, heterosexual love is contingent as much as gender is. Or, put another way, human relationships are all transsexual symbolically. The performance of the contingency of gender means that affect can function in non-normative ways independent of a cisgender, heterosexual original. As the song comes to a conclusion, Virginia begins to cry at the exact moment the words 'with you' are sung, suggesting that she is seeing (or will see) that heterosexual relations are as contingent as gender itself. This expression of affect implies a non-discursively defined idea of gender beyond stable gender definition, but it also implies a non-discursive relationality beyond heterosexuality. Puar asks in a well-known rhetorical question, 'is it the case that there is something queer about affect, that affect is queer unto itself, always already a defiance of identity registers, amenable to queer critique?' (Puar 2007: 207). I might say that in this case there is something queer not about affect but about affective relationality. After this expression of affect, the two characters look at each other without words, the final scene of the film rendered possible at this moment, even if neither character knows yet that they will be in a long-term, loving relationship that cannot be easily categorised in normative terms.

The drag scene is followed by a dance scene in the club, the song being Amanda Lear's 'Follow Me' (1978). As Virginia and Claire dance with the queer crowd, a woman who reads as lesbian slowly makes her way over to dance with Claire, who begins to dance with her but then moves away to dance with Virginia. She rejects the seduction of queer relationality founded on the recognised category of lesbianism in favour of a transed relationality. Lear sings that she is 'moving on, and from now on, address unknown, I should be difficult to find'. She is 'opened' as she undertakes this metaphorical trip. But the song is not simply about her change, it is about her asking someone else to come along on a gendered journey. Precisely because of the new place to which she is moving and her vague open-endedness, she invites someone else: 'Follow me. Just follow me'. It is 'unbelievable maybe', but the follower will change: 'You'll have a new identity'. The song is Faustian (Lear cites Faust as being without regrets for his deal with the devil), but the song – like the scene – invites Claire to follow Virginia into a world of new genders and of new relationalities, not into a more legible lesbian relation. Virginia is her 'fate', as Lear puts it, the direction in which she will necessarily head as she follows along.

Amanda Lear is an especially apt singer for this moment in the film, because she was widely rumoured to be transsexual, though this was not clear or confirmed in public discourse.[12] If a public unknowingness characterised her performances as a star, her song 'Follow Me' here suggests a lack of firm knowledge: we do not know who is asking to lead or who is being asked to follow. Is it the cis character or the trans one who leads? Virginia's transformation might be bringing Claire along, but Claire is also leading her friend as she supports and encourages her and as she takes a similar gender journey of her own. The very idea of trans is vague and unclear.

QUEER ADAPTATION

If these two key scenes highlight the dual nature of transition, Ozon's adaptation of the short story on which the film was 'loosely based', Ruth Rendell's 'The New Girl Friend' (1987), does something similar. In the story, Christine is afraid of being alone with men but learns that David – her female friend's husband – dresses as a woman. The two decide to go out for a night on the town as 'girl friends'. At the end of the narrative, Christine takes out a knife and stabs her friend as she fears that she will be raped or sexually abused by him as they are alone in a hotel room and he transforms back into a man. The story is notable for what it lacks: a gender dynamic or change in the characters. Gender remains stable: David's seeming cross-dressing turns out to be temporary transvestism as he proclaims: 'I'm not really like a woman, Chris' and 'I'm falling in love with you' (1987: 419). He asks Christine if she feels the same, but she is unable to speak, feeling violated as they start to have sex. She takes out the steak knife in her handbag and stabs him 'again and again' (1987: 420). Christine is unable to accept what she wants David to be, a man who lacks virility by virtue of dressing regularly as a woman. She fears men in general and feels 'awkward and apprehensive' with them since she is afraid that 'a man might make an advance to her and the thought of that frightened her very much' (1987: 412). She has 'a feeling of panic' (1987: 412) and stabs him because his male masculinity remains fixed and the gender dynamic between them remains a heterosexual male–female relation, not at all transed.

This final scene of the short story is adapted by Ozon in a scene late in the film in which Virginia and Claire begin to have sex, also in a hotel room. But the scene takes a different turn: Virginia articulates her relation to femininity as belonging in part to Claire: 'Only you can help me accept it ('assumer')' and 'You want it as bad as I do'. As the scene progresses, Claire touches Virginia's penis, jumps up from the bed unable to continue because he is 'a man'. If this scene lacks physical violence, it is because the violence of the original story is transferred onto the following scene in which, while crossing the street after leaving the hotel, Virginia is hit by a passing car and ends up in a coma. But she does not die, and the narrative does not end there. Claire comes to the hospital with Virginia's clothing and accessories, and sings the same song that they had heard together in the gay club ('Une femme avec toi' ('A Woman with You')) while dressing her. She becomes the purveyor of the contingency of gender (like Eva), but gender is contingent for Virginia as much as for her. Claire, too, becomes 'une femme avec toi' ('a woman with you'). The scene allows for the rebirth of Virginia 'finally' as a 'woman' just as it allows for Claire's rebirth as a devoted member of a cis-trans relation.

The film thus transes Rendell's short story and, more broadly, a gender model in which a man 'becomes' a woman temporarily to enter into a more seductive-seeming heterosexuality and not to destabilise gender normativity or stability.[13] Unlike Rendell's David who is a wolf in sheep's clothing, Ozon's David does not in any way become a woman to better seduce Claire. Together with David's transformation, Virginia's rebirth in the penultimate scene suggests a dynamic model of trans/cis subjectivities that rejects the gender model of Rendell's story. This queer adaptation corresponds to Ozon's use of adaptation more generally, as producing what Fiona Handyside describes as 'new relationalities and affective encounters beyond the heteronormative reproduction of the nation state' (Handyside 2011: 53).

NEW AFFECTS, NEW REPRESENTATIONAL MODES

In the final scene of the film, Claire and Virginia present as a long-term couple. With Claire pregnant, they appear to have a stable home life as they pick Lucie up from school. Ozon describes the two characters and their journeys: 'Ce sont deux chemins parallèles, deux personnes qui se cherchent, se font du bien l'une à l'autre et qui s'émancipent' (Pris 2014) ('There are two parallel paths, two people who are looking for themselves, who help each other out and who free themselves'). Their identitarian search for 'themselves' is at the same time a search for 'each other' (the reflexive 'se' in French denoting both 'themselves' and 'each other'). Delorme's review in *Cahiers du cinéma* notes the film's lack of coherence in terms of affects, but adds that what matters in the end is 'their relation, thus the birth of a unique affect' ('un affect particulier') (Delorme 2014: 706). It is significant that Gilles disappears at the end of the

Figure 8.4 A new family

film without explanation, a traditional heterosexual relation removed because it is not a unique affect. The final affective relation cannot be characterised in easily recognisable terms, rather it resembles what Williams terms a 'structure of feeling' (Williams 1977), not yet coded in culturally recognisable terms but on the verge of becoming legible. In an early scene, Claire speaks at Laura's funeral, citing a famous line from Michel de Montaigne: 'Because it was her, because it was me'. The essayist cannot describe his incomparable relation with his deceased male friend ('her' being 'him' in the original) except as a two-person relation between two selves. The discursive situation applies to Claire and Virginia as well, establishing what their relation will become in the remainder of the film – a new type of relation that does not have readily available language to describe it. Kate Ince studies Ozon's corpus as 'the emergence of new modes of relating from the social effects of non-normative queer sexualities' (Ince 2008: 115).[14] Reis reads this particular film similarly: 'By reframing the understanding of human behaviour outside the rigid hierarchies of heteronormativity, Ozon carves out a new ethico-political space for what may be possible, acceptable and understandable' (Reis 2020: 19) (Figure 8.4). What emerges in *Une Nouvelle amie / The New Girlfriend* is a new affective relation, a unique affect between two humans, without a tag to easily label it. Part of Ozon's queer mode, on a more abstract level, is a relation between a Baudrillardian 'transsexual' representational mode and transgender experience on the other, a relation in which each has an effect on the other. That new affect, in part at least, is produced because signification and lived experience are functioning hand in hand, like Claire and Virginia holding hands in the final scene of the film.

NOTES

1. Baudrillard's emphasis. An earlier, somewhat different version was published as 'Nous sommes tous des transsexuels' / 'We Are All Transsexuals' in the newspaper *Libération* on 14 October 1987.
2. Unless otherwise noted, all translations are my own.
3. The essay has provoked trenchant critical responses in Transgender and Queer studies. See, for instance, Felski (1996) or Stryker (1999), who rightly calls his tone 'vitriolic' (162) but notes that his transsexual does 'productively figure in attempts to make sense of recent as well as productive historical experience' (Stryker 162). For similar critical issues, see Chapter 1 in Prosser (1998); Love (2014). On Baudrillard's essay in a specifically French trans context, see Reeser (2013a: 10–12). Baudrillard states up front in his essay that he is using transsexual 'not in any anatomical sense, but rather in the more general sense of transvestism' (Baudrillard 1993: 20).
4. It is important however to raise the extradiegetic issue that Duris is a well-known cisgender male actor playing a trans character. Virginia's transformation thus remains entirely within the film.
5. 'Une femme avec toi' (1975), song, composed by Pierre Delanoë and Hubert Giraud, performed by Nicole Croisille. France: Sonopress.
6. Ozon mentions the film in an interview, as the kind of 'dramatic' and 'tragic' film that he did not want to make (2014). Later films with a similar tolerance narrative include Arnaud Sélignac's *L'Epreuve d'amour / The Test of Love* (2017) and Nadir Moknèche's *Lola Pater* (2017). See also Léonor de Récondo's novel *Point cardinal* (2017).
7. This dynamic interrogates presuppositions of French political universalism by implicitly revealing that all political subjects can be put into movement, and that universalism should entail more than the collective permitting the transgender citizen to be treated in the same way as, or to have the same rights as, cisgender citizens. On transing French cisgender citizens, see Reeser (2013a, 2013b).
8. Ozon's film is a rendition of Fassbinder's play *Tropfen auf heiße Steine / Drops of Water on Hot Rocks* (1966), which did not include the trans character (Véra is a cisgender woman).
9. Ozon notes that *Une Nouvelle amie / The New Girlfriend* follows on the model of the transformation of masculinity in Ozon's *Une Robe d'été / A Summer Dress* (1996). In both cases, a female character helps a male character undergo a 'rite of passage', 'deconstructing the idea of virility instilled in them' (Ozon and Cros 71: 2020). While making the short, Ozon already had in mind the idea to make *Une Nouvelle amie / The New Girlfriend*.
10. Ozon mentions in an interview (2014) that he got the idea of a man becoming a woman after the death of his wife from Chantal Poupaud's documentary *Crossdresser* (2009).
11. Reis links this scene to the famous train episode in Fanon's *Black Skin, White Masks* (2020: 12).
12. As an example of questions posed to Lear on television, see 'Amanda Lear, un homme?' (1987). See also Gibson (1997: 534) and Chapter 4 in Fallowell and Ashley (1982). (Thanks to Maxime Foerster.)
13. On this model, see Chapter 5 in Reeser (2010). In an interview (2014), Ozon notes that his film is meant to resemble the gender ethos of American films such as *Tootsie* and *Mrs Doubtfire* in which men play with the signs of gender. Such films, I would note, often inscribe this very model of a man who takes over femininity and becomes a better woman than the women, reaffirming male masculinity's gender dominance through cross-dressing.

14. As theoretical model, Ince cites '"new relational modes" envisaged by Leo Bersani and Ulysse Dutoit' in *Forms of Being* (2004). Ince also compares Ozon to Almodóvar in this respect.

WORKS CITED

'Amanda Lear, un homme?' (1987), *Le Divan d'Henri Chapier*, directed by Jean-Claude Longin, Paris: Institut National de l'Audiovisuel, 4 April, <http://www.ina.fr/video/I17089577> (last accessed 31 July 2020).

Asibong, Andrew (2008), *François Ozon*, Manchester: Manchester University Press.

Baudrillard, Jean (1990a), 'Transsexuel', in *La Transparence du mal: Essai sur les phénomènes extrêmes*, Paris: Galilée.

Baudrillard, Jean (1990b), *Seduction*, trans. Brian Singer, New York: St. Martin's Press.

Baudrillard, Jean (1993), 'Transsexuality', in *The Transparency of Evil: Essays on Extreme Phenomena*, trans. J. Benedict, London and New York: Verso.

Butler, Judith (1990), *Gender Trouble: Feminism and the Subversion of Identity*, New York: Routledge.

Coccinelle (1987), *Coccinelle*, Paris: Filipacchi.

Delorme, Stéphane (2014), film review, *Cahiers du cinéma*, 706, p. 47.

Donaldson-McHugh, Shannon and Don Moore (2006), 'Film Adaptation, Co-Authorship, and Hauntology: Gus Van Sant's "Psycho" (1998)', *The Journal of Popular Culture*, 39: 2, pp. 225–33, <https://doi.org/10.1111/j.1540-5931.2006.00230.x> (last accessed 31 July 2020).

Doty, Alexander (2000), *Flaming Classics: Queering the Film Canon*, New York: Routledge.

Fallowell, Duncan and April Ashley (1982), *April Ashley's Odyssey*, London: Jonathan Cape.

Felski, Rita (1996), 'Fin de siècle, Fin de sexe: Transsexuality, Postmodernism, and the Death of History', *New Literary History*, 27: 2, pp. 337–49.

'Follow Me' (1978), song, composed by Anthony Moon, performed by Amanda Lear. France: Ariola.

Gibson, Ian (1997), *The Shameful Life of Salvador Dalí*, London: Faber and Faber.

Grace, Victoria (2000), *Baudrillard's Challenge: A Feminist Reading*, London and New York: Routledge.

Hain, Mark (2007), 'Explicit Ambiguity: Sexual Identity, Hitchcockian Criticism, and the Films of François Ozon', *Quarterly Review of Film and Video*, 24: 3, pp. 277–88, <https://doi.org/10.1080/10509200500486387> (last accessed 31 July 2020).

Handyside, Fiona (2011), 'Queer Filiations: Adaptations in the Films of François Ozon', *Sexualities*, 15: 1, pp. 53–67.

Ince, Kate (ed.) (2008), *Five Directors: Auteurism from Assayas to Ozon*, Manchester: Manchester University Press.

Interview François Ozon et Anaïs Demoustier pour 'Une nouvelle amie' (2014), video. Strasbourg: Radio Arc-en-Ciel, 5 November, <https://www.youtube.com/watch?v=BjKGZO8nbn8&t=905s> (last accessed 31 July 2020).

Love, Heather (2014), 'Queer', *TSQ: Transgender Studies Quarterly*, 1: 1–2, pp. 172–6, <https://doi.org/10.1215/23289252-2399938> (last accessed 31 July 2020).

Marcuse, Herbert, Barrington Moore and Robert Paul Wolff (1970), *A Critique of Pure Tolerance*, Boston, MA: Beacon Press.

Ozon, François and Renan Cros (2020), 'Ozon et les garçons', *Têtu*, 223, pp. 70–3.

Pris, Frédérique (2014), '"Une nouvelle amie", un film follement romanesque de François Ozon', *Le Point*, <https://www.lepoint.fr/culture/une-nouvelle-amie-un-film-follement-romanesque-de-francois-ozon-05-11-2014-1878881_3.php> (last accessed 31 July 2020).
Prosser, Jay (1998), *Second Skins: The Body Narratives of Transsexuality*, New York: Columbia University Press.
Puar, Jasbir K. (2007), *Terrorist Assemblages: Homonationalism in Queer Times*, Durham, NC: Duke University Press.
Reeser, Todd W. (2010), *Masculinities in Theory*, Chichester and Malden, MA: Wiley-Blackwell.
Reeser, Todd W. (2013a), '*Trans*France', *L'Esprit créateur*, 53: 1, pp. 4–14, <https://doi.org/10.1353/esp.2013.0007> (last accessed 31 July 2020).
Reeser, Todd W. (2013b), 'Universalising Transgender Representation: Emmanuelle Pagano's "Les Adolescents troglodytes"', *Modern & Contemporary France*, 21: 3, pp. 265–79, <https://doi.org/10.1080/09639489.2012.736371> (last accessed 31 July 2020).
Reis, Levilson C. (2020), 'Goodbye, "temporary" transvestites – hello, new girlfriend! Ozon's transgenre and transgender crossovers in "Une nouvelle amie" (2014)', *French Screen Studies*, 20: 1, pp. 42–66, <https://doi.org/10.1080/14715880.2018.1535822> (last accessed 31 July 2020).
Rendell, Ruth (1987), *Collected Stories*, New York: Pantheon Books.
Schilt, Thibaut (2011), *François Ozon*, Urbana, IL: University of Illinois Press.
Schneider, Steven Jay (2000), 'A Tale of Two Psychos (Prelude to a Future Reassessment) – Senses of Cinema', *Senses of Cinema*, <http://sensesofcinema.com/2000/feature-articles/psychos> (last accessed 30 July 2020).
Stryker, Susan (1999), 'Christine Jorgensen's Atom Bomb: Transsexuality and the Emergence of Postmodernity', in E. A. Kaplan and S. M. Squier (eds), *Playing Dolly: Technocultural Formations, Fantasies, and Fictions of Assisted Reproduction*, pp. 157–71.
Williams, Raymond L. (1977), 'Structures of Feeling', in Raymond Williams, *Marxism and Literature*, Oxford: Oxford University Press, pp. 128–35.

CHAPTER 9

Sex Wars in *Potiche*: Womanhood Then and Now

Loïc Bourdeau

Released in 2010, François Ozon's *Potiche* is an adaptation of the famous French *Boulevard* play of the same name, created by Pierre Barillet and Jean-Pierre Grédy in 1980. Jacqueline Maillan played the lead role for 570 performances before two other comediennes took up the part for the subsequent French tour, thus attesting to the popularity of the play. In an interview with the filmmaker and the playwright for *L'Humanité*, Ozon explains:

> I met Pierre when I was still working with Fidélité Productions, but I was struggling to adapt the play ... In 2007, for the first time in French politics there was a [presidential] race between a man and a woman. That's when a new producer asked me to make a film in the same vein as Stephen Frears's *The Queen* but I thought that as a spectator I didn't want to pay to see Sarkozy in a film when we already see him every day for free on television. That's when I thought about the seventies ... a period of crisis, of unemployment, with a president who wants to modernize France, bring the voting age down to eighteen or legalize abortion.[1]

As is the case with most of Ozon's films, we witness once again an adaptation of a classic, which is made relevant again and speaks of the moment of production.[2] Indeed, while *Potiche* remains faithful to the original aesthetic, Ozon injects contemporary references that make the film pertinent and relatable to a 2010 audience. For instance, former president Nicolas Sarkozy may not have made it to the big screen, but some of his memorable declarations and political views have. With regard to the storyline, Ozon has also made a few changes which further anchor the film in the twenty-first century.

These observations aside, I should clarify that this analysis will not engage with questions of adaptation and the attendant rhetoric of fidelity and infidelity. Fiona Handyside already offers an excellent study on the subject in 'Queer Filiations: Adaptations in the Films of François Ozon', where she goes beyond that rhetoric and shows how 'Adaptation as process and product can produce normative texts that shore up cultural binaries, but it also contains the potential for radical rewritings and rereadings that can upset cultural hierarchies' (Handyside 2011: 58). The queering of cultural hierarchies is certainly at play in Ozon's work. It is at play in *Potiche*. By setting the film in the 1970s, Ozon forces the viewer to navigate between two different epochs and to constantly consider the past in relation to the present, and vice-versa. This temporal dialogue not only unveils a turning point in women's rights at that time, it also resonates with today's struggles. This chapter thus seeks to analyse Ozon's strategies to represent French womanhood and to bring forth his criticism of gender expectations and the political and queer dimension of the film.

In 1980, Jacques Siclier started his review of the play with the following sentence: '*Boulevard* theatre is above all entertainment; it aims not to change society but to laugh at it' (*Le Monde* 1980).[3] Interestingly, he goes on to show how transgressive Maillan's character is, how she 'quite simply leaves men powerless' (*Le Monde* 1980), yet he fails to see the empowering potential of the play. As this chapter will show, the female lead is in fact utterly feminist in more or less implicit ways. In particular, I argue that Ozon manages to empower the 'trophy wife' with the very means of her submission: credulity, candour and maternal responsibilities. By revealing her *jardin secret*, she also reveals liberating, non-normative sexual practices, desires and actions. At all times, Ozon relies on the ghost of the past to comment on contemporary matters and reminds us that cinema is political.

A WOMAN'S PLACE

Potiche takes place in 1977 France and follows the lives of housewife Suzanne Pujol (Catherine Deneuve) and Robert Pujol (Fabrice Luchini), CEO of an umbrella factory.[4] Together they have two children, Joëlle (Judith Godrèche) and Laurent (Jérémie Renier). When the factory workers go on strike, Robert loses his temper and falls ill. Communist Mayor-MP Maurice Babin (Gérard Depardieu) is called upon to help with negotiations. Suzanne soon becomes interim CEO, fulfilling the former role of her husband, and successfully runs the factory with the help of her children and her secretary, Nadège Dumoulin (Karin Viard). At the same time, past love affairs resurface and shake up the already unstable family dynamic.

As the titular character, Suzanne is at the centre of narrative gravity. Yet, the very qualifier of *potiche* seems to deprive her of any agency, subjectivity or power. Indeed, a *potiche* is a large vase, that is, a vessel, a recipient, on display. The film thus relies on this tension and posits the question of belonging at its heart. In the first few minutes of the film, having completed her jog outdoors, Suzanne comes out of the kitchen wearing an apron, and the following conversation with her husband ensues:

> Suzanne: Surprise!
> Robert: Serving breakfast now?
> Suzanne: It's their [the servants'] daughter's communion.
> Robert: You gave them more time off?
> Suzanne: Just a week. Portugal's far away.
> Robert: I pay servants so my wife doesn't have to work.
> Suzanne: It won't kill me. I like spending time in my kitchen.
> Robert: It's not your place. Don't forget you're Mrs Pujol.
> Suzanne: I know, Robert. Every morning I say, 'I'm Mrs Pujol, I'm Mrs Pujol...'
> ...
> Suzanne: I hear the girls are pretty there [at the Badaboum club]. Will you take me sometime?
> Robert: To the Badaboum? Are you mad? That's no place for you.
> Suzanne: The kitchen's not my place, the Badaboum's not my place. Where is my place?
> Robert: Don't ask stupid questions.
> ...
> Robert: Luckily I married you and set things right [at the factory].
> Suzanne: You did bring your energy ... And I brought the factory in my dowry.
> Robert: Enough chatter. (00:03:15-00:04:55)

The exchange highlights the couple's dynamic and, in particular, Suzanne's struggle to fit anywhere. Her husband constantly dismisses her and puts her back in her place: at home, not doing any house chores, not having an opinion. As *his* wife, she must stay in her place, lest she tarnish his reputation. Consequently, at the spatial level, she spends most of her time at home, at least for the first half of the film. It bears noting, too, that her place and duties are never stated nor are they clearly defined; viewers, like Suzanne, only know who she is *not*, or what she *cannot* do. She fills a negative space.

The house comes to represent her stage, on which she performs daily. I would argue that her repeating 'I'm Mrs Pujol, I'm Mrs Pujol ...' not only testifies to her performing to marital expectations, it also proves performative in that it gives way to her reality and its limitations. Because her own words are silenced and other words (or rather, the words of others) are put in her mouth, her very reality or world is in effect brought about through patriarchal discourse, according to which 'A man is socially an independent and complete individual . . . whose existence is justified by the work he does for the group', whereas women are confined to a 'reproductive and domestic role' (Beauvoir 1953: 416). The film further epitomises this opposition when Robert returns home briefly; Suzanne shares news about the son's new girlfriend, of whom the father does not approve. She attempts to share her opinion on the matter. Robert cuts her off and notes: 'Your opinion? What opinion? Your job is to share my opinion. Don't waste my time . . . Be a good girl and stick to your poems' (00:12:50). Upset, she sits down and deplores: 'I'm just a trophy housewife. Up on a shelf. Not allowed to speak my mind. Part of the décor. Worthless' (00:13:10). Initially, the shot tends to support her declaration. Her beige-coloured and plaid-printed clothes blend in with the surroundings. However, sarcasm saves her from mere object status. Asked what she has to complain about, she ironically retorts: 'True, I'm the queen of kitchen appliances' (00:13:22). While this comment, along with the previous one about the dowry, goes unnoticed by Robert, it does not go unnoticed by the viewer. As such, the film runs on a marital dynamic that, at first sight, undermines Suzanne. Yet her witty comebacks and ingenuous demeanour highlight a form of resistance to domination and constantly re-subjectify her. She may be denied the right to speak her mind, but she still benefits from language and its ability to produce a counter discourse – if not to her uncaring husband, to the audience.

Depicting such verbal battles, the film relies on and underlines not only the shifting nature of power but also the temporary and unstable nature of one's status as either dominant or submissive. This is no novel characteristic in Ozon's cinema. Andrew Asibong reminds us that the filmmaker often includes duelling duos of masters and servants and explains that his 'domestic figures seem designed not merely to illustrate the bourgeois status of the other protagonists, but rather as crucial players in their own right, catalysts for the main action in the narrative, the location of the very possibility for subversion' (Asibong 2008: 48). Although in the vein of Ozon's previous work, *Potiche* differs slightly from previous productions. While the film makes the bourgeois status of the Pujols quite clear, the servants never actually appear. One could also argue that the husband's secretary and the workers' strike allow for narrative development and subversion, but it is really Suzanne who delivers radical transformations. Indeed, portrayed early on as subservient, a servant to her husband, she embodies the promise and possibility of subversion.

The predominant space of the home is perhaps one of the main markers of her social and conjugal captivity. Unable to go anywhere, except for her jogs in the park, her pleasures and desires are likewise restricted to and by maternal and spousal duties. For instance, after Robert has left for work that morning, she waltzes around the kitchen in a lighthearted manner while putting dishes in the dishwasher. On the radio Michèle Torr's song, 'Emmène-moi danser ce soir' ('Take me dancing tonight') is playing as Suzanne sings along and unveils her own desires by proxy: 'Take me dancing tonight. Cheek to cheek, hold me tight. I want you to woo me and thrill me. Like the night when you popped my cherry' (00:06:20). She quickly stops when she finds out that Robert has forgotten to take his medication. The scene thus displays her different roles as housewife and caretaker and how they take precedence over her own pleasures, be it singing, going out dancing or physical love.

Furthermore, if the kitchen scene with its yellow colour scheme, floral wallpaper and decorative knick-knacks bolster the seventies aesthetic, the space also conjures up post-Second World War consumerism. Diana Holmes and Imogen Long explain that: 'Female bodies were highly visible in 1970s France, but represented in advertising, the press and popular culture primarily as either highly sexualised objects of desire or as maternal.' (Holmes and Long 2019: 37) Ozon relies on this dichotomy, placing Suzanne on the maternal side of the spectrum and other characters, such as the secretary, on the sexualised side. In addition, he adopts the commercial codes of the time to frame women and women's bodies within this limited binary opposition. Thinking back to commercials from the 1950s to the 1970s, women are usually portrayed at home, doing chores or cooking, waiting for their husband to come home. Domesticity is thus constantly relational; it is about pleasing one's (male) spouse or one's children. In *Potiche*, the kitchen scene resembles a commercial for appliances, providing everything a housewife/mother could hope for (according to patriarchal ideology); it is a space wherein she can prepare meals for her husband. And, as mentioned, that the musical scene be interrupted by Robert's urgent request for his medication attests to Suzanne's caring, maternal nature. Later on that day, she is shown preparing dinner for the entire family. The cinematic frame is but a mirror of social frames. At the opposite end of the spectrum, Suzanne recalls the baker's wife, Mrs Marquiset, whose daughter Laurent is supposedly dating. Using an opening iris transition, the film takes the viewer back to Sundays after church when they would stop at the bakery. The roundness of the iris shot echoes the baker's speciality dessert, the *bombe glacée*. Mrs Marquiset picks one up from the window, stands sideways and holds the breast-like dessert with its nipple-like topping by her own bosom. Behind the window whose luxurious golden design frames the woman like a painting, she becomes an object of desire; she is as desirable and edible as a cake on display. The brevity of the flashback and the absence of speech further denotes women's lack of agency, even when they are working (Figure 9.1).

According to Sylvie Schweitzer: 'women have always contributed to the nation's economy. But not always in exchange for pay . . . Society prefers them

Figure 9.1 Mrs Marquiset in the window

to be their husbands' helpers in the field or at the shop' (Schweitzer 2002: 61), which has led to their invisibilisation. Suzanne and Mrs Marquiset may be represented at opposite ends of the spectrum of patriarchal womanhood, but they are both objectified, and their social contributions are equally overlooked. Nevertheless, in the French context of the seventies, 'the modern consumer culture set up tensions that encouraged women to become critically aware of the restrictions on their lives' (Holmes and Long 2019: 34). Specifically in the context of the film, the framing, limitations and constant dismissals of women's bodies illustrate the need for an impending liberation. Indeed, within the first quarter of the film, Suzanne is forced to acknowledge the restrictions on her life. Such an awakening is triggered by her own daughter's harsh words: 'You accept everything . . . I don't want your dreary life. I'd rather divorce . . . The last thing I want is to end up like you, a trophy housewife' (00:10:17–00:11:06). The daughter is representative of 'the new youth culture that developed from the 1950s on . . . [and that] emphasised self-fulfilment, freedom from authority and a style of music, dress and behaviour that was . . . oppositional' (Holmes and Long 2019: 34). Intergenerational and empowering exchanges lie at the heart of liberation in *Potiche*. More importantly, perhaps, these exchanges are multidirectional and exceed notions of age, experience or progress.[5]

WOMEN'S LIBERATION

Towards the end of the first third of the film, the strike has put the factory to a halt. Robert loses his temper and is held hostage by the union representatives.

Under the cloak of night, Suzanne pays a visit to (communist) Mayor-MP Maurice Babin to ask him 'to use [his] influence to free [her] husband' (00:25:05). Invoking their affair as young adults, she persuades him to help in spite of his hatred for the bourgeoisie and in exchange for 'radical, urgent reforms' (00:28:30). Upon Robert's successful release, he is forced to appoint an interim CEO while he convalesces and recovers from a heart condition:

> Babin: He'll need to turn [the factory] over to his authorized representative.
> . . .
> Laurent: No way. I have no desire to run a factory.
> Joëlle: Me?
> Laurent: She'd be worse than Dad.
> Suzanne: Then who? Who?
> . . .
> Babin: Why not you, Mrs Pujol?
> Joëlle: Mom? Are you joking?
> Babin: Makes perfect sense. Founder's daughter, boss's wife.
> Suzanne: I know nothing.
> Laurent: You won't have to run the factory. Just sit in Dad's chair and weather the storm.
> Joëlle: They won't give you real responsibilities.
> Suzanne: Still, but I'm not sure I could. . .
> Robert: Suzanne. . . Do as you're told. Better you than someone else. We have no choice.
> Suzanne: If you say so, Robert. I won't make any decisions without you.
> Robert: I should hope not.
> Babin: So you accept?
> Suzanne: If it'll help the factory, yes. (00:35:06–00:36:10)

Following Babin's suggestion that Suzanne take over, the entire family and the secretary burst into laughter. They are not laughing because it is a socially transgressive idea. Indeed, since 1942, women had the right to 'represent their husbands and manage the funds needed by the household' (Schweitzer 2002: 48). In addition, the constitution of the Fourth Republic (1946) granted equal rights for women and men in all domains. Rather, they laugh because of Suzanne's *naïveté* and seeming inability to run a business. Yet, as noted in the introduction, her empowerment occurs through the means of her submission. Supposedly a figurehead who will simply sit in her husband's chair, Suzanne soon proves to be a fierce leader who establishes her independence. She will not do as she is told, but as she wants, in collaboration with the workers. Preparing her encounter with the union representatives, she shows new signs of rebellion and illustrates what her son calls 'a sign of the times, Mom. Women everywhere are taking power' (00:36:38). Babin coaches her before the meeting; she sits at the desk, while he stands behind and attempts to dictate her speech:

> Babin: I'd start with, 'Gentlemen, I come in the spirit of understanding. . .'
> Suzanne: Why 'gentlemen'? It's cold, snobbish. I'll say, 'My friends!'
> Babin: Bad idea. They're not your friends and they know it.
> . . .
> Babin: Let's continue. 'I come in the spirit of understanding. I may be just a woman, but. . .'
> Suzanne: I can't say that. They have eyes. I won't apologize for being a woman.
> Babin: I don't mean it in that way.
> Suzanne: I think you're a male chauvinist . . . I'll say, 'Yes, I am a woman.' (00:37:23-00:38:10)

Once more, this exchange brings forth the importance of naming and of speaking up. In this instance, Suzanne reappropriates language and posits herself as a true boss. Babin's use of the feminine word 'patronne' ('boss') also attests to the role that language plays in manifesting the real. For Schweitzer, gender neutrality (for nouns and job titles) may be grammatically correct, but 'it is also socially crushing and has long participated in the invisibilisation of women' (Schweitzer 2002: 11). Claiming 'Yes, I am a woman', Suzanne puts the process of her emancipation in motion. She then proceeds to change and puts on her best dress, a fur coat and expensive pearl jewellery. Babin notes: 'You can't go to the factory dressed like that. It's provocation.' She replies: 'No, it's to honour the workers! I'm wearing my best jewels. Without them, I wouldn't have any. It's only right to share' (00:40:20). While one might agree with Babin that she is overdressed for the occasion, her refusal to change, to let a man police her body, acts as counter discourse to social expectations. Outside of the kitchen and the home, her visibility happens on her own terms. After the successful union meeting, during which she used 'My friends', clear changes begin to take place. Perhaps the most important one is the new 'Pujol-Michonneau' factory sign: the old black sign is replaced by a bright red sign. Beyond the direct reference to communism, Suzanne's maiden name, Michonneau, becomes more visible (although it was already included in the old one). At the same time in the scene, viewers can hear Suzanne sharing business strategies ('Demand for umbrellas in Eastern India is up 14%. Increasing sales 25% over 3 years. . .' (00:50:58)), before seeing her walking through the factory with Nadège. The sequence epitomises her full transformation: from speech, to dress code and spatial belonging, she is a woman in charge of herself and of a large business.[6]

Suzanne's liberation occurs in a threefold way, with a clear focus on spatial transgression. For the remaining two-thirds of the film, she appears for the most part outside of her house and transcends the dichotomy between private and public. After the union meeting and dinner with her children, she goes out to celebrate with Babin in the very space Robert had denied her, the Badaboum club: 'If Robert could see me here . . . And with you. He'd have a heart attack' (00:46:18). A seductive dance scene between the two ensues, before they are joined by the other clients. Here, Ozon revisits his use of choreographed numbers, as seen in *8 femmes / 8 Women*; more importantly, however, the dance underlines the breaking down of restrictions on Suzanne's body and spatial belonging. At 01:08:05, Suzanne gives an interview for television in the middle of the factory, demonstrating, once more, her knowledge of the international market. In this instance, she has to some extent reached the last frontier of visibility – she is a competent businesswoman on television – and sends a message to French society and French men in particular. As such, *Potiche* offers an accurate portrayal of the radical and rapid social changes at play in 1970s France. Indeed, the 'explosion of effervescent feminist energy in the 1970s meant that women were now in the public eye and it was clear that the loud call from women for change needed to be taken seriously by the political establishment' (Holmes and Long 2019: 43).

When Robert returns from his 'god-awful cruise' (00:58:38), he finds a redecorated office and expresses sparks of desire for his wife. Yet he remains as dismissive as ever when she mentions how the factory is running smoothly thanks to the new changes. He notes: 'Always does, after a strike. And you did OK. You sat in my chair looking daft, generously granting every bonus and pay hike. Nice job, dear. Now it's time to hang up your CEO jacket and resume your domestic activities' (00:59:10). He refuses to believe in her abilities and now faces resistance instead of silence. Asking 'Who's the boss?', she confidently and firmly retorts, 'I am' (00:59:32). Sitting in her chair, at the centre of the shot, the scene asserts her authority as majority shareholder; she is visible and she will be taken seriously (Figure 9.2). The reversal sends Robert back to the domestic space, where she 'had a TV installed in [his] room' (01:02:45) and where he can watch 'Aujourd'hui Madame' ('Today's Woman').[7] Ozon incorporates actual footage of the show, where an interviewer asks men their opinion on women's work, and confirms that *Potiche* is more than a comedy, it is a historical testimony.

Beyond the case of Suzanne, whose centrality – from title, to shots and plot development – draws all the attention, the film makes room for a diversity of (white) womanhood. Suzanne, Joëlle and Nadège represent three different models and three different lived experiences. Collectively, they embody French feminism and women's emancipation, while offering an intersectional

Figure 9.2 Suzanne is the boss

approach, in that each woman articulates her identity in relation to class, age, marital status and personal needs. It is quite noteworthy, however, that they also illustrate 'post-1789 French feminism [and] the omnipresence of universalism . . . which assumes a male subject (Scott, 1997)' (Holmes and Long 2019: 3). Indeed, the women's liberation hinges on their ability to reverse the power dynamics with Robert (Suzanne's husband/Nadège's boss and lover), Maurice (Suzanne's former lover and political opponent) and Jean-Charles (Joëlle's husband).

The Suzanne–Nadège duo is of particular interest insofar as the former's privileged position allows for the liberation of the latter. Nadège, who has been having an affair with her boss, comes to appreciate Suzanne's new management style. At first, her dedication to Robert does not go unnoticed and extends beyond the office. During a heated exchange about working conditions and the strikers' demands, she reminds Joëlle: 'You don't clock in, you're the boss's daughter' (00:21:18). Joëlle's swift and unsparing response, 'Better than his whore!' (00:21:21), attests to everyone's awareness of the situation. After Robert's collapse, Joëlle eagerly brings him food and notes: 'You need my speciality' (00:32:04). Robert begins to undress, assuming that she speaks of her sexual specialty, before being shut down: 'I'm talking about my broth' (00:32:11). The intimate nature of their relationship is no secret to either family members or viewers. In such circumstances, Joëlle's emancipation can only manifest by severing sexual ties. From Suzanne, who values her hard work and opinion, Nadège learns to speak her mind and clearly state what she wants.

Upon Robert's return, the lovers quickly express their desire for one another; he takes Nadège to a corner and tries to initiate intercourse. Yet, she quickly refuses and stands her ground:

> Nadège: Why didn't you stay in touch?
> Robert: Didn't you get my mail?
> Nadège: One postcard in 3 months!
> Robert: My favourite secretary wasn't there to take dictation. Come on!
> Nadège: Enough!
> Robert: What? Not happy to see me?
> Nadège: Not like that, Robert. I've changed.
> Robert: What's got into you? Nadège!
> Nadège: I've changed. I'm a new woman. Thanks to my new boss.
> Robert: You're doing her too?
> Nadège: No need. She respects me.
> Robert: We have unfinished business. I'm so horny.
> Nadège: My mind's made up. If you want me, leave your wife . . . I'm sick of being in the shadows. I refuse to be a trophy mistress. (00:55:49–00:56:32)

Throughout the film, Nadège's character may seem unreliable and indeed her allegiance oscillates between Robert and Suzanne. In her capacity as secretary to the boss, her livelihood actually depends on her allegiance. Feminist ideals may well appeal to her, but other tangible factors come into play and supersede her ability to emancipate herself. Nevertheless, her collaboration with the new boss has allowed her to prioritise respect, recognition and visibility. Overall, *Potiche* brings forth

> the Mouvement de libération des femmes, formed in the early 1970s as a reaction to the subordination of women within organisations on the alternative and far Left. It adopted separatism so that the power relations which silenced women in these organisations would not be replicated. (Allwood and Wadia 2002: 218)

'THE PERSONAL IS POLITICAL THESE DAYS'

As other contributors to this volume show, Ozon has oftentimes been criticised for his lack of explicit political engagement, even though his films are all grounded in social problems and debates. Not only do such criticisms seem to ask too much of a filmmaker who is neither a politician nor an activist, these comments also overlook the very political nature of the arts in general, and of cinema in particular. The inclusion of an exchange on the matter in *Potiche* is not unintentional and asks that we see beyond the comedic effects. While Suzanne is getting ready to meet the workers, Laurent and Babin talk about the factory, arts and politics. Laurent notes that although he does not support 'man's exploitation of man' (00:39:07), he is not politically active, to which the Mayor-MP replies: 'The personal is political these days' (00:39:23). For Kate Ince, 'it is in and with comedy that Ozon goes the furthest towards showing new "modes of relation", new social formations' (Ince 2008: 123). Indeed, from the moment that Suzanne takes over, new social formations emerge in favour of women's rights as shown previously, but more broadly, queer modes of being-in-the-world come to dominate the social order. I would argue that, in this instance, queerness operates in subtle ways by constantly blurring the lines of desire and power dynamics, and by thwarting the heteropatriarchal order. Perhaps the context of the seventies and the ongoing social movements explicate the subdued queerness of *Potiche*. Yet, the film tackles women's reproductive rights, sexual freedom and political opposition to neoliberalism and capitalism.

In 2007, during the presidential elections, France saw for the first time in its history a woman candidate reaching the second round: Ségolène Royal (Socialist Party, left) faced Nicolas Sarkozy (UMP, right). Ozon has often mentioned the influence of this event, explaining that: 'I realized there was a kind of comeback of male chauvinism and misogyny. I thought maybe things haven't changed so much in 40 years' (Ackerman 2011). A closer look at the campaign, and in particular at the Royal–Sarkozy debate, provides striking echoes with the film. Béatrice Fracchiolla's study of the televised debate between the two candidates shows that '[Sarkozy] pleads for himself, whereas [Royal] pleads for others . . . she develops a discourse pattern to convince people that she is the best to defend them and their interests' (Fracchiolla 2011: 2483). The development of care ethics (Gilligan 1982) has shown women's relational approach to morality and the inclusion of *others* in their decisions. More recently, Lisa Downing, in her exploration of female selfishness, likewise reminds us that 'women . . . are supposed . . . to be life-giving, to be nurturing, to be *for the other*, and therefore literally *self-less*' (Downing 2019: 1, emphasis in original). From the 1970s to today, ambitious women have thus been forced to rely on essentialised and gendered traits to attain success; in particular they must present a maternal image and rely on caring strategies. Any other mode of (re)presentation would give way to resistance and pushback. While Sarkozy or Robert can be self-centred leaders, Royal or Suzanne cannot, because, as Downing explains, 'it is a far more serious transgression to be selfish while a woman – indeed it is a category violation of identity' (Downing 2019: 1). Suzanne's success at the head of the factory has much to do with her considerate and inclusive management style (which is arguably a positive thing) and her motherly demeanour with the workers.

Towards the end of the film, having been voted out, Suzanne elects to pursue a political career, wins Babin's MP seat and exhibits bigger, national ambitions. At all times, she resorts to a maternal rhetoric. Indeed, in the final scene, she delivers her victory speech, acknowledges the memory of her father and tells the audience:

> My dream today, as your MP, is to open an enormous umbrella, pull you all close to me, and shelter you, comfort you, pamper you. Because you are all children. My children! . . . That's what I want to be for you. A mother. For 30 years, I limited myself to running Robert Pujol's household. In a matter of months, I cleaned up the mess in his factory. Why not try the same thing with France. After centuries of oppression and slavery it is time for women to take back power. Time to go back to the matriarchal model, the grand era of the Amazons! (01:35:30–01:37:05)

Her speech resorts to helpful patriarchal and matriarchal figures. By first inscribing herself into her father's lineage – a rightful heir – and placing her audience in the position of children, she judiciously manages to assert her power and ambitions without any hindrance. Even her reference to a matriarchal model receives cheerful support because it is not in breach of expected conceptions of womanhood (Figure 9.3).

Then or now, it bears keeping in mind that '[t]he stakes of female ambition and female success are so much higher – and the chances of them so much more fragile that they are freighted with judgment and precarity' (Downing

Figure 9.3 Suzanne among her voters

2019: 116). Hiding her ambitions and personal success under the cover of collective and maternal care allows Suzanne new freedoms. It also allows her to empower her secretary – who will become her parliamentary assistant – and her children who join the factory and take part in its growth. However, when Robert challenges her leadership and calls for a new board vote, Suzanne is betrayed by her daughter who gives her shares to her father:

> Suzanne: Why, Joëlle? Why wage war with me? I'm your mother and I'm on your side.
> Joëlle: Want the truth, Mom?
> Suzanne: Of course.
> Joëlle: I voted against you for Jean-Charles.
> Suzanne: What do you mean?
> Joëlle: Dad agreed to give him my job for my 10%.
> Suzanne: You're giving up your job?
> Joëlle: Yes . . . So Jean-Charles will stop traveling and stay home with us. I can't be alone anymore. I'm pregnant, Mom.
> Suzanne: You mustn't sacrifice yourself and your job, for your husband. There's the pill. And abortion's legal now.
> Joëlle: Jean-Charles is against it.
> Suzanne: It's your body, honey, not his. It's your choice. (01:20:25-01:22:37)

The content of the exchange is certainly not anodine. Holmes and Long remind us that '[b]y 1975 contraception had only recently been legalised, and Simone Veil's law decriminalising abortion was finally passed in January of that year' (Holmes and Long 2019: 37). Set only two years after these landmark events in French history, *Potiche* offers a progressive older female character who is committed to women's personal choice, thus reversing the mother-daughter / older-younger / conservative-progressive dynamics. While Suzanne first deplores her daughter's lack of 'female solidarity', it becomes apparent that Joëlle's seemingly selfish vote was not so selfish after all; she cared for the good of her entire family.

Notwithstanding Suzanne's efforts at collective change and progress, it would be reductive to describe her as a selfless individual whose needs and desires are non-existent. In fact, the film also owes part of its comedic dimension to conjugal infidelity; a classic element of vaudeville theatre, it serves, in the case of *Potiche*, as a queering agent that brings forth non-normative sexual encounters. Early in the film, Robert informs Suzanne that he does not approve of Laurent's girlfriend because she might be his daughter, having had an affair with Mrs Marquiset. Later, surprised to learn that Laurent and is girlfriend are still dating, Suzanne confesses that Laurent is probably not his son. Having found an old locket with a picture of Maurice Babin in his wife's bedroom, Robert believes the Mayor-MP is the biological father. The latter takes Suzanne on a car ride outside of the town, where they first met, to clarify the situation:

> Babin: Your husband came to see me. Is it true that his son is mine? That my son isn't his?
>
> . . .
>
> Suzanne: I'd love to make you happy, but . . . He's not yours, Maurice.
> Babin: I see. So he's Pujol's after all.
> Suzanne: No Maurice. He's not yours or his.
> Babin: So whose son is he?
> Suzanne: Laurent's father could be Mr Balestra.
> Babin: The lawyer. . .
> Suzanne: He was a clerk at the time . . . Although . . . In terms of physical appearance, he looks much more like Gunnar. Remember him? That lovely Swede who taught tennis?
>
> . . .
>
> Babin: Were there many others?
> Suzanne: Not in May of 1952.
> Babin: Poor Pujol married a bourgeois nymphomaniac.
> Suzanne: You have no right to judge the folies of my youth. Just be glad you got your share. (01:09:50-1:11:55)[8]

At first, Suzanne's revelations might seem somewhat unexpected. Yet, from a broader perspective, it confirms that '[w]hat is problematized in Ozon's oeuvre is the fixity of things and people' (Schilt 2011: 38). Indeed, Suzanne's constant devotion, care for others and seeming candour hide a much freer woman who has sexual needs, too. And, if the exchange limits her affairs to her youth, she soon proves that age is irrelevant. Disappointed, Babin asks that she step out of the car. He leaves her alone on the side of the road. Suzanne starts hitchhiking and stops a truck. She and the driver quickly exchange flirtatious looks and smiles to the sound of Julio Iglesias's romantic song, 'CuCuRuCuCu' (Figure 9.4). The Spanish castanets hanging from the truck's rear-view mirror further add to the sexual dimension of the scene. The discussion with Joëlle and this scene with Babin not only speak of the 1970s – during which 'campaigns on reproductive rights and sexuality . . . performed an attack on the linguistic repression of female experience' (Holmes and Long 2019: 41) – but also of the contemporary moment of production. Under Sarkozy, women's rights and visibility stagnated and his sexist remarks have not gone unnoticed (Dejean 2015). His party showed some fierce opposition to gay marriage (a law proposed and passed by his successor, François Hollande) and the party continues to oppose medically assisted procreation for lesbian couples. Ozon's work, and *Potiche*

SEX WARS 177

Figure 9.4 Suzanne hitchhiking with a truck driver

in particular, criticises conservative positions (held by politicians such as Sarkozy) and very much aligns with 1970s liberation movements.[9]

CONCLUSION: 'THE RAINBOW'

Under Suzanne's leadership, political student and art enthusiast Laurent leaves Paris to join the factory as creative director. He designs new, colourful umbrella collections inspired by famous painters, as well as another one entitled 'The Rainbow'. Suzanne is very pleased with the modern looks and asks for Nadège's opinion:

> Suzanne: What do you think, Nadège?
> Nadège: A bit loud.
> Suzanne: No, it's all the rage! And so original.' (00:52:05-00:52:25)

The use of 'criard' – translated as 'loud' and derived from 'crier' ('to scream') – echoes a conservative rhetoric according to which social demands and actions from minoritised groups, such as the LGBTQ community (represented here by the rainbow reference), are too visible or too vocal. Here, the film pokes fun at such unsubstantiated discourse and attests to its awareness of contemporary debates. At the level of plot, this scene also performs a sort of coming out on the part of the son. Though he makes references to Floriane, his girlfriend whom we never see, Laurent's somewhat effeminate behaviour and creative penchants serve to signal his homosexuality. During the last third of the film, having broken up with Floriane, Laurent thanks his mother for helping him realise that Floriane was not the right person for him and notes: 'You've become the most important woman in my life' (01:26:53). He then proceeds to introduce her to a 'handsome young man canvassing for [her]' (01:27:03). Though it is clear to the audience that they are together, Suzanne is quite oblivious and remarks: 'He looks a bit like you. He's the lawyer Balestra's son' (01:27:019). Laurent may not be a central character but his development – which diverges from the play – inscribes the film further into the Ozonian oeuvre and his queer universe. Schilt explains that:

> [w]hen asked . . . whether he himself feared, because of his persistent tendency to depict homosexual desire on screen, being 'trapped in an image' . . . Ozon replied: 'I have no problem with the risk of being labelled . . . I never saw myself as making militant films, but when I realized that *Une robe d'été* had been reappropriated . . . for militant purposes, I was pretty happy about it. (Schilt 2011: 37)

In the case of *Potiche*, I have argued that the queering of social norms and desires is rather subdued, partially because of the bourgeois setting which prioritises silence. Naming proved a crucial element in the processes of domination and liberation – as it has been for civil rights movement which relied on identity politics. Yet, the absence of naming, with regard to desire and sexuality, successfully blurs the lines of heteropatriarchal expectations and forestalls binary models or oppositions.

As such, the film brings forth different models of womanhood and of empowerment that take into account one's context. Moreover, beyond feminist considerations, *Potiche* also promotes a societal organisation grounded in care, human connections, respect and emancipation. The inclusion of *sarkozysmes*, such as 'travailler plus pour gagner plus' ('work more to earn more') or 'casse-toi pauv' con' ('Get lost, you idiot'), and Joëlle's enthusiasm for the relocation of the factory abroad to save on labour cost, only serve to make Suzanne's conception of *vivre-ensemble* or togetherness more appealing. In the end, *Potiche* offers a portrayal of women's liberation and success and clearly highlights the many hurdles on the way. Yet, liberation will not be complete while the possibility and acceptability of women's ambition and success continue to depend upon maternal and caring qualities.

NOTES

1. In addition to these comments, let us remember 'the keen interest in the minutiae of quotidian conjugality that Ozon displayed in earlier films such as *La Petite Mort* and *Gouttes d'eau sur pierres brûlantes*' (Asibong 2008: 95), as well as in *5x2*.
   All quotes are included directly in English; all translations are my own. Regarding dialogue from the film, I am citing the provided English subtitles as they appear.

2. It is worth noting that most contemporary viewers, including Ozon, do not know much about the play; comparisons can easily be avoided. Barillet rightly points out that 'The play was very successful, but theatre is ephemeral. There are very few traces left of it' (*L'Humanité* 2010). Unlike classic novels, unpublished (*Boulevard*) plays have indeed few chances of remaining collective, cultural landmarks.
3. I would briefly add to Handyside's analysis insofar as Ozon does not simply adapt a literary classic, but, in this instance, a popular and bourgeois cultural production (in opposition to upper-class, classical theatre). There is here something definitely queer: *Boulevard* does not praise French cultural prestige, nor does it add to France's grand, aesthetic and intellectual ideals. As a result, Ozon's adaptation strays even farther away from (conservative) heritage cinema, its 'reproduction of the nation's image and [its] transmission of national memory' (Handyside 2011: 54). If *Potiche* is transmitting memory, as I argue, it is the (progressive) memory of women's fights, victories and liberation.
4. From an intertextual perspective, *Potiche* also conjures up Catherine Deneuve's famous performance in *Les parapluies de Cherbourg* / *The Umbrellas of Cherbourg* (1964). In today's context, the term umbrella also brings about references to queer, an umbrella term for sexual and gender minorities, which further foregrounds the film into concepts of fluidity, marginality and subversion.
5. From a comparative perspective and taking into account Thibaut Schilt's extensive work on Ozon, the father figure in *Potiche* echoes that of *Sitcom* or *8 femmes* / *8 Women* insofar as 'it is shown to be incompatible with queering and overall evolution of the family' (Schilt 2011: 78). That being said, the filmmaker offers multifaceted and contrasting representations of fatherhood, as is the case with his 'portrayal of women [which] is no less complex' (Schilt 2011: 78). *Potiche* is one such example where the identity category of woman is indeed broad and diverse.
6. The conditions that led to her nomination make Suzanne an exceptional case in the context of the seventies. Even if the decade is marked by a great number of pieces of legislation in favour of women's rights, such as the right to go to school, discrimination prevailed. School girls were trained for 'jobs oftentimes reserved to them only' (Schweitzer 2002: 58). Put otherwise, they were not trained to become CEOs and leaders, rather instruction prepared them for childrearing and domestic work.
7. 'Aujourd'hui Madame', which ran from 1975 to 1982, was the first daily afternoon show on French television. It dealt with societal topics of interest to women.
8. Ozon relies on the iris transition to introduce flashback scenes of young Suzanne enjoying her sexual encounters with the various men. The bright colours and sunny sequences showcase the positive and fulfilling nature of these moments. Later on, Robert attempts to reconnect with Suzanne to no avail. Yet, the thought of their first encounter triggers a flashback to a beach where both bodies embrace one another in the sea, thus reminding us of previous films such as *Une Robe d'été* / *A Summer* Dress (1996) or *5x2* (2004). For an analysis of the significance of beaches in Ozon's cinema, see Handyside (2012).
9. Holmes and Long note that '[t]he will to deconstruct language and forge the "words to say" women's experience resounds in the texts and films that marked 1975' (2019: 42).

WORKS CITED

Ackerman, Emily (2011), 'François Ozon: Potiche', *Tribeca Films*, 23 March, <https://tribecafilm.com/news/512bfdf51c7d76d9a9000097-francois-ozon-potiche> (last accessed 25 October 2020).

Allwood, Gill and Wadia Khursheed (2002), 'French Feminism: National and International Perspectives', *Modern and Contemporary France*, 10: 2, pp. 211–23.

Asibong, Andrew (2008), *François Ozon*, Manchester: Manchester University Press.
Atack, Margaret, Alison S. Fell, Diana Holmes and Imogen Long (2019), 'Introduction: Making Waves', in Margaret Atack, Alison S. Fell, Diana Holmes and Imogen Long (eds), *Making Waves: French Feminisms and their Legacies 1975–2015*, Liverpool: Liverpool University Press, pp. 1–15.
Beauvoir (de), Simone (1953), *The Second Sex*, trans. Howard M. Parshley, London: Jonathan Cape.
Dejean, Mathieu (2015), 'Les 5 déclarations les plus sexistes de Nicolas Sarkozy', *Les Inrockuptibles*, 24 April, <https://www.lesinrocks.com/2015/04/24/actualite/actualite/top-5-des-declarations-les-plus-sexistes-de-nicolas-sarkozy> (last accessed 25 October 2020).
Downing, Lisa (2019), *Selfish Women*, Oxford: Routledge.
Fracchiolla, Béatrice (2011), 'Politeness as a Strategy of Attack in a Gendered Political Debate – The Royal-Sarkozy debate', *Journal of Pragmatics*, 43, pp. 2480–8.
Gilligan, Carol (1982), *In a Different Voice*, Cambridge, MA: Harvard University Press.
Handyside, Fiona (2011), 'Queer Filiations: Adaptations in the Films of François Ozon', *Sexualities*, 15: 1, pp. 53–67.
Handyside, Fiona (2012), 'The Possibilities of a Beach: Queerness and François Ozon's Beaches', *Screen*, 53: 1, pp. 54–71.
Holmes, Diana and Imogen Long (2019), '1975: The Year of Women', in Margaret Atack, Alison S. Fell, Diana Holmes and Imogen Long (eds), *Making Waves: French Feminisms and their Legacies 1975–2015*, Liverpool: Liverpool University Press, pp. 33–50.
L'Humanité (2010), 'François Ozon: "Je voulais filmer la fin du monde"', *L'Humanité*, 10 November, <https://www.humanite.fr/francois-ozon-je-voulais-filmer-la-fin-dun-monde> (last accessed 25 October 2020).
Ince, Kate (2008), 'François Ozon's Cinema of Desire', in Kate Ince (ed.), *Five Directors: Auteurism from Assayas to Ozon*, Manchester: Manchester University Press, pp. 112–34.
Schilt, Thibaut (2011), *François Ozon*, Urbana, IL: University of Illinois Press.
Schweitzer, Sylvie (2002), *Les femmes ont toujours travaillé: Une histoire du travail des femmes aux XIXe et XXe siècles*, Paris: Odile Jacob.
Siclier, Jacques (1980), '"Potiche", de Barillet et Grédy Pour Jacqueline Maillan', *Le Monde*, 20 September, <https://www.lemonde.fr/archives/article/1980/09/20/potiche-de-barillet-et-gredy-pour-jacqueline-maillan_3074484_1819218.html> (last accessed 25 October 2020).

CHAPTER 10

Female Creativity, Selfishness and Monstrosity in François Ozon's *Angel*

Fiona Handyside

In 2007, François Ozon's ninth feature film, *Angel*, was released. Based on a book of the same title by a relatively unknown British author, Elizabeth Taylor, the film tells the story of Angel (Romola Garai), who aspires to become a rich and famous authoress despite her humble background as the daughter of a widowed grocer. Much to his cynical wife, Hermione (Charlotte Rampling)'s astonishment, publisher Theo Gilbright (Sam Neill) decides to publish Angel's pulpy romance novel *The Lady Irania*. Sure enough, Angel soon achieves fame and fortune, penning a flurry of similar books. She earns enough to buy herself Paradise, the stately home where her Aunt Lottie (Janine Duvitski) had once worked as a servant. The film charts Angel's meteoric rise and her entangled relationships with the Howe-Nevinson siblings: Nora (Lucy Russell), the plain failed poet and Angel's helpmeet and companion; and Esme (Michael Fassbender), the handsome womanising painter and Angel's husband. Waning popularity; the outbreak of war; and Esme's loss of a leg, infidelity, and eventual suicide coincide to leave Angel wretched and destitute. She discovers that Esme had an affair – and possibly a son – with Angelica, the young woman who lived at Paradise as a girl and had Angel's aunt as her nanny. Broken-hearted, Angel takes to her bed, and in her last moments, asks Nora if she had 'lived the wrong life'. She hugs Nora, telling her that she is the only one who ever truly loved her.

The film, which had been gestating in Ozon's mind since he read the novel in 2000, had a difficult production history. Ozon struggled to convince British producers of the appeal of an English-language Edwardian-era costume drama directed by a Frenchman. Furthermore, the book was unknown and Ozon hadn't attached a star to the project. He had initially proposed the role of Angel to Nicole Kidman, who accepted, but as he worked on the adaptation and realised that his film would need to cover a substantial period of Angel's adolescence, he decided he needed a younger actor for the part. With presumable understatement, Ozon reports that his producers 'ont un peu tiqué' ('raised an eyebrow') at his decision to abandon a star, although they followed his logic (Rouyer 2007: 23). The difficulties in raising money were such that production was delayed, and Ozon made use of the downtime to make his first short since *Regarde la mer / See the Sea* (1997), *Un Lever de rideau / A Curtain Raiser* (2006), based on a short play by Monthérlant.

After such a chequered production history, the completed film fared quite poorly at the European box office and did not receive a theatrical or DVD release in the USA. The critical response to *Angel* upon its release was mixed. Patrice Blouin, reviewing the film for trendy cultural review magazine *Les Inrockuptibles*, claims it is Ozon's most impressive film to date, but his description of the character of Angel as 'criard' or garish suggests too why the film struggled to attract a large audience (Blouin, 2007: np). Andrew Asibong, writing in 2008, argues that the film is a culmination of what he sees as an increasingly solipsistic turn in Ozon's filmmaking away from an earlier commitment to the creation of alternative communities outside patriarchal norms. He condemns *Angel* as an 'utterly alienating cinematic experience' (Asibong 2008: 138) that is the unfortunate product of a drift 'towards the eccentricities of a self-pleasuring and ironical cinematic baroque' (Asibong 2008: 142). He comments that in contrast to the earlier interest Ozon has paid to possibilities of transformation and metamorphosis, Angel remains resolutely unchanging in the face of the vicissitudes of her life and society. She fails to pay any attention to external reality, interested only in the Romantic visions of life as she wills it to be, to the extent that by the end of the film she has become a pathetic figure clothed in such old-fashioned witch-like garb that she terrifies small children. Although Asibong thus stresses how *Angel* differs from Ozon's earlier work, Philippe Rouyer notes the connections between *Angel* and some of his other films, most notably *Swimming Pool* (Rouyer 2007: 21–5). Generally, the preoccupation with the necessity of fantasy to alleviate shame, humiliation and loss is to be found repeatedly in Ozon's filmography, from Marie (Charlotte Rampling)'s traumatised response to her husband's disappearance in *Sous le sable / Under the Sand* (2000) to the fantasmatic friendship between Frantz (Anton von Lucke) and Adrien (Pierre Niney) in *Frantz* (2016). Through its main character's determined investment in her fantasy of fine living in Paradise, the film demonstrates Ozon's continued interest in the power and impact of imagination upon reality, and his conviction that 'a person is defined as much by her fantasies as her actions' (Piazzo 2003: np). This chapter on *Angel* argues that Angel's utter commitment to her fantasy life makes the film a study of female selfishness, as women are not expected to have such an investment in their interior world but to find fulfilment through human connection, community and family. Angel does not promise anything as radical as the Utopian communities ridded of patriarchal oppression that Asibong identifies in Ozon's earlier films. However, the film does offer a portrait of a deliberately unsympathetic female figure – the narcissistic, self-obsessed, childless woman. Through suggesting connections between his own creative impulses and those of Angel, Ozon offers a potentially politically complex and artistically self-reflexive film that foregrounds a mode of being that privileges individual selfish instincts over the kind of self-sacrifice that, as Lisa Downing points out, women have been trained to perform over millennia. Downing explains that:

> Given that men are supposed to be 'full of self' (assertive, confident, self-assured, driven), male selfishness is a minor infraction. For women, who are supposed in this binary logic that casts them as the mere compliment of men, to be life-giving, to be nurturing, to be for *the other*, and therefore literally self-less, it is a far more serious transgression to be selfish while being a woman – indeed it is a category violation of identity. (Downing 2019: 1)

Downing identifies the figure of the nineteenth-century female author as particularly able to comment on society's views of selfishness, opening her book with epigraphs from two of her favourite female Georges (Eliot and Sand). Women artists in eras unconducive to female autonomy, comments Downing, were 'positioned vis-à-vis power in such a way as to have an acute sense of which kinds of people, exhibiting what kinds of behaviours, and threatening what sorts of hierarchies, are likely to attract to themselves the label of "selfish"' (Downing 2019: 2). Philip Kemp's acerbic review of the film in *Sight and Sound* reveals, perhaps unwittingly, why the film aroused such ire, at least for British viewers, when he comments that the film's 'uncertainty of tone infects Romola Garai's performance; she opts to play Angel with wide-eyed steeliness, as if Margaret Thatcher were trying to morph into Charlotte Brontë' (Kemp 2008: 50). Kemp's rather peculiar and unlikely mash-up of Brontë and Thatcher locates two figures whom Downing identifies as key to cultural understandings of rebarbatively selfish women: the right-wing female politician and the nineteenth-century female author. Angel is clearly a writer, so the Brontë reference is easy to find in the film, but Thatcher does also hover over the character as an influence. Ozon efficiently sketches Angel's background as a grocer's daughter and her desire to transcend her class position through fantastical narratives in the film's opening few minutes. We begin with Angel being chastised in a schoolroom, with her teacher telling her 'you'll receive no marks for this essay, Miss. Deverell. Your homework was to describe where you live. Unless I am mistaken, you do not live in a great house cherished by the gods, but over your mother's grocery shop', as we hear girls' laughter on the soundtrack. Angel returns to her desk and moments later we see her walking through the shop having returned home from school. Thatcher's background as a grocer's daughter was very much part of her political persona, informing her choice of language to describe and justify a free-market, neoliberal ideology under the guise of the shrewd housekeeping of the British housewife who keeps a careful eye on budgets and does not spend beyond her means (Downing 2019: 81). Downing contends that Thatcher was a politician who provoked 'exceptional vitriol' not only because of her ruthless right-wing politics but also because she was an individualistic, selfish, bellicose woman, challenging cultural norms about womanhood demanded both by conservative society and progressive feminists (Downing 2019: 95).

Angel's pursuit of her own artistic vision and her creation of her fantasy life at Paradise show us both the exhilarating pleasure a woman can get in being free to pursue her own pleasure as well as the harsh price Angel pays, as she finishes the film completely dislocated from any kind of social connection at all. Asibong and Downing thus provide us with two productive perspectives from which to consider Angel's selfishness and solitude within a feminist reading of the film. How is it possible for women to live a strong fantasy life that does not end in their conformist complicity with limiting heteronormative romance? For Asibong, *Angel* shows us the damage inflicted by preferring 'the solidity of . . . moribund fantasies to the stimulation of living others' which he associates with many Ozon characters from the 2000s on (Asibong 2008: 83). Downing, however, in her discussion of selfishness, coins the term 'self-fulness', allowing us to imagine that for women, the fantasy of a self-centred existence might be exactly what is needed to counter patriarchal pressures. She proposes this term both as the exact antonym of what women are supposed to be – selfless – and as a value judgement-free alternative to selfishness. For, Downing argues, self-fulness is a strategically useful weapon in the feminist's armoury, allowing her to resist conformist pressures of what consists of 'a good life' and pursue her own goals. Angel's solipsistic narcissistic fantasy life might be alienating to viewers, but it affords her, for a while at least, wealth and the ability to construct a life that doesn't revolve around ministering to another's needs, such as her mother in the grocery or Aunt Lottie as a servant at the big house. In this vein, we might revisit the ending of *Angel* and ask ourselves whether Angelica, a married mother, is any happier than Angel. Her family life might too be based on a lie, as Esme could well be the father of the child she is raising as another man's son, because of the weight of social conventions. Ozon's significant rewriting of the novel is interesting here – in the novel, Esme's affair is with a woman called Laura, who is not linked in any way to Angel. Through making Esme have a connection to Angel's namesake, the girl who lived at Paradise, Ozon introduces into the narrative his love of the trope of doubling. This is a device common to noir thrillers and frequently deployed by Hitchcock, particularly in *Vertigo*'s famous splitting of the main female protagonist into a blonde and a brunette, revisited here in the contrast between Angelica's 1920s blonde bob and Angel's long dark hair. As Mark Hain comments in his discussion of Ozon's Hitchcockian leanings,

> the very ambiguity (what [Robin] Wood refers to as the resolution the films can never achieve on their own) in the films of both Hitchcock and Ozon speaks to the necessity of engaged and questioning viewership. What each filmmaker presents to us can be received as a didactic, prepackaged message, or as a vital and challenging critique: the difference is in the viewer. (Hain 2007: 288)

The film explores one of Ozon's pet themes: that fantasy necessarily leads to disappointment, because of the discrepancy between fantasy and reality. A feminist reading attentive to the different positions of male and female fantasy in a patriarchal society shows how, for women, however, fantasy is in particular a double-edged sword, leading to either loneliness and destitution, or banal self-sacrifice in the service of others.

SELF-REFLEXIVITY IN *ANGEL*

In his recent discussion of Ozon's cinema as part of a wider consideration of the impact of the New Wave on French cinema, Douglas Morrey argues that Ozon's films share with those of his fellow contemporary directors Oliver Asseyas and Christophe Honoré a tendency towards a highly referential (at times almost parodic) style that in some ways is indebted to the New Wave and its acute authorial self-consciousness about the act of filmmaking (Morrey 2020). Morrey undertakes a comparative analysis of *Swimming Pool* and *Dans la maison / In the House* (2010), drawn to how both of them understand writing as emblematic of the creative process and explore its addictive and obsessive qualities (Morrey 2020). In the character of Angel, then, Ozon could be seen to be creating a typically Ozonian figure, the self-obsessed narcissistic author who values creative self-realisation over the ties of family. The most powerful desires that animate Angel are not sexual but creative; her interest is not in reproduction through childbirth, but in ongoing, fruitful production of narrative. Although Ozon changes many aspects of the novel's narrative, most notably its denouement, he keeps verbatim the exchange where Esme identifies the heart of the appeal of Angel's (pulpy, badly written, overly sentimental) fiction for her audience. As she poses for her him to paint her portrait, Esme comments that he has read one of her books, lent to him by his landlady, and tells Angel 'I think that the secret of your power over people is that you communicate with yourself, not with your readers' (Taylor 2006: 133). As Morrey points out, Ozon's protagonists are rarely out homosexuals, and Ozon is not interested in documenting the process of coming out or confirming a sexual identity. 'Instead', explains Morrey, 'Ozon repeatedly demonstrates the power of desire to challenge and disrupt heteronormative social structures' (Morrey 2020: 196). In *Angel*, this desire is Angel's utterly self-absorbing investment in narrative production and her prolific production of fiction as a method of finding and celebrating herself. *Angel*'s mixed critical reception might come, then, from whether we judge it a highly self-conscious piece of art about the power of creative forces to challenge staid thinking, or a self-obsessed reworking of a clichéd and hackneyed portrait of the artist as master of transgression. Of particular interest for a more progressive reading of the film is Ozon's identification of his own artistic processes with a creator of the opposite sex. He suggested when asked about his identification with Sarah Morton in *Swimming Pool* that this cross-sex identification allows him to examine the selfishness of the artist 'with more cruelty and more lucidity' (Ozon 2003: np). Certainly, it foregrounds how women's selfish pursuit of their own artistic vision is one that challenges normative views of the female role.

Ozon explains, *pace* his decision to drop Kidman as the film's star, that when he is in the process of creating his storyworld, he has to think creatively rather than commercially and stay true to his vision. Such intransigence in his pursuit of creation gives Ozon something in common with Angel who also stubbornly and steadfastly refuses compromise. When she is asked by her publisher to change some details in her first novel, such as having a character open a champagne bottle with a corkscrew, she refuses, leaves his office, and returns to the train station, although she has no bargaining power at all, being an entirely unknown writer. Theo is touched by her tenacity and he invites her to dinner, agreeing to publish her book unchanged. This connection between Ozon and Angel, his producers and Theo, gives the film a parodic and self-reflexive relationship to Ozon's authorship. As Thibaut Schilt suggests, 'for those familiar with the trajectory of Ozon's career, the character of Angel feels a bit like the filmmaker's alter-ego' (Schilt 2011: 138). Ozon confesses that when he initially read the novel, 'I recognised myself in the story. You could say that *Swimming Pool* (2004) was born from my desire to adapt *Angel*. One could already find the relationship between the author and the editor, between fantasy and reality' (Rouyer 2007: 21). In an interview with *Le Devoir*, he explains that both Sarah Morton (Charlotte Rampling) in *Swimming Pool* and Angel in *Angel* function as 'hidden self-portraits' (Lévesque 2008). In aligning himself in this way with his creations, Ozon forms a filmic universe in which identifications occur between a straight woman and a gay man. The queerness of his cinema is thus not (only) predicated on his depiction of gay couples and homosexual activities, but rather through the creation of a space in which spectators are invited to take up positions of desire and identification beyond those based on

FEMALE CREATIVITY, SELFISHNESS AND MONSTROSITY 187

their assumed gender and sexuality. While *Angel* may not on the surface seem such an insistently queer text as the riotous *Sitcom* (1999) or the melancholic *Le Temps qui reste / Time to Leave* (2005), Ozon's insistence on the creative act as one that forges bonds above and beyond those assigned as identificatory essences in a heteronormative world opens up new modes of relation. In this universe, in Judith Mayne's words

> cinematic identification is never masculine or feminine, but rather a movement between the two. From this vintage point, positions may well be defined as masculine or feminine (or both), but they are taken up by spectators regardless of their gender or sexuality. (Mayne 1993: 71)

PASTICHE IN *ANGEL*

If *Swimming Pool* gives Ozon the opportunity to recognise the 'repressed spinster' aspect of his creative personality, *Angel* unflinchingly writes large the monstrous narcissistic ego that drives creativity. As Hilary Mantel explains in the book's introduction, Elizabeth Taylor reveals the tyrannical taming of reality that lies behind the act of creation – whether the art produced is good or bad. 'Writers are monsters she is telling us' (Mantel in Taylor, 2006: 6). Ozon uses clumsy and artificial devices to portray Angel's somewhat shaky relationship to reality, so that we see things through her romanticised perspective. Her trip through London with Theo and her honeymoon in Cairo, Athens and Venice are rendered through clunky back projections of famous vistas associated with each city that are obviously artificial (Figure 10.1)

Figure 10.1 Angel's honeymoon

The opening credits unfold in a sugary bright pink against a dark background while a syrupy Philippe Rombi score plays. Most egregious is the engagement scene. In a significant departure from the novel where Esme and Angel's engagement is a tacit agreement reached in his dingy studio, the film makes the engagement scene spectacular. Angel is hosting a lavish book launch at the Savoy Hotel, at which she also plans to unveil Esme's portrait of her as a surprise to him. Angry and humiliated by her desire to fool him, Esme leaves. Angel, wearing an enormous red dress with a flowing crinoline skirt and matching feather fascinator, runs down the staircase and into the courtyard to confront Esme. As thunder claps and rain pours, she tells him 'I'll go on loving you til the day I die' as the camera closes in to a tight close-up on her rain- and tear-splashed face. As the couple kiss, the camera draws back and tilts up so we see the sun bursting through the clouds and a rainbow appears framing them as violins play. Not since *Four Weddings and a Funeral* (Newell, 1994) has there been such an egregious rain-based love scene in an English-language film. Ozon explains 'For the proposal in the rain, I added a rainbow. I didn't hesitate to push certain clichés to their extreme. For me, there's no irony. It's done utterly sincerely ['très premier degré'], just to enter into her world' (Rouyer 2007: 24) (Figure 10.2).

Once Angel and Esme move into Paradise House together, the film's production design becomes quite extraordinary, showing a series of richly decorated rooms. We enter into Angel's imagined ideal of a stately home complete with peacocks (when reminded by Nora that she has to pay for the peacocks, however, Angel grumbles that she finds them disappointing and more like vultures). A conversation between Esme and Angel, invented by Ozon and not present in

Figure 10.2 Angel and Esme embrace in the rain

Taylor's novel, neatly encapsulates Angel's attitude towards the purpose of art. Esme is painting some flowers in the brightly lit studio Angel has created for him at Paradise. Angel asks him why his painting is so dark, telling him that his flowers look nothing like reality. 'Since when was my darling Angel so interested in reality?' asks Esme. 'Everything you write is complete fantasy.' 'But I am not interested in what's real, but what's beautiful', retorts Angel.

As Mantel explains, Angel's world is constructed through sheer force of will that blocks anything that might disrupt it, but it is riddled with cliché and melodramatic excess, identifiably bad art. Ozon reports that some viewers were shocked by the very idea of being interested in the production of bad art (Rouyer 2007: 23). The question remains for us as to whether Ozon's entrance into Angel's world is also bad art, or a deliberately trashy and camp pastiche that wants to allow us both to identify with Angel's longing to transcend banal everyday life and to criticise her inability to see beyond her own narrow concerns. Philip Kemp tends to the former view, commenting that 'the film is marred by clumsiness, or perhaps carelessness, including some shaky special effects' (Kemp 2008: 50). Ozon admits in interview to Rouyer that using back projection to show Angel's travels was obviously useful in terms of budget, but stresses also that it suited his aesthetic and narrative vision (Rouyer 2007: 23). Rear projection is achieved through a 'process shot', that is to say, one that mixes direct-to-camera action with other more or less synthetic elements. This special effect is achieved using transparencies (also known as plates) and represents an attempt to reconcile the desire for star performances with the need for action sequences. It is a technique associated especially with the Hollywood studio era, where it was routinely used as a cost-saving measure and can be found in films by such canonical directors as Hitchcock (*Marnie*, 1964) or Preminger (*River of No Return*, 1954). Landscape or cityscape footage, often filmed by a second unit or extracted from a studio library, was projected in a specialised studio onto a screen; then as the actors played their scene (with as little extra movement as possible), screen and studio would be filmed together.

As Laura Mulvey argues, 'nothing divides the history of cinema into pre- and post-digital so clearly as the world of special effects and nowhere is this clearer than in the disappearance of rear or back projection' (Mulvey 2007: 3). Mulvey goes on to comment that the technique thus introduces a 'dual temporality' into the image: two diverse registration times are montaged into one image (Mulvey 2007: 3). While this is true of any photographic superimposition, the dramatic difference between the documentary nature of the landscape footage and the artificiality of the studio scene heightens the sense of temporal dislocation. Furthermore, as the actors stay still, rooted to one spot, often facing artificial wind or water or vertiginous height, their performances become mannered and excessive: 'self-conscious, vulnerable, transparent' (Mulvey 2007: 3). Mulvey coins the term 'a clumsy sublime' to refer to the glaring artifice and implausibility of the sequences that invites a different kind of viewing response from the spectator. Mulvey's point is that rear projection was rarely intended to be noticed at the time of its production, but now, in hindsight, it has become evocative of the bygone studio era, rather like Technicolor, and that we cannot fail but notice its use and the clumsy effort of performance it demands from its actors. The clumsy sublime destabilises our ontological assumptions about how the image was made (indeed, its impact stems from our sudden awareness that the image we are watching is precisely an artificially manufactured image). Illusions originally meant as realistic representations that would lure the audience into the storyworld of the Hollywood film acquire with age a doubled resonance, inviting both an ironic awareness of the limitations of 1950s studio technology *and* an emotional revisiting of the aura of movie magic. Ozon's knowing use of anachronistic techniques holds in tension the different registers of the film, involving us in its storyworld while also distancing us from it through drawing our attention to its fictional, constructed nature. I have commented elsewhere on its particular suitability for a project that self-consciously plays with the costume drama, disowning the naturalist slant of most heritage cinema and literary adaptations, and rather drawing our attention to how our view of the past is always a kind of fiction (Handyside 2011: 63).

This combination of emotional identification with and ironic distance from the trials and tribulations of Angel resonates with Richard Dyer's argument about the function of pastiche. For Dyer, pastiche is not merely a second-rate imitation. The point of a pastiche is not to be indistinguishable from its source. Pastiche, argues Dyer, is able to mobilise structures of feeling. Discussing Todd Haynes's Sirk pastiche *Far From Heaven* (2002), Dyer argues that although 'there were moments where I could not see the screen for crying' (2007: 174), he was also 'fully conscious of the way the film was doing Hollywood melodrama, was pastiche' (Dyer 2007: 174). Our emotions are historically and culturally shaped, and pastiche makes us aware of how situated we are in relation to these. We simultaneously realise that films like this are not made anymore, and are grateful for an ability to indulge nostalgically in one. At the same time, the film is able to differ in terms of form and content from an actual 1950s melodrama.

For *Angel*, in terms of form, cinematography plays an important role. Cinematographer Denis Lenoir shot on 35mm but also makes use of digital colour grading, such as in the night-for-night sequence where Angel and Theo gaze at Paradise through dusk. Although the scene is nearly black-and-white, Sam Neill's face is flesh coloured, and the car headlights shine out yellow, which would be impossible without modern technology. In terms of content, consider the scene where we see Esme and Angel have sex on their return from honeymoon, and we subsequently see Angel sitting naked at her desk, writing about her happiness. There is no such discussion of sexual pleasure in the novel. Once Esme returns from war, Angel finds it difficult to re-establish their sexual intimacy. We see him drunkenly forcing himself on his wife, prising her legs open, with Angel terrified and disgusted by his violence; Nora resorts to hitting him with his cane to get him to stop attacking Angel. This is a scene entirely missing from the source text and graphic in its display of sexual violence. As Alice Stanley points out, the numerous comparisons critics make to *Gone with the Wind* (Fleming, 1939) is instructive here (Stanley 2009: 113). It is implied that Scarlett is raped by Rhett while he is drunk; the next day, realising that it was a vain attempt at intimacy, Rhett leaves her. Later, it is Rhett's impulsive, angry behaviour that causes Scarlett to fall down the stairs and miscarry her resulting pregnancy. Stanley comments that:

> *Angel*'s depiction of miscarriage and rape is far more explicit and underlines the fact that women's lives were not – maybe still are not – represented cinematically in a way that corresponds to female lived experience . . . [T]he story reveals that real women do not live in the world of 1950s melodrama; she is physically unwell and yearns for her husband, while at the same time not wanting to tell Esme about the miscarriage in fear that he will not understand this 'failure'. (Stanley 2009: 113)

While Angel might sincerely believe in her vision of beauty and the force of fantasy, Ozon's film reminds its viewers of women's relative lack of control compared to men as they are much more likely to be victims of sexual violence, an issue that the 1950s melodramas he pastiches can only tackle obliquely. While Stanley's reading of the film emphasises its indebtedness to the women's film, Sonia Amalia Haiduc studies it as a fictionalised biopic. Like the biopic, it follows its subject from childhood to death, but it also subverts the preferred narrative trajectory of the genre, showing a life that ends in failure rather than triumph. 'Along the way it asks the audience to question its assumptions as to who deserves to be elevated and allowed entrance into the pantheon of cultural mythology' (Haiduc 2020: 40). She draws our attention in particular to moments where Ozon uses one of the most familiar tropes of the literary biopic – that of written text superimposed over the body of the author as a means of signalling the similarities between the body of the author and the body of work (Figure 10.3).

For Haiduc, given we know how vacuous Angel's work is, this trope signals the lack of emotional weight and depth of the character. It is worth attending here to how Ozon edits this scene, however. We have Angel lying naked in bed, writing on a portable écritoire. A white sheet and a red blanket frame her slim waist rising from her barely visible buttocks, and we see the smooth curve of her breast. Nora comes into the room and nearly drops her tea-tray, overcome

Figure 10.3 Angel massaged by Nora

with desire for Angel. The next image is the most physical intimacy we ever see between the two women, as Nora massages Angel's buttocks and back as writing is superimposed over the image. While Angel and her writing might be silly and solipsistic, the edit of this scene also associates them with Nora's immense pleasure that the text is barely able to articulate, suggesting the powerful intra-feminine connections that might be established in works that on the outside seem only shallow folly.

CONCLUSION

The notion of a 'politics of form' with *Angel* might be most closely discerned in its obvious relationship to classic melodramas of thwarted female desire such as *Gone with the Wind*, *Letter from An Unknown Woman* (Ophüls, 1948) and *All That Heaven Allows* (Sirk, 1955). This is because melodrama remains one of cinema's most productive modes, rescued out of obscurity by feminist critics in a vast, still ongoing project of reassessment and redefinition as a coherent aesthetic system with definite features. Christine Gledhill's introductory chapter to the seminal *Home Is Where the Heart Is* identifies how melodrama's dismissal as 'bad art' at the beginning of the twentieth century enabled it to be 'the anti-value for a critical field in which tragedy and realism became cornerstones of "high" cultural value, needing protection from mass, "melodramatic" entertainment' (Gledhill 1987: 5). In a later discussion, she points to the term's continuing effect: 'melodrama provokes . . . anxiety of the establishment as to the cultural degeneration and insubordination of the lower orders' (Gledhill 2000: 222). This assessment demonstrates the suspicions of sentimental feminine culture aimed at women, seen as mawkish trash rather than anything akin to art. This work nourishes of course exactly the fantasies that women might indulge of love, sex, romance and marriage. In the double bind typical of patriarchy, women are offered a small amount of approved cultural space for the exploration of the tensions and compromises that heterosexual desire demands of them, and an even smaller arena for queer longings, then denigrated for their enjoyment of that very cultural space.

Ozon's film self-consciously plays with the gendered question of the relation between mass melodramatic entertainment and modernist high art through embodying them in the differences between Angel and Esme. Angel produces highly popular work that its audience laps up with a complete failure of necessary critical distance. In a brief montage sequence showing Angel's rapid rise to fame and prodigious production of new books, the audience at her book signing is shown as exclusively female. This general illustration of worshipping female adoration of Angel's cringeworthy fiction is particularised in the figure of Nora. Upon first meeting Angel at a reception hosted by her uncle, Lord Norley (Christopher Benjamin), Nora prostrates herself before Angel and kisses her hand. She gives up her own poetry writing to be Angel's (unpaid?) servant. By the end of her life, Angel's books have already been forgotten. In contrast, Esme produces austerely modernist painting in the style of Lucian Freud. Although he receives no recognition during his lifetime, after his death, a young male art critic visits Angel asking for permission to photograph his work and praising his 'restricted palette', saying that audiences are now ready for it. In a rather neat and enjoyable Ozonian twist, perhaps our response to his film might be to imagine Ozon himself as either Angel or Esme, producing either a lush overblown melodrama as light relief for silly women or a clever modernist work of art that its audience isn't yet quite ready for.

WORKS CITED

Asibong, Andrew (2008), *François Ozon*, Manchester: Manchester University Press.
Blouin, Patrice (2007), 'Angel', *Les Inrockuptibles*, 589, https://www.lesinrocks.com/cinema/films-a-l-affiche/angel (last accessed 25 October 2020).
Downing, Lisa (2019), *Selfish Women*, London: Routledge.
Dyer, Richard (2007), *Pastiche*, London: Routledge.
Gledhill, Christine (1987), *Home Is Where the Heart Is: Studies in Melodrama and the Women's Film*, London: BFI.
Gledhill, Christine (2000), 'Rethinking Genre', in Christine Gledhill and Linda Williams (eds), *Reinventing Film Studies* (London: Arnold), pp. 221–43.
Haiduc, Sonia Amalia (2020), 'Biopics and the Melodramatic Mode' in Deborah Cartmell and Ashley P. Polasek (eds), *A Companion to the Biopic*, Hoboken, NJ: John Wiley and Sons, pp. 23–44.

Hain, Mark (2007), 'Explicit Ambiguity: Sexual Identity, Hitchcockian Criticism, and the Films of François Ozon', *Quarterly Review of Film and Video*, 24: 3, pp. 277–88.
Handyside, Fiona (2011), 'Queer Filiations: Adaptation in the Films of François Ozon', *Sexualities*, 15: 1, pp. 53–67.
Kemp, Philip (2008), 'Angel', *Sight and Sound*, 18: 9, p. 50.
Lévesque, François (2008), 'François Ozon où l'imaginaire comme réalité', *Le Dévoir*, 7 June, <https://www.ledevoir.com/culture/cinema/193003/francois-ozon-ou-l-imaginaire-comme-realite> (last accessed 25 October 2020).
Mayne, Judith (1993), *Cinema and Spectatorship*, London: Routledge.
Morrey, Douglas (2020), *The Legacy of the New Wave in French Cinema*, London: Bloomsbury.
Mulvey, Laura (2007), 'A Clumsy Sublime', *Film Quarterly* 60: 3, p. 3
Piazzo, Philippe (2003), 'François Ozon: "On se définit aussi par ses fantasmes"', *Le Monde*, 21 May.
Rouyer, Philippe (2007), 'Entretien avec François Ozon: L'ironie et l'émotion', *Positif*, 553, pp. 21–5.
Schilt, Thibaut (2011), *François Ozon*, Urbana, IL: University of Illinois Press.
Stanley, Alice (2009), 'Representations of Sexuality in the films of François Ozon', Unpublished PhD thesis, University of Warwick.
Taylor, Elizabeth (2006 [1957]), *Angel* [with an introduction by Hilary Mantel], London: Virago.

CHAPTER II

From *Faits Divers* to *Grandes Affaires*: Giving Voice to Sexual Abuse Survivors in *Grâce à Dieu*

Levilson C. Reis

> 'Ce film est une fiction, basé sur des faits réels'.
> *Grâce à Dieu / By the Grace of God* (2018)

The critical assessment that François Ozon has been gratuitously transgressive in his treatment of human sexuality and iconoclastic in his engagement with social issues and institutions, deliberately shirking any sense of social responsibility, is a commonplace in film reviews and academic criticism of his early works. To cite one such example, Alice Stanley observes that Ozon is wont to 'allude to a hotly debated topic only then to fail to engage with the issue in a politically committed, some might say responsible, or "realist" manner' (Stanley 2009: 43). This reluctance to explicitly express a political stance on a current social problem is indeed idiosyncratic, but, as Asibong (2005), Ince (2008) and San Filippo (2016) argue, it does not mean that Ozon's films are apolitical. Those familiar with contemporary French culture cannot ignore the dialogue that Ozon's latest productions have held with *faits divers* (sensational news items) and especially those which have turned into national socio-political issues or *grandes affaires*. *Jeune & jolie / Young & Beautiful* (2013) and *Une Nouvelle amie / The New Girlfriend* (2014), for example, re-enact previous dialogues with national debates surrounding prostitution and same-gender marriage, respectively.[1]

Tackling the child abuse scandal in the French Catholic Church, *Grâce à Dieu / By the Grace of God* (2018) stands as the latest example of Ozon's engagement with *faits divers* turned *grandes affaires*. Based on the case of Father Bernard Preynat, a Lyonnais priest who molested over eighty boys under his leadership at the Scout Group Saint-Luc in Sainte-Foy-lès-Lyon, *Grâce à Dieu* tells of the struggles faced by three fictional sexual abuse survivors as they seek to bring to justice the priest who abused them and his superior, who had allegedly failed to report their cases to the civil authorities. By situating this story in the director's filmography and the ongoing growing Catholic Church's paedophilia scandal, this chapter aims to limn an evolution in aesthetics and representational politics instead of a sudden change of direction. In *Grâce à Dieu*, Ozon uses the power of film narrative not only to transform the secretive and unspeakable experiences of sexual abuse into an accessible story but also to give voice to those who have been silenced.

Although sexual abuse has been a recurrent theme in a number of Ozon's shorts and early features, two episodes from *Sitcom* (2003) and *Les Amants criminels / Criminal Lovers* (2001) offer the most relevant context for *Grâce à Dieu*. In *Sitcom*, after Nicolas (Adrien de Van) announces at the dinner table that he is gay, Abdu (Jules-Emmanuel Eyoum Deido), one of the dinner guests, a black gym teacher, is sent to talk to the teenage boy and assess the situation. In the bedroom, Abdu ascertains that Nicolas has never had sex with a man and offers himself for experimentation. Abdu undoes his bow tie and snaps his tuxedo shirt open to reveal his muscular chest: 'Moi, je te fais de l'effet?' ('Do I turn you on?').[2] The scene follows the script of a homoerotic scene: 'Ça te plaît?' ('Do you like what you see?'). He tells Nicolas to touch his chest and, while holding the boy's hand in place, Abdu kisses the young man passionately on the mouth. Maria (Lucia Sanchez) would later disclose that her husband, Abdu, lost his teaching job because he was accused of molesting his students.

In *Les Amants criminels / Criminal Lovers*, Luc (Jérémie Renier) plans and executes the murder of a fellow student, Saïd (Salim Kechiouche), to avenge his girlfriend Alice's (Natacha Régnier) reported gang rape. After having disposed of Saïd's body in the woods, Alice and Luc get lost and chance upon a cottage which they break into to find food and water. The owner (Predag 'Miki' Manojlović) surprises them and keeps them prisoner in his basement until he expresses a sexual interest in Luc. One day, he orders Luc to give him a bath in the tub at gun point and then they switch roles. In another sequence, the woodsman tells Luc to get into bed with him, as Alice watches from the basement. At the end of the film, the woodsman ties Luc to the bed and forcibly sodomises him. As the woodsman sleeps after the sex scene, Luc and Alice make a run for it only to be hunted down by the gendarmes who are looking for them. Luc is subdued, Alice is shot down, and the woodsman is taken away as Luc screams from the police wagon that 'il n'a rien fait' ('he didn't do anything').

In *Grâce à Dieu*, Ozon abandons such tendentiously fantasy-driven *mises-en-scène* of sexual abuse and engages with real-life cases in the context of social, political and institutional debates. The treatment of sexual abuse is premised on the child abuse scandal in the Catholic Church of Lyon that surfaced in

2014 as a result of a complaint by Alexandre Hezez, one of the sexual abuse victims of Father Bernard Preynat. Although allegations of sexual abuse in the French Catholic Church have been documented since 2000, the magnitude of the problem did not come under the national spotlight until the scandal broke out worldwide. In France, the tv news magazine 'Cash Investigation', in collaboration with *Mediapart*, an online news magazine, conducted a year-long investigation to unearth a systemic cover-up of allegations of sexual abuse by priests in the French Catholic Church since 1960. Their investigations were aired on 21 March 2017, in a programme entitled 'Pédophilie dans l'Église: le poids du silence' ('Paedophiles in the Church: The Burden of Silence') in which it was revealed that twenty-five bishops were aware that a priest in their respective dioceses had been accused of sexual misconduct and, instead of reporting them as the law requires, they routinely reassigned the culprits to other parishes in France or abroad.[3] Philippe Barbarin, Cardinal of the Archdiocese of Lyon, is the latest to be convicted for the same charge and remains arguably the most notorious, given his status as the Primat des Gaules (Primate of Gaul), the media coverage and the release of *Grâce à Dieu*, a partly documentary partly fictional representation of the Catholic Church's paedophilia scandal in Lyon.

FICTIONAL DOCUMENTARY: 'EMPLOTTING' REAL-LIFE AND SCREEN STORIES

As the film's epigraph announces, *Grâce à Dieu* presents itself as a fictional adaptation of a true story. The struggles faced by Alexandre Guérin (Melvil Poupaud), François Debord (Denis Ménochet) and Emmanuel Thomassin (Swann Arlaud) are accordingly based on Alexandre Hezez's, François Devaux's and Pierre Emmanuel Germain-Thill's real-life stories and their joint efforts to get Father Bernard Preynat prosecuted for sexual abuse and Philippe Barbarin for 'non-dénonciation d'aggressions sexuelles sur mineurs et non assistance à personne en péril' (CAL 2019: 13; 'not reporting sexual abuse of minors and not providing assistance to persons in danger'). The fact that Ozon changed the victims' surnames but kept the real names of the accused belies the claim that *Grâce à Dieu* is an exclusively fictional adaptation of a true story, however.

In fact, Ozon draws rather closely on the facts of the case and the personal stories of three survivors to 'emplot' the film narrative of *Grâce à Dieu*. 'Emplotment', as Hayden White (1978: esp. 84) and Paul Ricœur (1991) conceptualise it, entails bringing together conflicting sides of historical and personal facts into a narrative with a plot. In the film, Ozon does indeed bring together 'a multitude of written and oral words – emails, letters, testimonies, complaints, minutes, expert reports, interviews, confessions, press conferences, hearings'

(Ozon 2019: 5). As Ricœur goes on, this type of emplotment also 'organises together components that are as heterogeneous as unintended circumstances, discoveries, those who perform actions and those who suffer them, chance or planned encounters, interactions between actors ranging from conflict to collaboration' (1991: 21). The film narrative accomplishes all that while situating each one of the three survivors in his respective social, economic, ideological and familial milieu. It shows the effect that experiences of sexual abuse have on the young men's lives and how they cope both individually and collectively (in the context of their familial and professional lives) when they discover that their predator is back in office. To better understand the interplay between reality and fiction in *Grâce à Dieu*, it would be helpful to establish a baseline against which one may assess how Ozon makes screen stories out of real lives.

Alexandre Hezez has kept his personal life private. The little we know about it is gleaned from his LinkedIn account, personal interviews, newspaper articles and court documents. From 1986 to 1995, he started out as a boarder at the Lazaristes school, and later attended the Lycée Sainte-Marie, specialising in mathematics. He then pursued a degree in financial and actuarial sciences at the Université Claude Bernard Lyon 1, and in 1998 received a master's in actuarial science from the Institut de sciences financières et d'assurances. Since then, he has worked in the field of finance and actuarial science, most recently at investment firm Richelieu Gestion. For professional reasons, Alexandre always kept a low profile as he fought against the Catholic Church's cover-up of the Saint-Luc sexual abuse.

Of the three survivors, Alexandre has always been the most faithful to the Church. Up until 2014, he had been a devout Catholic, avid reader of the Bible, and an assiduous churchgoer. In an interview, Alexandre admitted that, although he did not agree with Cardinal Barbarin on some issues, 'he admired [Barbarin's] sermons and his service to Orthodox Christians. He had personally officiated the confirmation of my two children. For me, he was someone I found to be honest' (Mongaillard 2019). The reference to Barbarin's confirmation ceremony of Alexandre's oldest children depicts the Hezez as a practising Catholic family with close contacts with the Church's highest office. Accordingly, when Alexandre found out that Father Preynat was back in office at a nearby parish, he trusted that Barbarin would resolve the issue.

In July 2014, Alexandre emailed Philippe Barbarin via Pierre Durieux, the cardinal's cabinet manager, to reveal for the first time that 'during almost two years of boy scout service, between the ages of nine and eleven, I was repeated molested by the priest who was in charge of the boy scouts' (CAL 2019: 9–10). He ended his email by asking Pierre Durieux very pointed questions: 'How is it possible? Were you aware of it? Was he punished? Were his actions condemned? Why is this man still taking care of children?' (CAL 2019: 10).

When he realised that none of his questions and demands would be answered, Alexandre filed the complaint that would launch the investigation and provide the source of inspiration for *Grâce à Dieu*.

François Devaux stands as the most outspoken survivor. François was ten years old when Preynat molested him, according to his testimony on the 'Parole Libérée' website.[4] Back at home, François told his older brother that Father Preynat had kissed him on the mouth. He immediately told his parents and, on 14 February 1991, M. and Mme Devaux wrote a letter to the then cardinal Decourtray to denounce the 'perversions sexuelles' ('sexual perversions') that Father Preynat 'exerted on the some children of the Saint-Luc parish scouts group' (CAL 2019: 12) and to demand that Preynat be removed from the Saint-Luc scouts group immediately. A week later, Father Preynat responded to François's parents by mail.[5] All things considered, Preynat was more concerned about the urgency of their demand for his departure than the gravity of the situation.

When he found out, as a result of Alexandre's complaint, that Father Preynat was still in contact with children after his parents had reported him decades earlier, François decided to contact the media. He was behind some of the earliest media reports on the case in *Le Progrès* and the *Tribune de Lyon* (see Breuil 2015; Comte 2015). With the help of social media networks, he led an all-out effort to locate classmates that may have been abused and whose cases had not yet fallen under the statute of limitations. When Bertrand Virieux came forward, François founded (with Bernard) the sexual abuse survivor group 'La Parole Libérée'. On 12 January 2016, as the president of the association, François organised a press conference to publicise the sexual abuse case and to call the current cardinal to task.[6] François and his group therefore played a vital role in helping other victims (including Alexandre Hezez) come forward and open up publicly about what happened to them.

Pierre-Emmanuel Germain-Thill may have had the least stable life of the three survivors. He never told his parents about Father Preynat's sexual abuse because he was never able to, as he put it, 'really explain the priest's actions towards him to his mother when he was a little boy, and that he lived since with this memory buried deep within him' (CAL 2019: 15). Even if he'd tried, he thought nobody would have believed him. Therefore, he kept his experiences of sexual abuse to himself.

The traumatic experience impacted several aspects of his life. As Pierre-Emmanuel intimates in a *Euronews* interview, '[t]hat led me to challenge authority, since there is a spiritual abuse, and an abuse of the priest's authority. As a result, I then rejected the authority of my parents, my teachers, and my employers' (Gauriat 2019). Because of the chaos that such a recalcitrance caused, as he puts it in his personal website, he dropped out of high school without getting his baccalaureate (Germain-Thill 2018). As a result, he had a number of business-related odd jobs, working as a cashier, usher, deliverer, accountant and manager in some well-known companies (Carrefour, Euronews, Staübli, Bureau Véritas, LAB S.A., Contenur and La Poste).

The abuse Pierre-Emmanuel suffered also affected his social and sexual life: 'It's difficult for me to have a relationship [. . .] to think about someone touching my body or me touching someone else. It's things like that that still penalize me in my life today' (Gauriat 2019). It was not until he joined the survivors' group 'La Parole Libérée' that Pierre-Emmanuel found a more stable path. As he confesses, '[i]n January 2016, the biggest drama of my life came out into the open, as it did for many men, and allowed me to free myself from an immense weight' (Germain-Thill 2018). In 2018, he went back to school to become a certified personal, life, and business coach. He has his own coaching business in Lyon, while teaching part-time at Coaching Ways France, from where he graduated.

Father Bernard Preynat was a charismatic man, adored by the parents of Saint-Luc's boy scouts. After the Devaux's complaint, Cardinal Decourtray transferred Preynat to 'La Petite sœur des pauvres', a senior-citizen church facility, where he would not have any contact with children. It was discovered that he was back in the Lyon area six months later, ministering in pastoral schools.

If Father Preynat had only recently gained notoriety as the allegations of sexual abuse became public, Cardinal Philippe Barbarin, the Archbishop of Lyon, had been nationally known as a staunch opponent of marriage for all and of adoption, and as a defender of a heteronormative family structure.[7] When Ozon was making *Une Nouvelle amie / The New Girlfriend*, Barbarin was already a notorious opponent of same-sex marriage and a fierce advocate for the right of a child to have a mother and father and not same-sex parents. In *Une Nouvelle amie / The New Girlfriend*, when Claire finds out that David cross-dresses, David begs Claire not to tell his ultra-Catholic mother-in-law, fearing that he will lose custody of little Lucie. In *Grâce à Dieu*, Barbarin plays, contrapuntally, an equally notorious intra-diegetic role, accused of covering up Bernard Preynat's sexual abuse by failing to report the incidents to the authorities.

THE IDEOLOGICAL APPARATUS OF *GRÂCE À DIEU*

Before the screen stories of Alexandre, François and Emmanuel begin, the film foregrounds the power of the Catholic Church of Lyon as both an ideological and repressive state apparatus. As Louis Althusser (1976) theorises it, the ideological state apparatus (ISA) uses ideology to interpellate and repress subjects. The 'religious ISA' relies on not only ideology (its system of beliefs, its iconic representation, its mode of communication, and the imaginary relationship that this ideological apparatus forges between individuals and their life styles), but also its practices and rituals. In Christian religious ideology, the Church exercises power through the word and discourse. As Althusser puts it, it interpellates its subjects through 'what it "says" not only in its two Testaments, its Theologians, Sermons, but also in its practices, its rituals, its ceremonies and its sacraments' (Althusser 1976: 116; Brewster 2001: 120). The religious individual 'goes to Church to attend Mass, kneels, prays, confesses, does penance . . . and naturally repents and so on' (Althusser 1976: 106–7; Brewster 2001: 113). This archetype of the faithful subject of the religious ISA informs the fictional character of Alexandre Guérin.

Sandwiched between the film's epigraph and Alexandre's testimony, the establishing shot shows Cardinal Barbarin using the Blessed Sacrament to tell the story of Christ's passion and the power of redemption. The film opens with a prayer from Cardinal Barbarin (François Marthouret) in voiceover as he walks to the parapet of Notre-Dame de Fourvière's esplanade, holding up the Blessed Sacrament:

Seigneur Jésus-Christ,
Dans cet admirable sacrement, tu nous as laissé le mémorial de ta passion.
Donne-nous, de vénérer d'un si grand amour, le mystère de ton corps
    et de ton sang.
Que nous puissions recueillir sans cesse le fruit de ta rédemption.
Toi qui règnes pour des siècles et des siècles. Amen.[8]

The voiced-over prayer reiterates the power of the religious state apparatus, making its ideology (and discursive mode) weigh upon its flocks, even if its secondary repressive function remains, as Althusser would qualify, 'attenuated, concealed, even symbolic' (Althusser 1976: 85; Brewster 2001: 98). The religious ideology of the power of redemption, always accompanied by prayer, becomes a leitmotif in Father Preynat's and Barbarin's interactions with Alexandre and his family.

The first sequence situates Alexandre Guérin as the patriarch of a very Catholic family. He is married and father to five children: Victor (Nicolas Bauwens), Gauthier (Max Libert), Gaspard (Timi-Joy Marbot), Côme (Zuri François) and Lila (Zéli Marbot). They are named after traditional biblical figures or saints. The opening scene shows Alexandre sitting in the apartment's living room, reading the local newspaper, next to his son Gaspard who is reading a book while a non-diegetic sonata plays in the background. The newspaper and the paratextual date of 'June 2014', visible on the lower third of the screen, add a reality effect to a narrative that seamlessly weaves real-life facts and fiction (Figure 11.1). In the next shot, Alexandre gets up, telling his wife Marie (Aurélia Petit) that it is time to leave for church. The camera pans right to show his daughter Lila sitting at the dinner table and Marie summoning the older boys (Victor and Gauthier). As soon as Marie comes into the picture, Alexandre introduces himself and the premise of the film via a non-diegetic voiceover, as he and his family walk to church:

> Je m'appelle Alexandre Guérin, j'ai 40 ans, je suis marié et père de cinq enfants qui sont scolarisés aux Lazaristes à Lyon, où ma femme est elle-même enseignante . . . J'ai croisé il y quelque temps le père d'un petit garçon dans la même école que mes fils. Comme . . . il était aux scouts de Saint-Luc à Sainte-Foy-lès-Lyon, nous nous sommes rappelé nos souvenirs d'enfance, l'école, les camps de scouts. . . et il m'a posé cette question qui trotte toujours dans ma tête: 'Toi, aussi, tu t'es fait tripoter par le père Preynat?'[9]

Despite the abuse, Alexandre continues to be a practising Catholic. He got married in the Church and has raised his family 'in the love of the Lord'. His children go to the local Catholic school. He attends mass at Notre-Dame de Fourvière at least once a week. Mirroring the confirmation of Alexandre Hezez's children in real life, Ozon stages Victor's and Gauthier's confirmations in the film to paint the Guérins as a practising Catholic family, although, by 2014, Alexandre Hezez had in reality began to distance himself from the Church (Gauriat 2019). As we have seen, when Alexandre finds out that Father Preynat, who (he thought) had been relieved of his duties in 1991, is still ministering in the Lyon area and possibly still in contact with children, he writes to Philippe Barbarin, the current Cardinal of Lyon.

Figure 11.1 Alexandre reads a newspaper

The opening shot's voiceover narrative turns into Alexandre's reading of an email he is writing to Cardinal Barbarin, where he confesses to having been sexually abused by Father Preynat: 'For almost two years at the scouts group, between nine and twelve years old, I was sexually abused by priest Bernard Preyant' (CAL 2019: 9–10). This sentence echoes almost exactly what Alexandre Hezez wrote to Cardinal Barbarin in 2014, as the transcript of the trial documents show. So does the ending of the email, as Alexandre Guérin's final questions mirror those that Alexandre Hezez posed to Pierre Durieux, the cardinal's secretary.

In subsequent meetings with cardinal's secretary and the cardinal himself, Alexandre Guérin begins to question religious ideology on principle. Despite the power of the religious ideological apparatus, as Althusser affirms:

> [E]very 'subject' endowed with a 'consciousness' and believing in the 'ideas' that his 'consciousness' inspires in him and freely accepts, must '*act* according to his ideas' must therefore inscribe his own ideas as a free subject in the actions of his material practice. (Althusser 1976: 107; Brewster 2001: 113)

The one time they meet, Alexandre and Barbarin end up disagreeing over the terminology that would best characterise Preynat's sexual misconduct. When Alexandre calls it paedophilia, the cardinal cuts him off to tell him not to use that term. He draws Alexandre's attention to the etymological and ideological senses of 'paedophile', reaffirming that it means 'aimer les enfants' ('to love children') and that, according to the Lord, 'il faut aimer les enfants, pas trop évidemment' ('one must love children, but not too much, obviously'). Resorting to the latest neologism, Alexandre proposes the term 'pédosexuel' ('pedosexual') instead, which Barbarin deems a suitable compromise. In a follow-up meeting with Pierre Durieux, Alexandre makes a more intelligent distinction between homosexuality and paedophilia, drawing a line between sexual orientation and criminal perversion. These passing remarks echo similar distinctions made by Ozon between sexuality, sex work, and prostitution in *Jeune & jolie / Young & Beautiful*, and gender and sexuality in *Une Nouvelle amie / The New Girlfriend*. It is the Church's intransigence that brings us back to the matter at hand, as Durieux categorically affirms that Preynat would always remain a priest, and it is precisely that which finally leads Alexandre to file a complaint with the state attorney.

With the exception of François Debord, the Catholic flock in *Grâce à Dieu* is aware of the repressive power of the Catholic Church of Lyon and appears to harbour an internalised fear of the institution, of Philippe Barbarin, and of his influence. Unlike the faithful and dutiful Alexandre Guérin, François Debord incarnates the archetype of the free-willed religious ISA subject who believes in justice. As Althusser informs us: 'If he believes in justice, he will submit unconditionally to the rules of the Law, and may even protest when they are violated, sign petitions, take part in a demonstration, etc.' (Althusser 1976: 107; Brewster 2001: 113). When François Debord finds out in 2015 that Preynat is still in office working with school children, he decides to testify and alert the local media.

Before François meets Captain Courteau, his mother warns him that 'they' (the Church) are 'puissants' ('powerful'), so does his attorney, comparing the Church to 'une grosse machine' ('a big machine'). At the same time, François resorts to social networks such as 'Copains d'avant', LinkedIn and Facebook to get in contact with potential victims.[10] When Gilles Pérret (Éric Caravaca) comes forward, François proposes the creation of a sexual abuse survivors' association, 'La Parole Libérée', and a website as a platform for finding other victims. When Alexandre Guérin, tracked down by Gilles, meets François and learns about the plan to alert the media, he remains cautious, given his conservative professional field and the fact his wife still works for the Lazaristes Catholic school and his children are still pupils there.

Others voice a similar concern. After François appears on the news, Odile remarks that her Catholic bridge friends would not take her son's accusations lightly. After asking about François's 'Parole-Libérée' wrist band, the son of the biggest baker family in Lyon – his curiosity begging the question – declines to admit to François that he was also molested by Preynat, presumably for fear of having his business boycotted. Other sexual abuse victims remain unafraid, however. Gilles admits that half of his clients are, as he calls them, 'ultra-catho, tradi, ils soutiennent tous Barbarin à fond, "La Manif pour tous"' ('ultra-Catholic, traditional people, staunch supporters of Barbarin and the "Demonstrations for All"'), but he does not believe that he would lose his Lyon patients by standing up against paedophilia in the Catholic Church.

As a result of the media attention surrounding the case, Emmanuel Thomassin was the third victim to come forward, joining hands with François to press charges against Father Preynat. The last part of film narrative turns therefore to this youngest survivor, Emmanuel Thomassin (Swann Arlaud), who becomes the third full-time member of 'La Parole Libérée'. This segment's opening shot introduces the 34-year-old as something of a mummy's boy. The sequence starts with his mother, Irène (Josiane Balasko), clipping some newspaper articles. In the next sequence, a long shot of a motorcyclist type walking towards the entrance of an apartment building introduces Emmanuel, who comes to visit his mother and get his mail, under which he finds the newspaper articles his mother has clipped from the *fait divers* section of the local newspaper *Le Progrès* (Breuil 2015: 13). Here Ozon used the real article published in *Le Progrès*, blurring any distinction between fiction and reality. Soon after Emmanuel recovers from the shock, he clicks on the contact button of the 'La Parole Libérée' website and leaves an e-mail message, confirming that he

SEXUAL ABUSE SURVIVORS 205

was abused by Father Preynat from 1988 to 1991 and that he is eager to testify against him.

MORE TELLING THAN SHOWING

Ozon recounts the three men's individual experiences of sexual abuse in a quasi-documentary fashion but falls short of *showing* them on screen (Figure 11.2). After getting in contact with Cardinal Barbarin, Alexandre meets with the church psychologist Régine Maire (Martine Erhel) to tell his story and share two episodes of sexual abuse. He tells her about the Saturday afternoons in the parish church's photo lab:

> C'était sombre, tranquille. Il fermait la porte . . . me prenait dans ses bras. Il passait sa main dans mon short bleu marine, je ne bougeais pas. Il me serrait fort, très fort. Il m'embrassait dans le cou, se frottait contre ma jambe. Il me disait 'je t'aime'. Il respirait fort, très fort et puis plus rien.[11]

He also tells her what happened in a tent during the scout camp trip to Portugal in 1986:

> [L]e père Preynat me suit dans ma tente. Il m'allonge, se couche à côté de moi. Je sens son poids et son gros ventre sur moi. Et ça recommence . . . Il m'embrasse avec la langue. Il descend ma braguette. Il met sa main. Il se frotte. Il respire fort. Il amène ma main sur son sexe.[12]

Figure 11.2 Flashback to boy scout years

It is surprising that these very traumatic personal stories do not trigger flashbacks, the textbook 'mimetic representation of thought processes looking to the past, whether they may be [shown as] dreams, confessions or memories' (Hayward 2006: 156). Instead of the conventional flashback, Ozon relies more often on voiceover not only to convey back stories, but also to show characters releasing stored repressed memories. Character voiceover functions as a form of testimonial and confessional narrative device that creates a diegetic continuum between the sexual abuse survivor and the Church as an institution, Alexandre being the victim and Régine Maire the institution's representative.

It is an unexpected over-the-shoulder view (shot) of Father Preynat sitting in the church right before the mediation that Régine has arranged which makes Alexandre flash back to the tent episode in Portugal. The analeptic sequence is, however, for the most part silent (no accompanying testimonial voiceover), except for the diegetic noise of kids playing soccer, the dramatic non-diegetical musical score as Alexandre walks to his camp tent, and the audible (diegetical) noise of a zipper closing after Preynat follows little Alexandre into the tent. The sexual acts that Preynat imposes on him in the tent, which Alexandre recounts to Régine blow by blow, are not shown on screen, and neither are those that would take place in the photo lab on Saturday afternoons.

In his deposition to head of police Captain Courteau (Frédéric Pierrot), François recalls several similar instances of Preynat's snuggling him at the Saint-Luc church or during weekend outings, which he did not find out of the ordinary as he received similar attention from his father. The last contact was different, however. François tells Courteau how on one occasion at cub scouts ('aux louvetaux'), after cuddling with him, Preynat fondled his buttocks: 'We were alone, both of us. [. . .] He hugged me and, all of a sudden, he lifted my thigh to put his hand under my shorts and caress my buttocks.' In the film, François Debord's recollections are consistent with François Devaux's real-life experiences, as posted on the 'Parole Libérée' website (under the 'Témoignages' ('Testimonies') tab). The film never shows Preynat sexually abusing François, however.

Emmanuel's deposition finally synchronises flashback and (diegetic) voiceover seamlessly. After framing the circumstances of his moving from Strasbourg to Lyon in 1988 and joining the Saint-Luc boy scout group, the story flashes back to the beginning of 1989, when Emmanuel was eight years old. He narrates the flashback sequence as Captain Courteau's assistant types his deposition: 'He [had] asked me to come over to help him bring some stuff back to his office. I came in through the lower entrance on the right.' As the voiceover stops, the screen shows Emmanuel going up the stairs and then knocking on the photo lab door. Father Preynat opens up, lets him in, and closes the door. In the next shot, inside the dark photo lab, the camera shows Father Preynat sitting in front of little Emmanuel (standing up), and then jump cuts from a medium to a close two-shot as the father begins to touch Emmanuel's scarf. Right before the flashback stops, Emmanuel resumes his voiceover: 'Ça durait cinq à dix minutes, pas plus' ('It lasted 5 to 10 minutes, no more than that'). This is the most revealing of all the flashback sequences, for it shows Preynat fondling young Emmanuel's body.

The nature of these real-life sexual abuse cases recalls the two episodes in *Sitcom* and *Les Amants criminels / Criminal Lovers* in which an adult man takes advantage of a situation, however fantasy driven it may be, to make sexual advances towards a much younger partner. In *Sitcom*, the bite of a rat that drives everyone's latent desire to the surface may have led Abdu to offer himself to Nicolas, not because he genuinely meant to give the boy a sense of what it felt like to be gay but because he was a closet paedophile. In *Les Amants criminels / Criminal Lovers*, while the ogre-ish woodsman may feel justified to punish the intruders, forcing the boy to have sex with him at gunpoint or tethered to the bed constitutes a criminal act. One distinction to be made between the woodsman and Luc, and Preynat and his victims concerns the victims' ages, which also defines the nature of the crime, according to the French penal code, even though some scholars have qualified the woodsman and Luc's relations as 'paedophiliac' (Asibong 2005: 211; Schilt 2011: 54). That may very well explain why the flashbacks were cut short, since the French penal code also forbids filming of minors in a sexual context.

I would argue that Ozon uses François Debord's memories to draw attention to M. and Mme Debord's reactions to Preynat's sexual abuse and the actions that they took to stop him from further hurting their son. In a classic flashback, the camera goes from a close-up of François as an adult to François as an eleven-year-old boy scout, walking towards his parents, who waste no time in laying down the law, forbidding him to go on the next camping trip to Ireland:

> M. Debord: 'François, est-ce que tu peux venir, s'il te plaît?'
> Mme Debord: 'Ce que t'a fait le père Preynat, c'est mal et c'est interdit par la loi. Un prêtre n'embrasse pas un enfant sur la bouche et ne lui touche pas les fesses. Il peut aller en prison pour ça.'
> Little François: 'Je ne veux pas qu'il aille en prison.'
> M. Debord: 'Oui, François, mais on ne peut pas y rien faire! Il n'avait pas le droit de faire ce qu'il t'a fait.'[13]

In reality, M. and Mme Devaux write a letter to Cardinal Decourtray on 14 February 1991, to report Father Preynat and demand that he leave the parish immediately (CAL 2019: 12). The Devaux's complaint led to the ousting of Father Preynat from the boy scout group of the Church of Saint-Luc in Sainte-Foy-lès-Lyon.

M. and Mme Debord's complaint brings us full circle on the fictional–documentary continuum. When Alexandre files a complaint with the state attorney (le Procureur de la République), the police investigation reveals that, six months after being dismissed from ministerial duties, Bernard Preynat was officiating in a number of local parishes in the Loire and Rhône departments (Neulise [Loire], Cours-la-Ville [Rhône], Le Coteau [Loire], and Saint-Priest-la-Roche [Loire]), and had been working at the École Saint-Marc, a private Catholic school in Le Coteau. The *Tribune de Lyon* newspaper publishes two follow-ups of its own investigation in October 2015 and January 2016, when Bernard Preynat was finally charged for sexual abuse of minors (Comte 2015, 2016). The civil trial was deferred to a later date but, in the meantime, the Catholic Church's ecclesiastical court found him guilty of sexual abuse on 4 July 2019. According to the communiqué, the facts of the case, the recurrence of the abuse, the number of victims and Preynat's abuse of a leadership position weighed heavily on the decision to defrock him of his ecclesiastical status (ECL 2019).

As the release date of Ozon's *mise-en-scène* of the whole affair in *Grâce à Dieu* neared, both Bernard Preynat and Régine Maire tried to block the premiere of the movie for being portrayed in the film by their real names. Bernard Preynat's attorney claimed that the direct implication of his client in the affair could prejudice his trial and requested that the movie not be released until the trial was over. Ozon argued that everything the movie presented had already been publicised in the media. The court eventually rejected the request for the injunctions.[14] In the meantime, Philippe Barbarin was also charged for not reporting Father Preynat to the civil authorities. His trial took place on 7–10 January 2019, and *Grâce à Dieu* premiered on 20 February 2019, before the court released the verdict on the case. On 7 March 2019, Lyon's high court sentenced Barbarin to a six-month suspended sentence, which a local appeals court reversed on 30 January 2020, acquitting the cardinal of all charges and finding no intentional cover-up in his handling of sexual abuse. Bernard Preynat was convicted of sexual abuse and sentenced to five years in prison on 16 March 2020.

CONCLUSION

While Ozon's previous treatment of prostitution, cross-dressing and paedophilia had been limited to the imaginary universe of his film narratives, *Jeune & jolie / Young & Beautiful*, *Une Nouvelle amie / The New Girlfriend* and *Grâce à Dieu* enter into a dialogue with real-life contemporary iterations of these social problems and the socio-political debates surrounding them, all revealing the symptomatic aspect of individual, social and religious crises.

In *Grâce à Dieu*, however, Ozon takes an unprecedented political stance on the social issue that inspired him in ways that he had not done in *Jeune & jolie / Young & Beautiful* or *Une Nouvelle amie / The New Girlfriend*. This time, *Grâce à Dieu* is used as a medium for not only the victims but also the director himself and the cast to speak up, openly militating against the Catholic Church's silence during the film's premieres and interviews. The *avant-première* at the Commoedia cinema in Lyon brought the director, the three victims the film depicts and their fictional doubles together to engage with the public debate on the issue of sexual abuse in the Catholic Church.

If the Catholic Church's *omertà* on sexual abuse hinges on the individual and popular fear of the Church as a repressive state apparatus that has silenced victims of such abuse, in *Grace à Dieu*, Ozon focuses on those aspects of the film narrative that reaffirm the power of speaking publicly and openly about one's experiences. Although the use of some flashback sequences was necessary to show what the victims experienced, the film privileges the adult characters' use of voiceovers to tell their own stories. For the most part Ozon relies on character voiceovers to play up the power of a confessional narrative, however subversive it may be, without overlooking the many forms it may take in modern times. The email voiceovers that Alexandre enacts to provide a back story, for example, infuses the film narrative with a sense of immediacy and urgency, as do François's creation of the 'La Parole Libérée' website and his reliance on social networks such as 'Copains d'avant' and LinkedIn to enable other victims to come forward and speak up.

In the end, narrative agency proves to be more powerful in creating change than the real facts themselves. However impactful, the Devaux family's letters in 1991 and Alexandre's emails in 2014 to church officials did not and would not by themselves bring Preynat to justice. It was the ability of the victims to come forward and speak up that would make the difference. *Grâce à Dieu* not only showcases this process but offers solutions to the problem as Alexandre's opens up at the dinner table about what happened to him to his own children. If it ever happened to them, he says, they should never now be afraid to speak up. François goes even further and says that, in matters like these, our duty is to inform. All in all, *Grâce à Dieu* stands as a *film citoyen*, a social justice film.

NOTES

1. For an existing study on prostitution in *Jeune & jolie*, see Wallenbrock (2015), pp. 419–21; on transgenderism and marriage for all in *Une Nouvelle amie / The New Girlfriend*, see Reis (2020).
2. Unless otherwise noted, all translations are my own.
3. Available at <https://www.youtube.com/watch?v=xJuzr--zKKc&li=> (last accessed 27 October 2019).

4. Available at <https://www.laparoleliberee.org/les-temoignages-des-victimes-du-per> (last accessed 30 July 2019).
5. Available at <https://www.laparoleliberee.org/les-aveux-du-pere-preynat> (last accessed 30 July 2019).
6. Available at <https://www.youtube.com/watch?reload=9&v=FQNLnVuxOls> (last accessed 29 August 2020).
7. Barbarin attended the 17 November 2012, the 13 January 2014 (Paris) and the 14 February 2012 (Lyon) demonstrations of 'La Manif pour tous' ('Demonstrations for All'). Cf. 'Mgr Barbarin: "Nous sommes tous nés d'un père et d'une mère"', *CNews*, 11 January 2013, <https://www.cnews.fr/france/2013-01-11/mgr-barbarin-nous-sommes-tous-nes-dun-pere-et-dune-mere-331828> (last accessed 30 July 2019).
8. 'Lord Jesus Christ, in this sacrament, you have left us the memory of your passion. Give us, as we venerate such a great love, the mystery of your body and blood. May we be able to always receive the fruit of your redemption. You who reign for ever and ever. Amen.'
9. 'My name is Alexandre Guérin, I am 40 years old, I am married and the father of five children who go to school at the Lazaristes in Lyon, where my wife is herself a teacher . . . I crossed paths with the father of a little boy in the same school as my sons some time ago. As . . . he was with the scouts of Saint-Luc in Ste-Foy-lès-Lyon, we recalled our memories of childhood, school, scout camps . . . and he asked me this question that is still running through my head: 'You, too, were fondled by Father Preynat?''
10. Devaux's 'Copains d'avant' profile is available at <http://copainsdavant.linternaute.com/p/francois-devaux-782766> (last accessed 20 June 2019).
11. 'It was dark [inside]. He closed the door . . . took me in his arms. He ran his hand through my navy-blue shorts, I didn't move. He was holding me tight, very tight. He kissed me on the neck, rubbed against my leg. He used to say to me "I love you". He was breathing hard, very hard and then nothing.'
12. 'Father Preynat follows me into my tent. He lies down, lies down next to me. I feel his weight and his big belly on me. And it starts again . . . He kisses me with his tongue. He unzips my fly. He puts his hand inside. He rubs himself. He is breathing hard. He leads my hand toward his penis.'
13. Mr Debord: 'François, can you come, please?' Mrs Debord: 'What Father Preynat did to you was wrong and is against by law. A priest does not kiss a child on the mouth and does not touch his buttocks. He can go to jail for that. Little François: I don't want him to go to jail'. Mr Debord: 'Yes, François, but there is nothing we can do about it! He was not allowed to do what he did to you.'
14. 'French priest loses bid to block Ozon's child abuse film', *France24*, 18 February 2019, <https://www.france24.com/en/20190218-france-priest-block-church-child-abuse-film-ozon-grace-god-berlin> (last accessed 24 September 2020).

WORKS CITED

Althusser, Louis (1976), 'Idéologie et appareils idéologiques d'état (Notes pour une recherche)', *Positions (1964–1975)*, Paris: Éditions Sociales, pp. 67–125.
Asibong, Andrew (2005), 'Meat, Murder, Metamorphosis: The Transformational Ethics of François Ozon', *French Studies*, 59: 2, pp. 203–15.
Breuil, Xavier (2015), 'Prêtre accusé de pédophilie: 25 ans après, les questions d'une victime', *Le Progrès*, 26 October, <https://www.leprogres.fr/faits-divers/2015/10/26/pretre-accuse-de-pedophilie-25-ans-apres-les-questions-d-une-victime-ijkg> (last accessed 15 March 2020).

Brewster, Ben (trans.) (2001), *Lenin and Philosophy and Other Essays*, New York: Monthly Review Press, pp. 85–126.
Comte, Antoine (2016), 'Le père Bernard Preynat mis en examen', *Tribune de Lyon*, 27 January, <https://tribunedelyon.fr/salade-lyonnaise/article/le-pere-bernard-preynat-mis-en-examen> (last accessed 10 January 2020).
Comte, Antoine (2015), 'Qui est Bernard Preynat, le prêtre lyonnais visé par des plaintes pour pédophilie?', *Tribune de Lyon*, 28 October, <https://tribunedelyon.fr/2015/10/28/qui-est-bernard-preynat-le-pretre-lyonnais-vise-par-des-plaintes-pour-pedophilie> (last accessed 10 January 2020).
Cour d'Appel de Lyon (CAL) 2019, 'Jugement Correctionnel', Lyon, France: Tribunal de Grande Instance.
Église catholique à Lyon (ECL) 2019, 'Communiqué du Tribunal ecclésiastique en charge du procès pénal de l'abbé Bernard Preynat', 4 July, <https://lyon.catholique.fr/actualites/textes-et-communiques/2019/07/04/abbe-bernard-preynat-jugement-du-tribunal-ecclesiastique> (last accessed 3 March 2020).
Gauriat, Valérie (2019), 'Pédophilie: les victimes brisent le silence', *Euronews*, 6 January, <https://fr.euronews.com/2019/01/06/pedophilie-les-victimes-brisent-le-silence> (last accessed 7 March 2020).
Germain-Thill, Pierre-Emmanuel (2018), 'Qui suis-je?', <https://cohadel.com/coach-pierre-emmanuel-germain-thill> (last accessed 2 February 2020).
Hayward, Susan (2006), *Cinema Studies: The Key Concepts*, London: Routledge.
Ince, Kate (2008), *Five Directors: Auteurism from Assayas to Ozon*, Manchester: Manchester University Press.
Mongaillard, Vincent (2019), 'Alexandre Dussot-Hezez, l'homme qui a fait chuter le cardinal Barbarin', *Le Parisien*, 8 March, <https://www.leparisien.fr/societe/alexandre-dussot-hezez-l-homme-qui-a-fait-chuter-le-cardinal-barbarin-08-03-2019-8027223.php> (last accessed 30 July 2019).
Ozon, François (2019), *Grâce à Dieu: Trois actes et un épilogue*, Besançon: Éditions Les Solitaires Intempestifs.
Reis, Levilson C. (2020), 'Goodbye, "Temporary" Transvestites – Hello, New Girlfriend! Ozon's Transgenre and Transgender Crossovers in *Une nouvelle amie* (2014)', *French Screen Studies*, 20: 1, pp. 42–66.
Ricœur, Paul (1991), 'Life in Quest of Narrative', in David Wood (ed.), *On Paul Ricœur: Narrative and Interpretation*, London: Routledge, pp. 20–33.
San Filippo, Maria (2016), 'Female Trouble: Representing Transwomen in *The Danish Girl* and *The New Girlfriend*', *Journal of Bisexuality*, 16: 3, pp. 403–5.
Schilt, Thibaut (2011), *François Ozon*, Urbana, IL: University of Illinois Press.
Stanley, Alice (2009), 'Representations of Sexuality in the Films of François Ozon', PhD dissertation, University of Warwick, <http://go.warwick.ac.uk/wrap/3195> (last accessed 10 May 2019).
Wallenbrock, Nicole Beth (2015), 'The Screen Student-Prostitute, a Twenty-First-Century Discourse: *Mes chères études* (2010), *Elles* (2011), *Jeune et jolie* (2013)', *French Cultural Studies*, 26: 4, pp. 415–25.
White, Hayden (1978), *Tropics of Discourse: Essays in Cultural Criticism*, Baltimore, MD: The Johns Hopkins University Press.

Filmography

OZON AS DIRECTOR

Shorts and documentaries

Photo de famille, short film. François Ozon (producer): France, Paramount, 1988.
Les doigts dans le ventre, short film. François Ozon (producer): France, Paramount, 1988.
Mes parents un jour d'été, short film. François Ozon (producer): France, Paramount, 1990.
Victor, short film. Fémis (producer): France, Paramount, 1993.
Une rose entre nous / A Rose Between Us, short film. Fémis (producer): France, 1994.
Action vérité / Truth or Dare, short film. Olivier Delbosc and Marc Missonier (producers): France, Fidélité Productions, 1995.
La petite mort / Little Death, short film. Olivier Delbosc and Marc Missonier (producers): France, Fidélité Productions, 1995.
Jospin s'éclaire, documentary. No known producers: France, Elma Productions, 1995.
Une Robe d'été / A Summer Dress, short film. Olivier Delbosc and Marc Missonier (producers): France, Fidélité Productions, 1996.
Regarde la mer / See the Sea, short film. Olivier Delbosc et al. (producers): France, Fidélité Productions, 1997.
Scènes de lit / Bed Scenes, short film. Nicolas Brevière (producer): France, Local Films, 1998.
X2000, short film. Olivier Delbosc and Marc Missonier (producers): France, Fidélité Productions, 1998.
Un lever de rideau / A Curtain Raiser, short film. Cécile Vacheret (producer): France, Foz, 2006.

Feature-length films

Sitcom. Olivier Delbosc and Marc Missonier (producers): France, Fidélité Productions, 1998.
Les Amants criminels / Criminal Lovers. Olivier Delbosc and Marc Missonier (producers): France, Fidélité Productions, 1999.

Gouttes d'eau sur pierres brûlantes / *Water Drops on Burning Rocks*. Olivier Dubosc et al. (producers): France, Fidelité Productions, 2000 & USA: Zeitgeist Films, 2001.
Sous le sable / *Under the Sand*. Olivier Dubosc et al. (producers): France, Fidélité Productions, 2000.
8 femmes / *8 Women*. Olivier Delbosc et al. (producers): France and Italy, Fidélité Productions, 2002.
Swimming Pool. Olivier Delbosc et al. (producers): France and UK, Fidélité Productions, 2003.
5 x 2. Olivier Dubosc et al. (producers): France, Fidélité Productions, 2004.
Le Temps qui reste / *Time to Leave*. Olivier Delbosc and Marc Missonier (producers): France, Fidélité Productions, 2005.
Angel. Olivier Delbosc et al. (producers): France, UK and Belgium, Fidelité Productions, 2007.
Ricky. Claudie Ossard et al. (producers): France and Italy, Eurowide, 2009.
The Refuge. Chis Bolzi and Claudie Ossard (producers): France, Eurowide, 2009.
Potiche. Eric Altmayer and Nicolas Altmayer (producers): France and Belgium, Mandarin Films, 2010.
Dans la maison / *In the House*. Eric Altmayer et al. (producers): France, Mandarin Films, 2012.
Jeune & jolie / *Young & Beautiful*. Eric Altmayer and Nicolas Altmayer (producers): France, Mandarin Films, 2013.
Une Nouvelle amie / *The New Girlfriend*. France, Mandarin Cinema, 2014.
Frantz. Eric Altmayer et al. (producers): France and Germany, Mandarin Films, 2016.
L'Amant double / *Double Lover*. Eric Altmayer et al. (producers): France and Belgium, Mandarin Films, 2017.
Grâce à Dieu / *By the Grace of God*. Eric Altmayer and Nicolas Altmayer (producers): France and Beligum, Mandarin Films, 2019.
Été 85 / *Summer of 85*. Eric Altmayer and Nicolas Altmayer (producers): France, Mandarin Films, 2020.

Index

Aaron, Michele, 16, 82
abuse
   and child, 138, 195–6
   and psychological, 18
   and sex, 2, 9, 156, 196–200, 202–9
   see also cruelty, justice, violence
adaptation, 5–6, 15, 35–6, 38, 52–4,
   62–8, 110, 150, 156–7, 162–3, 181,
   186, 190, 197; see also Handyside,
   pastiche, play
aesthetic, 4, 16, 36, 39, 43, 46,
   62, 72, 77, 81, 120, 162, 166,
   189, 192
   and queer, 17, 68, 80, 109, 115
affect, 17–19, 22–32, 47, 100, 103,
   126, 135, 155, 157–8
AIDS, 1, 4, 32
Almodóvar, Pedro, 4, 35, 43
ambiguity, 55–6, 59, 77–81, 84, 103,
   113, 120, 185
   and ambivalence, 73–5
   see also Blur
Amin, Kadji, 3
angle, 23, 26, 31, 59, 79, 82, 132
Asibong, Andrew, 1–2, 4, 15, 35, 39,
   43, 73, 115, 118, 120, 128, 148, 165,
   182–4, 195, 207;
   see also bourgeois, servant
Augé, Marc, 102
auteur, 3, 5, 9, 64, 88–9, 91, 128;
   see also Ince, New Wave Cinema,
   Morrey

Baudrillard, Jean, 143–5, 154, 158; see
   also transgender
beach, 4, 72, 73, 77–8, 81–3, 88, 95,
   102, 126–9, 131–2, 134, 137;
   see also Handyside
belonging, 43, 62, 102, 164
   and nation, 63
   and space, 169–70
   see also community
black-and-white, 44, 52, 55–6, 190
blur, 39, 73, 109–10, 173, 204;
   see also ambiguity
bourgeois, 19, 37, 39–41, 43, 55–6,
   61, 63, 88, 91, 93, 98, 102–3, 116,
   119, 127, 165, 168, 178;
   see also Asibong
Breillat, Catherine, 16
Buñuel, Luis, 90, 94
Butler, Judith, 55, 153–4

Cahiers du cinéma, 39, 157
camera, 17, 19, 22–3, 26–8, 31–2, 41–2, 59–60, 79, 81–3, 87, 128, 130, 135, 139, 151, 188–9, 202, 206–7
camp, 7, 17, 23, 26, 32, 56, 72, 88, 133, 189
Chabrol, Claude, 41
child, 18, 28, 45, 57, 117–18, 126, 131–6, 138–40, 148, 163, 166, 170, 174–5, 182, 184, 195–6, 198–204, 209; *see also* education
choreography, 17, 47, 170
close-up, 17–19, 21–9, 31–2, 41, 43–4, 59, 75, 84, 87, 96, 131–2, 134–5, 188, 207; *see also* frame
colour, 24, 52–3, 55–6, 61, 66, 166, 190
  and saturation, 17, 32
community, 1, 59, 64, 109, 148, 177
  see also belonging
Connell, R. W., 58; *see also* masculinity
costumes, 19–20, 32, 92, 181, 190
cruelty, 15, 18, 20–1, 24, 186;
  see also abuse, violence

Dawson, Leanne, 111, 122
Deleuze, Gilles, 17–19, 73–4, 76–9, 84, 90, 146
Deneuve, Catherine, 64, 102, 125, 163
Depardieu, Gérard, 64, 163
desire, 2, 23, 54, 75, 173, 175, 183
  and creativity, 185–6
  and family, 18, 41, 109, 116–18, 121
  and film, 36, 100, 113
  and gender, 146, 163, 165–6
  and queer, 4, 120, 128, 178
  and sex, 19, 26, 39, 42, 47, 60, 110, 121–2, 148, 192–3

dialogue, 17–18, 21, 26, 28–9, 55, 64–5, 95–6, 111–13, 121, 128, 130, 150, 163
Downing, Lisa, 173–4, 183–4;
  see also selfish
Dyer, Richard, 63, 190; *see also* pastiche

Edelman, Lee, 57, 61, 67–8
editing, 17, 21, 191–2
education, 112
  and French, 90, 111, 114–15
  see also child
excess, 17, 35–9, 43, 47, 189

fabric, 2, 22, 41
family, 2, 38, 40–3, 46–8, 52, 54–5, 58–60, 87, 92, 94, 103, 109–10, 115, 117–18, 121–2, 126, 136, 139–140, 148, 163, 166, 168, 171, 175, 182, 184–5, 200, 204, 209
  and bourgeois, 37, 93, 116, 119, 127
  and Catholic, 198, 201–2
  and French, 42, 44–5, 119, 136, 140
  and homosexuality, 40
  and nation, 63–4
  and nuclear, 58, 63, 109, 116–20, 122
  and patriarchy, 36, 91, 119
Fanon, Franz, 44, 46; *see also* race, Thomas
Fassbinder, Rainer Werner, 4, 7, 15–22, 27, 29, 31–2, 35;
  see also play
fatherhood, 126, 134–5, 138–9;
  see also reproduction
femininity, 24, 31, 41–2, 109, 117, 145–6, 151–3, 156, 169, 187, 192–3

feminism, 1, 9, 39, 125, 134, 163, 170–2, 178, 184–5, 192
Fémis, 91, 129
fetish, 48, 62, 132
filmmaking, 17, 36, 82, 89–91, 93, 109, 115, 129, 182, 185; see also New Queer Cinema, production
flashback, 53, 55–6, 59, 65–6, 81–2, 166, 206–7, 209
fluidity, 2, 16, 83, 84, 109, 126
and fluid, 35, 75, 80, 82–3, 153
and gender, 17, 39, 154
and sexuality, 17
Fox, Alistair, 6, 89
frame, 18–24, 26–7, 40–4, 79, 82, 88, 166; see also close-up
Freud, Sigmund, 58, 117, 122

gaze, 42–3, 48, 152, 190
and male, 16, 46, 150
see also Mulvey, voyeur
Genet, Jean, 3, 16
Genre, 5–6, 35–6, 37–8, 40–2, 53, 62, 66, 68, 82, 85, 89, 92, 94, 128, 140, 191; see also heritage cinema
ghost, 9, 52, 72, 74–5, 81
globalisation, 87, 89, 91, 100–1
Grethlein, Jonas, 111, 118, 122

Handyside, Fiona, 4, 6, 8, 9, 22, 54, 62, 63–4, 66, 73, 77, 80–1, 92, 132, 134, 140, 157, 190
and adaptation, 6, 66, 110, 163
and beach, 73, 77, 78, 81, 88, 126
see also adapation, beach, play, theatre
Hardy, Françoise, 22, 90, 93–7, 100
Haynes, Todd, 16, 35, 190
Hayward, Susan, 63, 206
heritage cinema, 53–4, 62–6, 68, 190; see also genre

heteronormative, 20, 35–6, 39–40, 45, 48, 52–7, 59, 62, 66–7, 109, 116–17, 121, 126, 133–5, 140, 144, 147, 150, 155, 157–8, 184, 186–7, 200
history, 16, 35, 65–7, 181–2
and cinema, 41, 146–7, 189
and Europe, 64, 67
and France, 44, 62, 90, 110, 140, 173, 175
and painting, 57
see also memory, time, trauma, war
Hitchcock, Alfred, 4, 41, 149–51, 184–5, 189
Homo Porno, 16

Ince, Kate, 4–6, 8, 35, 89–91, 102, 109, 115, 119, 128, 140, 158, 173, 195; see also auteur
intertextuality, 3, 15, 40, 56–7, 67, 87, 93–4, 100–3, 117, 128
intimacy, 3, 17, 40–1, 47, 55, 92, 113, 121, 171
and sex, 26, 113, 128, 134, 191–2
irony, 16, 27, 37, 40, 43, 68, 94, 97, 102, 188

Jameson, Fredric, 100–3
justice, 196, 204, 209; see also abuse

liberation
and emancipation, 56, 169–71, 178
and sex, 43
and women, 167, 170–2, 177–8
light, 44, 75, 82, 131, 137

mainstream, 5, 7, 36, 42, 64, 94, 146
marginality, 2, 42–3, 48, 53, 62, 66, 148; see also queering
marriage, 60–1, 117–8, 193
and same-sex, 39, 126, 135–6, 140, 146, 176, 195, 200
see also reproduction

masculinity, 45, 53, 55, 57–8, 61–2, 67, 109, 151, 156, 187; *see also* Connell, Silverman, trauma
memory, 64, 66, 174, 199
　and nation, 63
　see also history, mourning, nation
mirror, 21–2, 24, 31, 96, 112–13, 132, 151–2, 176
　and image, 65, 76, 78–9
mise-en-abyme, 66, 110–12, 116–18, 121–2
mise-en-scène, 7, 37, 40, 43, 115, 208
Morrey, Douglas, 3, 4, 5, 6, 185–6; *see also* auteur
motherhood, 125–6, 128, 131–5, 138, 163, 165–6, 173–5, 178; *see also* O'Reilly, pregnancy, reproduction
mourning, 52, 60–1, 66, 68, 73, 81, 97, 125–7, 131–3; *see also* memory
Mulvey, Laura, 16, 31, 189–90; *see also* gaze, voyeur
music, 2, 4, 19, 22–4, 26–30, 35, 43, 47, 63–4, 75, 81, 87, 89, 95–7, 113, 119, 121, 127, 130, 133, 137, 166–7, 206

nation, 40, 62–4, 101, 136, 157; *see also* republic
New Queer Cinema (NQC), 5, 7, 16, 35, 82; *see also* filmmaking, Rich
New Wave Cinema, 3, 5, 90, 120, 185; *see also* auteur, Morrey

O'Reilly, Andrea, 133–4; *see also* motherhood

pastiche, 8, 16, 35, 38, 102–3, 110, 189–91; *see also* adaptation, Dyer
patriarchy, 46, 165–6, 178, 182–4
　and culture, 37, 109
　and family, 36, 38, 42, 47, 58, 60, 91, 116, 119, 133–4, 201
　and gender, 58, 117, 148, 167, 174, 193
　and society, 67, 173, 185
perversion, 36–7, 39, 44, 47, 199, 203
play, 9, 15, 17–24, 26–32, 53, 55, 61, 64–5, 67, 110, 162–3, 178, 182; *see also* adaptation, Fassbinder, Handyside, theatre
politics, 1, 3, 53, 62–3, 65, 67–8, 100–1, 113–14, 126, 158, 172, 184, 195–6
　and film, 9, 46, 163, 173, 183
　and form, 5, 7, 36, 192
　and French, 39, 90–1, 115, 162, 170, 177
　and identity, 36, 178
　and representation, 109, 196
postmodern, 35–6, 52, 54, 65, 87, 93, 101–3, 111, 143–4, 147
Poupaud, Melvil, 127–8, 135, 138
power, 38, 43, 47, 54, 66, 68, 112, 118, 120–1, 140, 163, 165, 167, 173–5, 185–6
　and Church, 200–4
　and economy, 46, 101
　and fatherhood, 135
　and film, 39, 182, 196, 209
　and Foucault, 120–1
　and gender, 36, 143
　and voice, 1
　and women, 134, 163, 164, 168–9, 171–2, 178, 183, 192
pregnancy, 125, 127–9, 131–4, 139, 145, 157, 175, 191; *see also* motherhood
production, 2, 5, 35, 62, 72, 89–90, 128, 140, 162, 165, 181–2, 186, 189–90, 195
　and design, 20–1, 32, 188
　and meaning, 74, 80, 84
　see also filmmaking

queering, 21, 32, 36–7, 43, 52, 53–4, 62, 67–8, 81, 92, 111–12, 115–16, 118, 120, 122, 135, 163, 175, 178; *see also* marginality, Rees-Roberts

race, 46
  and postcolonial, 44
  see also Fanon, Thomas
Rampling, Charlotte, 72, 77, 79, 94, 102–3, 133, 181–2, 186
reception
  and film, 3–4, 186
Rees-Roberts, Nick, 1, 5, 16, 109; *see also* queering
Reis, Levilson C., 128, 146, 151, 155, 158
reproduction, 42, 61, 135, 140
  and nation, 63, 157
  see also fatherhood, marriage, motherhood
republic, 1, 100, 140, 168; *see also* nation, universalism
Rich, Ruby, 16, 35, 65; *see also* New Queer Cinema
Ricoeur, Paul, 197–8
Royal, Ségolène, 173

Sarkozy, Nicolas, 1, 162, 173, 176–8
Schilt, Thibaut, 2–6, 15, 18, 24, 35, 39–40, 73, 80, 89, 92, 94–5, 109, 116–19, 122, 125–6, 128–31, 138, 148, 176, 178, 186, 207
selfish, 173, 175, 183–4, 186; *see also* Downing
servant, 21, 164–5, 181, 184, 193; *see also* Asibong
sex, 18, 23–4, 26, 31, 118, 120–2, 134–5, 147, 156, 193, 196
  and change, 20, 143–4, 153, 203
  and prostitution, 98
  and reproduction, 57
  and violence, 17, 207

sexuality, 2, 6, 35, 44, 57, 65, 67, 84, 92, 121, 149, 155, 157, 158
  and bisexuality, 61, 120
  and gender, 17, 39, 111, 187, 203
  and homosexuality, 5, 20, 38, 46, 53, 56, 58, 60–1, 65, 67, 80, 109, 177–8, 195, 203
  and transsexuality, 143–4, 147, 154
  and women, 176
short
  and film, 2–4, 60, 72, 125, 182
  and scene, 23, 26
  and story, 138, 156–7
signature, 5, 126; *see also* style
Silverman, Kaja, 53–4, 58, 62; *see also* masculinity, war
space, 17–19, 21–2, 24, 26, 28, 32, 41–2, 53, 73, 78–80, 85, 101–2, 121, 138, 151, 158, 164, 170, 186, 193
  and domestic, 47, 52, 88, 117, 165–6, 170
  and liminal, 78, 87, 111, 114
  and memory, 63
  and queer, 126
  see also time
style, 7, 16, 31, 35–6, 39–40, 42, 74, 81–2, 85, 109–10, 122, 126, 130, 151, 185; *see also* signature
suicide, 15, 20–1, 25, 31–2, 46, 52, 56–8, 65, 67, 74, 81, 83, 181
Szaryk, Evelyne, 19, 24

Teorema, 37–8, 117, 119
theatre, 15, 38, 40, 53, 102, 163, 175; *see also* Handyside, play
Thomas, Dominic, 44; *see also* race
time, 7, 77, 80, 82–3, 85
  and filmmaking, 125, 129, 146, 190
  and songs, 95
  and space, 19, 73, 97
  see also history, space

tradition, 42, 55, 87, 89, 94, 139, 158, 204
and cinema, 35, 55, 62, 90, 92, 101, 120, 130
transgender, 18–20, 143–7, 151–3, 158; *see also* Baudrillard
transgression, 15–16, 64, 122, 168, 186, 195
  and sex, 17, 26, 37, 92
  and space, 121, 170
  and women, 163, 173, 183
trauma, 7, 31, 53–5, 57–8, 60, 67–8, 182, 199, 206; *see also* history, masculinity, war
Truffaut, François, 120

universalism, 5, 36, 90–1, 171; *see also* republic

violence, 2, 5, 17, 43, 57, 67, 98, 121, 157
  and race, 46
  and sex, 191
  see also abuse, cruelty, war
Vincendeau, Ginette, 8, 63, 73, 88–9, 91, 98, 102–3
voiceover, 2, 27, 111, 113, 116, 121, 128, 138, 201–3, 206–7
voyeur, 4, 16, 32, 113, 117–18, 120–1

water, 83–4, 127, 189, 196
Waters, John, 4, 35
Waters, Sarah, 100
war, 52–8, 60, 62, 64–5, 67, 166, 181; *see also* history, Silverman, trauma, violence

EU representative:
Easy Access System Europe
Mustamäe tee 50, 10621 Tallinn, Estonia
Gpsr.requests@easproject.com

www.ingramcontent.com/pod-product-compliance
Lightning Source LLC
Chambersburg PA
CBHW070352240426
43671CB00013BA/2469